THE TRUE AMERICAN

THE TRUE AMERICAN

✳

MURDER AND MERCY IN TEXAS

Anand Giridharadas

W. W. NORTON & COMPANY

NEW YORK | LONDON

For information about permission to reproduce selections from this book,
write to Permissions, W. W. Norton & Company, Inc.,
500 Fifth Avenue, New York, NY 10110

For information about special discounts for bulk purchases, please contact
W. W. Norton Special Sales at specialsales@wwnorton.com or 800-233-4830

Manufacturing by Courier Westford
Book design by Chris Welch
Production manager: Devon Zahn

ISBN 978-0-393-23950-8

W. W. Norton & Company, Inc.
500 Fifth Avenue, New York, N.Y. 10110
www.wwnorton.com

W. W. Norton & Company Ltd.
Castle House, 75/76 Wells Street, London W1T 3QT

1 2 3 4 5 6 7 8 9 0

TO PRIYA,

an American, and
my forever girl, my witness

CONTENTS

AUTHOR'S NOTE

This is a true story. Although my movements as an author remain invisible in the text, the book has been carefully and densly reported from a wealth of records and testimonies that I am grateful to have tapped. These include dozens of hours of taped interviews that I conducted with the characters in, and witnesses to, the drama; video footage and text from the interviews done by others; personal correspondence; news reports; many thousand pages of legal documents spanning court transcripts, academic records, medical and psychological assesments, police and probation reports, among other things; a large volume of photographs and videos; and more. Of course, this story, like so many stories, relies so much on the memories of its subjects; in this case, a group of people mostly unknown to one another—living around Dallas, Texas, but from the world—who, through some strange permutation of fate and choices, found themselves tossed into this storm.

THE TRUE AMERICAN

Leavings

Every so often, a customer walked into the mini-mart at South Buckner and Elam Road and offered Raisuddin some reassurance. Perhaps they noticed his olive T-shirt and bright sneakers, and interpreted them as he had hoped: as the dress of a rising man, not a typical gas station worker. Or perhaps they heard in one of his newly crafted conversation starters some unexpected flair. In these moments, they might speak to Raisuddin or simply smile in a way that pleased him. They knew he was not of this place.

It was 2001. He had arrived in Texas at the start of the summer. He came from Dhaka, in Bangladesh, by way of two years in New York City. Here on the fringes of the Dallas metroplex, he began his days at 5 a.m., dressing quickly at his boss's house, where he was living, and rushing to get behind the counter before dawn. He sold Country Time lemonade and Tahitian Treat punch, Coors Light and ten-cent candies, Gillette razors and Copenhagen tobacco products until midnight or 1 a.m., mining the *Dallas Morning News* for sports scores and other flint for counter chatter, trying out on customers the pleasantries he was still learning, squeezing in as many of the five prayers as he could manage. Then he returned home to shower, eat, and catch his winks before the cycle resumed.

Selling Americans three tamales for a dollar was a strange landing for a twenty-seven-year-old who had trained to command fighter jets and qualified as a Microsoft Certified Systems Engineer. But so it is with the many who leave their native soil and find that to rise, they must first sink into the fresh earth below. Raisuddin was no longer a Bangladesh Air Force man. He was a Buckner Food Mart man.

✻

THE MINI-MART WATCHED over a barren corner of a luck-starved neighborhood. It lingered in the badlands between the central Dallas whose gentry regard the city as a second Los Angeles and the more rustic neighborhoods to the east. Drive one way out of the store, and it was easier to find vegan and Ashtanga than barbecue and two-step. Drive the other way, and within minutes the setting could be more redolent of Mississippi: the RVs turned home extensions, the Confederate-flag license-plate holders, the fenced-in horses, the slouching wooden cottages, the outdoor exhibition of those possessions that failed to fit inside.

To an immigrant like Raisuddin, the economy around the mart might have appeared rather desolate. It wasn't the economy of the legendary firms where third-world boys like him fantasized about working, of Boeing, IBM, Procter & Gamble—names whose appearance on a business card one day might be enough to soothe the pain of leaving home. The commerce in these parts was of consumption more than production: a repeating chain of gas pumps like his, tire shops, cheap eats, and financial agencies offering to move money across gradients of space and time—turning $100 cash here into $83 in Oaxaca or the $350 paycheck you were due on Friday into $300 right now.

Like much of the world, Raisuddin grew up with America on his television screen, so that he felt he knew it before he set foot there. As a young man, he thought of the place in exalted terms: "It's like one of the happiest, the richest, countries in the world, without any problems—that was the image. It's the land of opportunity. Whoever goes there, you can be whatever you want to. The tools are there; you use the tools. It's up to you. Not like Bangladesh, where there is limited opportunity, and there are millions of people fighting for a small opportunity."

His first two years in the U.S., in New York, had grayed this black-and-white schema. There was misfortune in America; there was misfortune in Bangladesh. But to be poor together, as people were back home, seemed to Raisuddin to be different from being poor alone, as people often were here on the edge of Dallas.

He came from an often brutal country, no doubt: the electricity that sizzled off whenever it wished, the rain that withheld itself until it arrived with lethal gusto, the factories that imploded and buses that soared off mountainsides and swollen barges that drowned. But in these things, as in life generally, you were rarely alone—even when you wanted to be. People lived thickly in one another's business, their presence at once invasive and soothing. The constant din of parents and siblings and in-laws staved off self-pity. The customary ways of eating and marrying and caring for elders held communities together and kept hurting people on the path. People threw weddings that took a lifetime to pay off, because they knew they would need a tribe even more than the money.

Of course, this connectedness hadn't been enough to keep Rais— the shortened name by which he introduced himself to Americans— in Bangladesh. Still, he was struck by how people in Dallas seemed to lack for each other far more than for bread or bus passes or a roof overhead. "So much lonely, so much alone, even detached from their own family," he said of the lives around him. They drove up to the food mart in their boat-cars, alone. They ate in their quickie restaurants, alone. They pinned what hopes they had of tranquil aging on scratch-off lottery tickets, not ardent children.

A fearsome wildness could thrive amid this isolation. The people around Rais seemed to him to live largely unobliged to their parents, their teachers, even in many cases their God. They had no one to answer to. Every man for himself, they sometimes called it. Four months at the Buckner Food Mart was plenty of time to discover what a terrifying idea that was. He was coming to see how the poverty of a place that is breaking can differ from the poverty of a place still being made.

Just since May, on more than one occasion, Rais had been behind the counter, waiting, when the front door would open and a customer appear. He would hand Rais a credit card for gas, then go outside to fill up. As the man pumped, Rais would be inside swiping the card over and over, wondering what he was doing wrong—until he realized that it was a dead card, that the man had no intention of paying and had already fled with $40 worth of liquid loot. This in the richest country in the world. Or there were the boys, still young enough to sit on their mothers' laps, who sauntered into the Buckner Food Mart and stole candy and gum. Or the recurring—and, on one occasion, strangely fastidious—condom thieves.

One night, after the time of the Isha prayer, around nine or ten, Rais saw two young men huddled in the corner. He came out from behind the counter to check on them, which made them scamper for the exit. He ran to where they had been hiding and there saw a three-pack of condoms ripped open, with two of the rubbers missing. At least they had the grace to steal only what they needed that night. Rais followed them out of the store and insisted that they pay for what they'd taken. They told him to "back off." He promised to do so once they paid. After all, things cost money, and Rais was answerable to his boss—didn't they see? Then one of the boys flashed what looked like a gun and reiterated his advice to back off. Rais reconsidered his stance: "After that—whoa, I don't wanna lose my life for a pack of condoms—I said, 'OK, you don't have to pay.' "

One afternoon near summer's peak, a man walked into the mart, fetched a soda from the cooler, and gave Rais a dollar bill. When the register opened, the man pulled out a gun. Rais, who took pride in the evenness of his keel, knew there was nothing to be alarmed about: "Many a times in the gas station, people used to come and sell their personal belongings—computer monitor, TV, this kind of thing—all the poor people in the neighborhood. So I thought this guy wants to sell that gun as well. Because he's a customer; it's two o' clock. In my mind, robbery happens in the dark. Robbery happens at night—in a less crowded place, but not in a gas station at two o' clock in the afternoon. And, plus, he bought a drink, so he's a customer."

Rais began the negotiation: "You wanna sell? How much?"

"No, amigo, give me the money," came the puzzled reply.

"Yes, I will give," Rais said. "How much you asking for?"

"No, no, amigo, give me the money," the man repeated, growing agitated.

Rais tried again: "Yes, I will give, but how much you want for the gun?"

The man cocked the pistol and pressed it into Rais's forehead, which roused the dormant soldier within him: "From my military experience, I knew he's about to shoot, because he cocked the gun. And I said, 'OK, OK, don't shoot me. Here's the money.' " Rais removed some modest green stacks from the register and handed them over. The incident left him irritated with himself, because Bangladeshi military training specifically covered one-on-one gunfights.

From time to time, Rais's mind darted back to the life he had left. What was he, man of burning promise, doing in a miserable gas station in Texas? But he never dwelled there long. "I know this is not my life," he told himself. "It's just temporary right now—for the time being, just to survive. I'm working on a bigger goal." It was not his first gas station, and he believed that in all work was dignity. If anything had stuck from those Thursdays in childhood, sitting on bedsheets stretched over the drawing room carpets, beneath the godly verses adorning the walls, swaying to his grandfather's recitations of the Prophet's sayings, it was that Muhammad was a shepherd whose day job obscured his destiny. Rais's days at the mart were steps in a carefully laid plan. Before year's end, inshallah, he would fly home and, with the gas station money, make good on a long-ago promise to Abida. After the wedding—to be held, if he could arrange it, in the Air Force mess in Dhaka—he would bring her to Dallas in proper style. He would enroll in a computer course at the University of Texas at Dallas or Richland Community College (he was still calculating the cost of each in dollars per credit). If things went according to plan, as surely they would, he would be a bona fide systems engineer at a prestigious company downtown.

Rais could suffer the Buckner Food Mart because he knew he'd be leaving it. His short life had already been full of leavings. Islam was his constant; other things he could renounce with an ease that eluded most beings. It was part of what made him a natural aspirant to America.

Not to mention his doggedness, his power to ignore voices not his own, and his focus on what he believed to be his God-given luck. What a casual visitor to the mini-mart could not see was that his presence there was the product of a great run of victories. Rais Bhuiyan's arrival in Dallas was, by the grace of God, the most merciful and compassionate, the seventh triumph in that run.

$*$

THE FORTUNE REACHED back half a generation, to the middle 1980s, in the years before the great cyclone. It fell on a young man from a household well prepared for it: an educated and devout upper-middle-class family that pursued its this-world and next-world ends with comparable devotion.

Rais's father was an engineer for Bangladesh Telephone and Telegraph. He rose steadily through its bureaucracy, where he performed various duties, including helping less capable countries build their communications infrastructure. The work gave his family a comfortable, gated life. His forebears came from Sylhet, to the northeast, and Assam, in what was now India. In Dhaka, he had been one of the early settlers of an area called Dania—a tranquil suburb of the teeming, honking, sweaty capital, just south of the Chittagong highway. The father had arrived in the neighborhood well before the '71 war of independence, back when the area remained full of paddy. He was ever engaged in the community, and this commitment became important to Rais's conception of his father: a man who was so much more than his day job, who was always asking what else could be done—whether working to set up a primary school in Dania, or aiding candidates for Parliament, or running the neighborhood welfare trust, which kept the streets clean and the drains swallowing.

Rais's parents had married in the traditional, arranged way. At least compared to the father, Rais's mother was of a more religious bent. Rais described her in the generic, uncontroversial way that women in her milieu were so often cast. She was soft-spoken, modest, deferential to others. If she had a flash of pride, it was about being unlike those housewives who went over to neighbors' sofas at the merest impulse to gossip and judge. But her network stretched far into the city, where her family had been settled for generations. Her ever sweeping radar maintained hourly awareness of such facts as whose daughter was marrying and whose father had fallen and whose roof had caved in and brought unpayable bills. Rais idolized her, and perhaps the highest praise he could offer was that no one could detect that three of her eight children weren't really hers: they belonged to her husband's first wife, who had left prematurely for heaven.

Though the Bhuiyan family's self-conception was of simplicity and piety, they lived in relative privilege, in a walled house on a quiet street. Rais remembered only three-wheel rickshaws plying it, not the belching trucks and buses that polluted the capital's less rarified streets. In the springtime, Dania offered that thrilling rarity in Dhaka: bird chirps you could actually hear. Mindful of their advantages, fearful of God, devoted to His way, the Bhuiyans sought to please Him and ward off envy through ceaseless charity to the world beyond the walls.

This charity was not of the United Way variety. Sometimes it took the shape of distant relatives—or "relatives"—showing up, sitting in the drawing room and, over snacks and juice, telling stories that inevitably landed in an explanation of, say, why they couldn't afford the wedding that was nonetheless happening next week. A wad of cash might then be given, or a spare sari, or a table no longer in use. In the style of their part of the world, they said it was their honor. It was, of course, also a way of ensuring that, if God ever changed His mind about you, you too would have drawing rooms to sit in and people to tell your story to. When the family didn't know the seekers, they would wait at the front gate. Rais or one of the other children would stand inside and listen to the visitors' tale, vetting it, bringing it to the parents, and ferrying back any offerings.

Rais grew up on a Gregorian calendar heavily punctuated by special days from the lunar Islamic one. The dates of exams to study for and school applications to fill out mingled with the dates of rites and sacrifices and family get-togethers. Rais liked to emphasize that many of these days involved charity, and especially the giving of food. On the tenth day of Muharram, for instance, the family would cook a vat of khichdi in the front yard, enough for many dozens. Rais remembered the smell attracting a queue of the hungry, who, when it was ready, were admitted through the gate—and allowed, when they asked, to take some for their families as well. On Thursdays, Rais's grandfather Hassan Ali led the household through a ritual of self-purification and prayer. It was important to do it on that day,

Rais believed, because Thursdays were when the angels whom God sent to check on us beamed their reports skyward. The family performed ablutions, then sat in a circle listening to the grandfather speak from the hadith. They would rinse their hearts, as Rais liked to think of it, through whispered repetition of the dictum that there were no gods but theirs.

Little Rais was known to his family as Ripon. He was born in September 1973 and was the seventh of eight children, easily lost in the family bazaar. But he often behaved, even as a boy, as though in possession of a secret understanding that he was special, somehow marked—much as he came across in a story he told about his brother and the cadet college.

As Rais recounted it, one of his elder brothers had dreamed of studying at a prestigious military boarding school. But the Cadet College of Sylhet saw thousands of applications each year, and just a tiny fraction passed through the filters of the written, oral, and medical tests. Rais's dada applied and failed. Rais remembered watching his mother dim with despair. The brother was a very good student, and if he couldn't make it, the prospects of her whole flock became questionable.

"I don't see who can do it," she snapped one day.

Rais was too ambitious and too dutiful not to recognize an opportunity. "Mom, don't give up," he said. "I think I can do it." He vowed to calm her by avenging his brother's rejection. And this vow, as he narrated it, spoke of Rais's emerging character: on one level, the sacrifice and self-denial, the willingness to shelve any plan and scale any mountain for the family; and, on another, his early intuition that the strings tying down others need not bind him. He was in the fourth grade.

Two years later, it was time to act on that old promise. Rais studied for the exams for as many as sixteen hours a day in searing heat, with two of the family's fans deployed to cooling him. He attended a coaching class in the winter and stuffed himself full of the lessons found in textbooks custom-made for aspiring cadets. He took the exam early in the new year. When at last the verdict came, it offered admission. Rais hoped the news would restore the family's confidence.

"I remember the day I was selected, I told my mom, 'Never give up. That my brother couldn't do, that doesn't mean that no one can do. You should not give up. You should try. I tried, and God helped me.' " These were Rais's lessons from the incident: to try and try; and, no less, never to confuse the fate of others with his special own.

When he got into Sylhet, the first victory in his streak, his mother could have filled a teacup with her tears. They were of joy, but also of anxiety about her Ripon's moving a full day's train journey away. "You are happy; I am happy, too," she said. "But I'm going to lose you."

✳

AMONG THE COMPLICATIONS of Rais's approach to life was this: chasing a thing with such fervor could distract you from considering what the thing, once captured, would be like. On joining day at the Cadet College of Sylhet, in the spring of 1986, little twelve-year-old Rais sobbed. A seventh-grader and brand-new cadet was beginning to realize what he had committed to in trying to please his mother. Like a stack of old family letters, precious but without use, he would be lock-and-keyed away in this cupboard for six whole years. Rais's dada, the rejected one, must have had his own complicated feelings about having to accompany Rais on the Surma Mail train to Sylhet, 150 miles to the northeast.

The cadet college was a universe unto itself, insulated from the larger country, with its own cinema, mosque, hospital, and dormitories—not to mention courts and fields for basketball, soccer, hockey, tennis, and volleyball. Its rituals were designed to harden boys and, equally, to apprise them of their mutual dependence. They awoke before six every morning, starting out with calisthenics and a run on some days and mock military parades on others. After the younger boys went to class, their dorm rooms underwent inspection by the seniors, who made sure that bedsheets were tucked tightly-tightly under mattresses and shoes lined up heel to heel to heel. Failure on this score or various others brought swift and bracing punishment: perhaps frog jumps while holding your ankles, or push-ups in the hallway, or rolling yourself across an open soccer field. For the crime of speaking out of turn in the classroom, the penalty might be a tugged ear or thwacked buttock.

"Military school taught me lot of things: discipline, team-building, leadership, patience," Rais said. He remembered everything being very precise. After classes and athletics, the boys had two hours, and only two, for homework. Then came dinnertime, to which they had to walk in formation, as Rais recalled it: "Not just walk on the street, holding hands or gossiping, chatting loudly—not like that. You go in a nice formation on the side of the street, where you walk in a line, and the leader"—typically, one of the seniors—"he makes sure the discipline is maintained and nobody makes any kind of chaos."

In general, the cadets left the campus only on Thursday mornings, for a race of about three miles up Airport Road, past the small airfield, into some tame hills and back. Guards stood along the route to protect the future soldiers of a newly independent republic and to ensure that they weren't making too much mischief.

Rais sought to be guarded in his self-admiration, but he made an exception for his prowess as a runner at Sylhet. "From grade seven, I used to always come at the beginning of the race," he said. He still remembered the seniors taking wary note of a boy many years their junior finishing within a few feet of them: "It was amazing thing. They said, 'Wow, this kid is something.'" Rais grew slightly embarrassed by his retelling: "I should not be talking more on this, but I got attention by that. From seventh grade to twelfth grade, I was always on the first row."

He recalled with special fondness the day when he was in seventh grade and an eighth-grader injured himself and had to pull out of the 600-meter run. Somebody suggested Rais as a substitute, despite his relative youth. The cadets belonged to rival "houses," which competed to accumulate points through the school year. Rais's Shahjalal House needed him to come in fourth, fifth, or sixth to secure enough points to win the day. Rais convinced an eighth-grader in the race to take a junior under his wing and help him achieve that goal. The eighth-grader agreed, and so Rais followed him around the track for most of the race. On the homestretch, with the finish line drawing within sight, Rais decided to sprint, even as his eighth-grade buddy languished, "completely out of his stamina."

"I came first," Rais said. "That was a disaster and that was a happiness as well, because it was a shock to the entire school that a seventh-grader who was sitting on the sidelines—he came first." He still chuckled thinking of the eighth-graders who confronted him back in the dorms: "Who told you to come first?" He said, "It was a shame for the eighth grade; it was a joy for the seventh grade. People are holding me above and laughing and dancing, saying that, 'You broke the history today. No seventh-grader did this in history.'"

When Rais told a story like this, sometimes he would catch himself and tell another, contrary one. Thus the tale of his 600-meter upset led to one about the limits of talent.

Rais said he learned, while ascending into seniority, that running his fastest kept his house from winning. He would finish early and secure applause and sometimes a medal, but the late finishers on his team prevented personal triumph from becoming collective victory for Shahjalal House. He found that if he ran more slowly, he could stick with them and galvanize them as they ran, goading them toward the finish line. Very often it worked. "If I give up my medal, if I bring these kids in front, it made my house go up," he said.

This was one of Rais's major lessons from that time—and it related to another lesson once imparted to him by a harsh teacher. The teacher pulled his ears and spanked him because of a noise in class that was in fact bleated by Rais's neighbor. When Rais later went to the teacher to protest the injustice, his teacher responded that, as with a contagious house fire in a congested quarter of Dhaka, in life sometimes you get burned for no sin of your own, simply because of where you're standing.

After six years at the college, Rais graduated. He came out feeling pulled this way and that by rival goals. He had dreamed of being an airplane pilot at least since he accompanied his father to Dhaka airport as a boy and watched the sky swallow him up and take him away to the Arab Emirates. In time the dream had grown more vivid: he wished to attend the Bangladesh Air Force Academy. But this vision now had to compete with another, inspired more recently by returning alumni of Sylhet, who visited the school to give pep talks about the world beyond it. The most impressive of them had gone off to America for higher studies. This appealed to Rais, too. The best approach, he felt, was to pursue both ambitions at once and defer to God's preferred timetable. "If I don't get to this dream, maybe that's the next one," he said. If not piloting here, then studying in America.

Rais cast his entry into the Air Force Academy as another story of improbable triumph. He reckoned himself to be among the shrimpiest of his classmates, short and slender, which he imagined would make it difficult to pass the academy's extensive scrutiny and testing: "It's very hard to go to Air Force, because it's very limited openings. You have to have a very good health, very good vision, and also have to be highly talented. Your IQ has to be more than 175." Setting aside that possibly inflated figure, the Air Force did have a reputation for difficulty, which led Rais to this observation about his peers: "Those who want to escape the military, they choose the Air Force, because they will be kicked out."

But Rais made it through the exams, and then three months of grueling joint-force training in southern Chittagong, where he lost so much weight—his cheeks looked sunken, his eyes darkly recessed—that his visiting mother wept at the sight of her little skeleton. Rais fractured his wrist two months into the three-month program, but he told no one. He was stubborn, and he feared falling behind in the daily points tally or being removed; the important thing was to keep moving. He pushed himself ever harder in the mile tests and, as at Sylhet, found success: "I was coming first every single day." Once again, it seemed to Rais proof of some special destiny.

When at last he saw a doctor for his wrist, two weeks before the training's end, he received a scolding and some damning news: "Your hand will never be OK. You took such a long time to come back and the fracture has spread so much, it's very unlikely that you'll be able to get it back the way it was before."

But this was, as ever, just the prelude to the story. The wrist did heal, and after three months in a plaster cast and a suspension of his training, Rais formally enrolled in the Air Force Academy.

The next victory involved the undoing of the last. Rais put in two and a half years at the academy in Jessore, studying aerodynamics and navigation and meteorology, collecting dozens of flight hours learning to pitch, roll, and yaw in Chinese-made PT-6A prop planes. He received his commission as a pilot officer. Then, a few months in, while undergoing further training in radar and air defenses, he simply changed his mind. If not this dream, then the other one, he had once said. The other dream—studying in America—had again begun to nibble on and whisper in his ear.

Rais described the change as a natural evolution of his ambitions. Still, it was an abrupt and uncommon shift: men trained up by the military system seldom left it so quickly. Rais couldn't fully explain what had come over him, even years later. It just became clear that this life wasn't for him, he said. Maybe it was the two plane crashes— one killing a teacher Rais knew, the other a fellow student. Or maybe the sense he suddenly had of whiling away his life cut off from the world—first in Sylhet, then in Jessore, now on base after base. "I was out of my house at age of eleven," he said. "I missed all the good times from my family—missed all the programs. Now I'm in the military last two and a half years: missed my sister's wedding, my brother's wedding, this and that. So now when I am going to have my personal time, some free time—what I wanted to do?" A military future would bring what he called a "tight life." He asked himself: "Do I really want to lead a life like this?"

As it happened, getting out of the Air Force was harder than getting in. His comrades tried to deter him. One senior officer warned that his likely career alternative was the venal life of a businessman: "If you do business, you have to be dishonest." Rais would fall from the height of prestige—from the pride of defending Bangladesh, from those government cars and colonial club memberships and foreign educational courses, from that look people give an officer—to its depths. Nothing seemed to convince Rais. Shortly, as per procedure, the air secretary of the country contacted Rais to inquire about his request for a discharge. He asked the young man to come to headquarters and bring his father along.

At the meeting, the official looked to the father: "Can you ask your son what we can do for him to stay?"

Rais was impressed by his father that day. "You raised my son," Rais remembered his father telling the air secretary. "You made my son an officer the last two and a half years through vigorous training. You made him a gentleman. And I think you also made him enough responsible to take his own decision. As a father, I think I did my part. And now you're the guardian, and I think you trained him enough. So I leave it unto you and him."

The official looked to Rais for his final answer. He wanted to go. Within six months, he had his release papers. Rushing to fill the void, a new striving took over: "Next goal: come to U.S.A."

Before that bit of fortune could arrive, however, another would complicate it. Rais, now twenty-two, had known Abida for years, but only as an acquaintance from the neighborhood. Their relationship had consisted of passing in the galis and saying hello-hello-hi-hi at most. On auspicious occasions, his family might call on hers, or vice versa. But Rais had been out of sight at boarding school for years. When he returned home, in the middle of 1996, thinking of higher studies, he bought a computer and became taken with programming. He was into dBase and FoxPro in particular and figured they might help him get to America. One day, in one of their passing encounters, he learned that his neighbor Abida was a computer junkie in her own right and had been dBasing and FoxProing for much longer than he. They exchanged programming books, which led to Abida trouble-shooting for Rais over the phone, which led to her coming over from time to time to help him in person.

"That computer brought us together," Rais said. One day Abida, unprompted, told Rais that she used to have a crush on him back in childhood, but he was always gone, and she never had her chance. It would be an unusually forward move for a woman in that setting, but Rais insisted that this was how it happened. He asked her: "Do you still have the feeling, or is it already gone?" And he remembers that dazzling look on her face that made a man like him rush to seek his mother's approval.

Abida soon began telling her own mother that she had classes on days when she really didn't. She and Rais would linger at an ice cream parlor or a snack bar, or at a waterfront place called the Harbour Inn, which was owned by a retired Air Force man and where Rais was thus confident of getting service that would impress Abida. Their courtship went on for more than a year in this manner.

He found Abida "beautiful, friendly, romantic, talented, and religious-minded." As with his mother, he struggled to describe her with richer specificity; in his corner of the world, women were often characterized in this way, judged by their skills at blending and smoothing, not by how they stood out. He did say that she was ever "in a jolly mood" and that she could "make any situation easy." Even without talking, each knew what was running through the other's head. "We had that kind of mental adjustment," Rais said. The courtship was of the hybrid traditional-modern kind now gaining acceptance in Dhaka—a few droplets of allowable romance, fast merged into the rapids of arranged matrimony. It was unlike what Rais would later observe in America: "There was no checking out whether the chemistry works or not. The chemistry already worked. We are in love. It's not that, OK, check out ten girls and find one girl. It's not like that. We were already in love, and love is respect."

Rais did what he believed an upstanding man in his place must do: solicit his mother's view. "My mother is on one side of the scale and the entire world is other side of the scale, but still my mother's side is heavier," Rais liked to tell people. His mother was fond of Abida from what she'd seen of her growing up and from her more recent tech-support visits. Early in 1999, Rais arranged a small get-together at a restaurant for him and Abida, his brother, and his mother. The couple wanted Rais's mother's blessing for their relationship, and at the restaurant she formally gave it. While Abida's mother was known to feel differently about the match, thinking Rais unworthy of her godly daughter for reasons unsaid, the young couple decided to proceed. They promised their lives and hands to each other. They would coax, outwit, and bypass dissenting elders as needed.

The fifth victory concerned a visa. Even as his relationship with Abida blossomed, Rais had been consumed by that recurring need of his: to leave. It wouldn't be enough to fly fighter jets all his life, and wouldn't be enough to be some plump, routinized salaryman. He wanted more—to study in America, learn computers, get in on this IT boom that had the world vibrating in the late 1990s. Or at least he could study commercial aviation over there and return home to be a pilot for Biman Airlines. He had heard, from schoolmates who emigrated and came home to tell about it, tales of abundance and greatness in places with names like St. Cloud, Minnesota.

Morning after morning, sometimes at 4 a.m., Rais joined the visa line outside the American embassy compound. Sometimes, three or four hours in, with the line finally slithering forward, he would learn that he was too far back. On other occasions, he got into the building, only to have his interviewer scoff at the notion that any young, unmarried Bangladeshi would actually study and come back to his country. To work for Biman? Yeah, sure. Visa rejected. Then again. And again. And again. And again. And again. And again.

In the meanwhile, Rais took advantage of his early adoption of technology, writing a pleading e-mail to a U.S. State Department official whose name he found on the Internet—one Cynthia Haley. His bureaucrat uncle helped him draft the message in the government-sounding language that such people use, and it elicited an encouraging but noncommittal reply: something circular and elusive along the lines of "We encourage you to go again if you feel you still have enough reason to go and apply for a visa." Still, the fact of a reply did impress him. And when he returned to the embassy for his eighth visa interview, he found that the man of seven rejections was gone, replaced by a new officer who seemed impressed by Rais's military background and his score on the TOEFL, or Test of English as a Foreign Language. He asked about the young man's dream. To study aviation, Rais said. All the wiser for his previous visits, he downplayed the IT idea and added, "So I can return to fly for Biman."

"Well, good luck with your dream, Mr. Bhuiyan," the officer said. Visa approved.

Rais came out of the embassy into the syrupy Dhaka air and went to the home of relatives who lived close by. He asked for their prayer rug, dropped to the floor, and gave God his thanks. At home later that day, he realized that he would have to give his mother two pieces of news. The first was that he had continued pursuing a visa even after he ceased to tell her about it, since the rejections had pained her. The second was that he had gotten it. He bent and touched her feet. His father seemed skeptical at first, then incredulous at his son's way of operating.

Wonderful news—for everyone but Abida. Now she would join the trail of people, places, and things floating in Rais's wake. The first thing she said was "You did it!" But her feelings were "sweet and sour" at best, Rais admitted. "You're leaving me," she said, after behaving with due pride. She was afraid that her mother would exploit her loneliness and turn her away from Rais. He remembers her warning: "I'm not saying that I'm negative, but I'm just feeling that maybe I won't be able to see you anymore. I'm having this feeling in the back of my mind that something's going to happen and then we'll never be able to be together."

To a man of Rais's disposition, this fear could seem like just another hurdle to jump. The anxiety seemed normal to him, even necessary. "That's a good concern," he told her. "Because you love me so much, you don't want to lose me. So that's why it's coming in your mind. But you know me: I'm not going to go there and just forget about you. I'm coming back." He would return, inshallah, within half a year to visit, he pledged. When he finished studying, he would fly home, persuade her mother just as he had the air secretary, and marry Abida grandly for the community to witness, maybe at the Air Force mess, perhaps on New Year's Eve, and in the particular way they'd discussed, with lots of food given to the poor and no gifts accepted. And there in Dhaka they would weave their nest.

Then again the plan changed.

The change began in a cramped apartment in New York, on the immigrant landing strip of Woodside, Queens. The area was thick with newcomers and with the longing for other places, the stores hawking phone cards and flags and nostalgic home-style sauces. Rais lived with a group of other men from Bangladesh, on one floor of a house near the corner of 59th Street and 37th Avenue. It was under the flight path into LaGuardia's Runway 4-22, and Rais often found himself unable to sleep after 5 a.m. or thereabouts, thanks to the roaring, house-quaking engines above. He and his three flatmates, whom he'd met through Bengali circles in New York and two of whom he happened to know of back home, first rented the basement for about $1,000 a month for all of them. Then they upgraded to the top floor for $1,500 or so.

The guys teased Rais for his phone calls to Abida, seeking what Rais jokingly called "cook support." When it was his turn to feed the house, he would sometimes dial her from in front of the stove, asking for help. Abida taught him how to curb the pungency of buffalo fish or tilapia using turmeric, lime, and water. She instructed him to hold his knife above the stove flame before cutting onions, in order not to cry.

He had finally arrived in New York in 1999, twenty-five years old, with a vague interest in IT but firm plans to study commercial aviation, which was more in keeping with his background. At first, he worked a series of part-time jobs to make ends meet. His flat-mate who worked at a gas station told Rais about an opportunity doing the graveyard shift there: Rais could take daytime classes and study behind bulletproof glass at night. So Rais did that for a few months, changing buses twice to get to work, sleeping just two or three hours a night. When that job drained him, he found another short-lived one at a copy store in Manhattan. He also tried being a busboy at a thriving French restaurant in Midtown but burned out after a single twelve-hour shift spent entirely on his feet.

Even before Rais could enroll in an aviation class, a friend of his, also ex–Air Force and now in New York, tried to convince him to switch to IT. He knew Rais loved computers and coding. He argued to Rais that technology was turning so many professions, including in aviation, obsolete. Why train to be a pilot when computers will soon fly planes? Much better to learn how to operate those computers.

When Rais had a goal clenched in his jaw, no one could tear it from him. But for someone so gritty, he was also easily persuaded by advice not to release an ambition so much as upgrade to a juicier one. So it was with his friend's suggestion: "I thought that would be nice, if I could go start a different career, different track." Rais was one of those fleet-footed men who look in the mirror and see only future incarnations of themselves. He decided to enroll in a full-time course in computer studies at Pace University, housed in a giant concrete compound near City Hall in Lower Manhattan.

But the visa that Rais had—the M-1, for vocational training—was different from the F-1 he needed to enroll as a full-time student. He had to leave the country and reapply. When he did so, after crossing over to Vancouver late in 1999, the embassy rejected him. He returned to New York for a few months, stranded in his plans.

Some friends of his had applied for something called the Diversity Visa. It was part of a program to admit immigrants from places that sent relatively few people to America. The program employed a lottery, choosing about fifty thousand winners out of several million applicants. The chance of making it was, on average, less than 1 percent. For those who did, the visa paved the way to a green card and permanent residency. Rais decided to apply.

Application submitted, he returned home to Bangladesh in February 2000. He had hoped it might be possible to marry Abida at this time. However, Abida's sister had died during childbirth just before he arrived. "That's not the time for going to wedding approach," Rais concluded.

Rais sensed that Abida's feelings for him remained strong, but her mother continued to lobby her otherwise. It was strange: Rais went over to their house on this trip, and the mother fed him and was unfailingly kind to his face. Behind the scenes, for reasons he never could understand (or perhaps didn't want to), she was pulling Abida in another direction. Abida, though, seemed resilient in her devotion. The young couple pined for each other, and on this visit a day without meeting gave them a sinking feeling. Rais's bedroom window looked into the kitchen window at Abida's, and Rais often checked to see if he could find Abida cooking and say hello through the layers of glass. On this visit, as before he left, Rais hung a few magnets on a nail on his door, where Abida could see them, as his signal to her that he was out of the house. He would remove the magnets when he returned, so that she knew he was safe. Abida, too, placed magnets—on the iron bars girding the kitchen window—and removed them upon returning home.

Their love renewed but a wedding date still elusive, Rais returned to New York. Out of nowhere, he soon learned that he had won a Diversity Visa. "A new chapter opened that day for me," he said. It was more than just a visa. In the hands of a man so ready for reinvention, it was an invitation to a wholesale change of life plan. Student visas, by definition, only allowed one to study in the country. Rais would have had to return home after finishing, or get an employer-sponsored visa in order to work and remain in the States; and, since they were unmarried, it would have been hard to get a visa for Abida. The Diversity Visa created a path both for his spouse to join him in America and for him to work indefinitely. And because Rais so easily reimagined himself, he resolved now that he would make a life in America. He would forget about Biman, fly home to marry Abida late in 2001, whisk her to New York, and make an American existence with her.

Without Abida's having much say in the matter, her life trajectory was swerving. And now it swerved again.

Back in New York, Rais decided to go on a trip. Before leaving for Dhaka, he had received a phone call from a man it took him a moment to place. The man called himself Salim and said he'd been a few years ahead of Rais at Sylhet. Rais remembered now: he'd been a friendly guy. Salim had heard of Rais's living in America from a common friend. On the phone Salim was instantly familiar in the American way, and he suggested that Rais pay him a visit in Dallas, Texas. Rais didn't know it yet, but in Salim's line of work, one was ever seeking fresh, hardworking immigrants whom you could trust.

The thing about Dallas, Rais found when he visited Salim, was that the bathrooms there were as big as his bedroom in New York. The city somehow enchanted him. New York was, if you thought about it, not unlike Dhaka—full of life, yes, but basically an overgrown bazaar, suffocating and dense. It was great for a single man who wanted only to work. But Dallas offered what Rais had begun to dream of as he drew closer to becoming a family man: space, freedom, twelve-lane roads. Rents were cheap and taxes low. Computer classes were abundant. It might not have appealed to him had he not won that Diversity Visa, but his calculations were now for building a family and for the long haul. America was no longer a training ground; it was home. In Texas, he could afford to study and pay his rent while working on the side; he could build a life for two and, with luck, more.

Not long after his visit, he called Salim from New York. "If I move to Texas, what I have there?" he asked. "How you can help me?" Salim, as it turned out, had much to offer. He and his brother were businessmen in Dallas, and they were opening a new gas station there. If Rais moved down, he could work as one of Salim's partners; if he did well, he might own a gas station of his own before long. It was not glamorous, perhaps, but it would earn Rais money for the wedding and his studies. "Like a team, we'll help each other," Salim told Rais. There was enough trust between them that they didn't talk about money. Rais planned to live in Salim's house upon arriving.

The Dallas opportunity was Rais's seventh victory in a row. What a streak it had been: Sylhet, then the Air Force, then the escape from the Air Force, then Abida, then a first visa and an improbable second, and now Dallas, Texas. All this helped Rais not to mind the long, smelly month of purging trash and scrubbing floors at the Buckner Food Mart, which had tumbled into disrepair before Salim bought it. Rais didn't mind the petty thieves and the deadbeat refuelers; he even got used to the guns. His eyes were, as ever, on the horizon. He would save up for the flight back to Dhaka in October, and finally the wedding would happen. He told Abida, "You do some groundwork with your parents, so that they should not be blocking and blocking. Once I come, it should be, 'OK, then let's get the business done.' "

Even amid this excitement, Abida wanted Rais to know of her very real concerns. "First thing she was telling that, 'That's too far from

New York. Do you really want to go to Texas?' Back home, Texas was always wild, wild, with lot of gunshot, cowboys, this and that—from all the Western movies." She urged him to rethink it: "Do you have to go? Can't you stay in New York?"

But she also knew how little she knew, and Rais was adamant that this was the right move for them. He would have preferred New York were he thinking just for himself, he explained to her. The whole point of moving south was to build a life suitable for a family—their family. Rais had convinced himself, if not yet Abida, that he was going to Texas for her.

✳

Rais was handsome in a way that didn't impose on a room, with a commanding nose, a full head of jet-black hair, a prominent forehead, and pecans for eyes, which stared intensely even when they smiled. His shoulders plunged humbly instead of spreading out, as though wary of hogging space. He was solidly built, but slender in the way that makes mothers want to cook things.

On the second Tuesday of September, four months into his Texan life, he was at home on a rare day off. He learned that jetliners of the kind he once dreamed of commanding had pierced into that pair of towers he knew so well. Rais was a movie buff who had the ability to see the cinematic analog to almost anything, and the sight of the first tower aflame made him marvel at what those Hollywood types can do. When the second was hit, it chilled him. He thought of how often he had tried to ascend those buildings but been thwarted by the lines.

For the next many days, Rais watched the television throb with rage. He overheard customers venting their anger at people from places whose names they had never pronounced. He remembered them saying things like "Foreigners are taking over our country" and "Kill all the Muslims in the Middle East." Some of them, seeing a brown-skinned man behind the counter, pressed Rais for his opinion of recent events. He sought to affirm their outrage and partake of it, without getting into too much discussion. What he thought, above all, was that the men who did this were not Muslims, but—and to him the distinction mattered—"people who practice Islam." They claimed to be Muslim and chanted "Allah" when they prayed and had maybe even gone to Mecca. But in Rais's vision of faith, they were automatic heathens, disqualified by their deed.

Some long, hot days passed. On the morning of September 17, scanning the *Dallas Morning News*, Rais saw a story that tensed his chest, under the headline "Fatal Shooting Draws FBI." A man grilling burgers over at Mom's Grocery, two and a half miles down on Elam, had been shot and killed under a WE APPRECIATE YOUR BUSINESS sign. He was the owner of the store, this man, and apparently he was a Muslim—a Pakistani named Waqar Hasan. The bullet had entered his right cheek, pierced through his skull, and stopped in the neck muscles behind his left ear. That much the police knew, but they had little else. "No motive, no robbery, no suspects, no witnesses," the police report said. Or, as Rais put it, "No one knew who did, and how, and why did."

In the nights after the murder, Rais's mind churned with violent dreams. The setting was always the Buckner Food Mart. He went to Salim with some constructive suggestions. Why not install a real security camera in the store, instead of the fake one they used as a deterrent? Why not maintain two employees in the store at all times?

"It's just a dream," Salim said. He sought to calm Rais down. He and his brother knew what they were doing, and they weren't millionaires. Who would pay for these refinements? It was natural that some angry customers would visit the store. They'd been attacked, after all. They didn't mean any harm. The best thing was to keep your head down. Salim gave Rais some easy-to-follow advice: "Try to stay away from any kind of conversation with people." The boss made his friend a deal: no more nights, OK? From now on, Rais would only work mornings. That sounded doable. In Rais's hierarchy of sentiments, loyalty trumped fear.

✳

SEPTEMBER 21 DAWNED dreary. The monsoon from back home seemed to have followed Rais to Dallas. The big Texas sky crouched low and gray over the station. Unpleasant as it was to people, the half inch of rain brought the soil tremendous relief after a summer that had baked it mercilessly.

Rais had opened the store that morning and would ordinarily have worked until noon. Then a colleague would take over, and Rais could go off to Friday prayers. That colleague had quit a few days earlier, though, so Rais was stuck there all day. So much for the mornings-only deal. Salim was in and out of the store. On a typical day, he might help Rais during the busy morning shift, then drive over to his brother's construction site, returning to the store in the evening. On this particular day, he came in for less than an hour, then left to pick up some inventory.

Around half past noon, at last, a customer appeared. It was the barber from the Strictly Cuts next door. A tall guy—six foot six or thereabouts. He did his usual American-style lunch of chips and a soda; on occasion, he threw in cookies or candy for a treat. He said something to Rais about all the tension in the city: a lot of people were coming into the barbershop and saying bad things about other people and groups. "Stay safe, man," the barber said.

The barber appeared to bring luck. Within a minute of his parting, the door opened again—yet another customer defying the rain. The man in the entrance immediately seized Rais's attention because of the red bandana around his mouth. He wore a wife-beater, shorts, a black baseball cap, and wraparound sunglasses that concealed the very parts of his face Rais might otherwise have probed for context. His arms were like massive hams, painted 360 degrees around with inscriptions. He was holding something black and shiny, which he seemed to wish to conceal from the people outside but reveal to the man inside—to Rais. Rais's institutional memory was improving: "I knew that this time he was not going to sell it to me, because nobody sells guns in the store. They come to rob you."

Now the man was walking into the store, toward the counter; now he was just feet from Rais on the other side. Proximity revealed that, yes, that shiny black thing was a gun—a double-barreled pistol, it seemed. The man pointed it at Rais's head.

"Oh, no. Again robbing today?" Rais thought. Oh, Texas—it was becoming a major irritation. "I know the drill," Rais said, "that I have to open the cash register, open the cash, give him the money, and just stay safe." *Click-whoosh*: the register opened. Rais removed $150 or so and placed it on the counter. He made the perfunctory noise about please-take-the-money-but-don't-hurt-me. He knew his lines by heart now; he was getting good.

But in this play the other player seemed not to know his part. The money did not faze him. All he said was "Where are you from?"

It was obvious to Rais that this question had very little to do with robbing. Maybe he hadn't heard the man right through his bandana. "Excuse me?" Rais asked faintly. Even as he said this, he felt his spine become an icicle. "Oh my gosh, he's not here for money," Rais said to himself. He took a step or two backward and turned his face away from the man.

Then millions of bees came out of nowhere and, as though their last earthly hive had just been destroyed, began what felt like a syn-chronized mass stinging of Rais's face. He heard the explosion after-ward. The melody of his "Excuse me?" had been revealing enough. At first, he couldn't bring himself to believe it was a gunshot. "I wanted to give myself benefit of doubt that I was not shot," he said. Rais tried to reassure himself: "Maybe he shot some drink or some-thing. Not me; I was not shot." He briefly wondered if he might be hallucinating.

It took the sight of blood, pouring from his head as if from a faucet, to know what had happened. He screamed "Mom" to no one. He had the wherewithal to cup his hands around his head: "I thought that my brain was going to come out any moment—first blood, now the brain." But the soldier within him couldn't stop telling himself that this didn't make any sense. Blood was spilling out of his head, which meant he'd been shot, but a bullet fired into a man's head from an arm's length or two away will end him at once. Not only was Rais alive; he was somehow also standing. Why in God's name was he standing? He considered the notion that he had already died and this was the transition to the Afterward.

Rais now saw that the tattooed man was still in the store, just standing there, gazing at his prey. What had somehow failed to occur the first time would surely occur the second. "If I don't pretend I'm dying, maybe he might shoot me again, to make sure that I'm dead," Rais reasoned. He had to play dead. He plunged to the floor, into a small pool of his own blood.

His mind was spinning through a reel of images: his beloved mother and father, his seven brothers and sisters, his lovely Abida. He had promised her he wouldn't be gone long. Each picture lingered for a few seconds, as though in one of those laptop slideshows. The faces were somber and drooping, looking at him but unable to help, darkly resigned. They seemed to be on the other side of an invisible wall, watching him die. That he recognized this flickering of images from the movies—much as his icicle spine had accurately forecast danger a short while earlier—left Rais especially worried: this was the Hollywood sign for looming death. He was vanishing. He could tell. He saw the pointed tombstones of a Muslim graveyard. He saw his own grave. The horizon drew closer. How many seconds were left? What a life it had been. Where-all it had taken him.

He was thinking of his God. A part of him wanted to believe that this, like everything else, was just a trial. He wondered which of His verses God most longed to hear right now. He decided to hedge his bets: "I wasn't sure which one is more effective at this moment. Just keep on reciting one by one all the verses." He whispered to God, from a floor wet with his own juices, lines from surahs known since childhood:

He is Lord of the two Easts and Lord of the two Wests:
Then which of the favors of your Lord will ye deny?
He has let free the two bodies of flowing water, meeting together:
Between them is a barrier which they do not transgress:
Then which of the favors of your Lord will ye deny?
Out of them come Pearls and Coral:
Then which of the favors of your Lord will ye deny?
And His are the Ships sailing smoothly through the seas, lofty as mountains:
Then which of the favors of your Lord will ye deny?
All that is on earth will perish:
But will abide forever the face of thy Lord—full of Majesty, Bounty, and Honor.

Could this God be bargained with? Was this God like the shops in America or the ones back home? Rais wanted to cut a deal. He was a sinner, he confessed into the sky, but in the name of his Prophet and for the sake of his mother, he begged for mercy. "At least don't make my mom sad," he asked God. His draining mind offered a quid pro quo: "If you give me my life back today, I will definitely dedicate my life for others, especially for the poor, the deprived, and the needy—I will, I promise. But give me a chance. There are a lot of people that love me. It will be too hard for them to get this message, to see that I'm gone today. Even for the sake of them—for the sake of my mother—please give me a chance."

The door made its closing sound. The tattooed man was gone. Somehow Rais found the vigor to stand, although he was fading: "I was thinking that I don't know how many seconds I have before I pass away." He thought about calling 911, but once again his knowledge of Hollywood returned to him. Weren't there so many films where some guy is dying and calls 911 and, before he can give full details, collapses? "If I call, staying in the store, and if I pass out, then many a times I saw in the movies that they took the phone but then never could call. Someone saying, 'Hello, hello. This is 911.' So I was thinking that I should not stay." He needed someone nearby to help him. He seized a cordless phone and staggered out of the door, on which his hand left a red imprint. A blood trail followed him to the adjoining Strictly Cuts. When he entered, the sight of him caused customers to panic, some of them running for the back door. Rais managed to grab a barber and begged him to call for an ambulance.

While the barber called, Rais caught a glimpse of himself in the mirror. He saw now that he had been destroyed. His face was perforated in what felt like a hundred places and oozing from every hole. His right eye was shut, caked with blood: "I looked at the mirror and I saw, it's like all those horror characters in the horror films, with blood pouring, bleeding all over my face. This olive-colored T-shirt was blackish with the blood." Because vanity is among the more resilient organs, Rais was astonished by his appearance: "I said, 'Wow—the way I look right now.' I was a beautiful young guy." He kept telling himself Death was mistaken. It was too early to bow.

He feared that sitting down and waiting for the ambulance could be fatal. "Now what?" he thought to himself. "I don't know how many minutes—how long they will take for an ambulance to come. In the meantime, should I just sit down on the floor? Should I just lie down? If I lie down, sit down, it means that's it—I'm giving it up, and maybe I will pass away. So instead of sitting tight, I should keep myself positive, energetic, and keep on doing something besides reciting Koran—also do some physical thing that will keep me energized. So I was running in the parking lot, back and forth—as if the ambulance is coming from this way, if the ambulance is coming from that way. Which way is the ambulance coming? I was in a craze—that ambulance, where is ambulance? Because I know I have to get treated. I have the phone in my hand—the cordless phone from the store—thinking that they might even call."

When the ambulance arrived minutes later and its back doors opened, Rais was standing just outside them waiting to board. Then he was on a stretcher inside under the medics' faces, twirling through the city's pretzel highways. He remembers worrying that the medics weren't doing enough quickly enough. "Please, start treating me faster," he begged. He was fighting the urge to sleep. Sleep, he knew, was the shortcut to death. The pictures of his family kept cycling through his brain, but sometimes now he saw just gray. He could feel that his eyes were dimming, swollen shut by the scalding pellets; his mind was dulling. He was losing the power to think. He couldn't see. He forced himself to stay conscious for as long as he could. He was aware of being in a hospital. Voices above him spoke urgently about him. Then the world faded to black.

✳

A TELEPHONE RANG IN Dhaka. Rais's father was bound for the bathroom when he fetched the cordless handset. Your son has been shot, a voice said. The voice sounded far away, but it spoke Bengali. Your boy was shot in the face. He is in hospital. Please continuously pray. Dial tone.

The father, an aging diabetic whose control of his body was starting to desert him, took a moment to process what he'd just heard. His bladder was telling him that he needed, no matter what, to proceed with his bathroom visit. Then he would come out and inform the family about the call. In the bathroom, he collapsed. It was a stroke, triggered by shock, and it took more than an hour for the family to notice his absence. When they found him, the panic about his condition was interrupted by some dark and cryptic news he wanted to share.

It sounded—coming as it did from a frail, unwell man—like some kind of mix-up. Then the reality of it sank in. Then tears and screaming. In the ensuing days, Texas sent them no more news, and the family realized that they stupidly had no phone numbers there besides Rais's, which wasn't working. They could only assume the worst: the boy had been shot in the head, after all. The news rippled out through the neighborhood. Friends and relatives began to arrive at the house, seeking updates, offering words of consolation to go with the beef curries and rice they brought to spare the family from cooking in sorrow. Slowly the Bhuiyans pivoted from waiting to grieving. Little Ripon was lost, torn from his sweet bride before she could know him. *Why did we let him go?* they kept asking themselves, until the question spent itself.

The Chore

Here sits the Arab Slayer, for what he did we
Should make him our mayor.
He has no regret for what he has done,
Killin Arabs is just half the fun.
Patriotic yes indeed, a true American, a special breed.
Did what other's wanted to do, did the chore for me and you.
They said he was blue, but all he could see was Red, so he shot one
  of them Arabs in the head.
So all you American's let's stand tall and let's not forget the man
  who's dream was to kill em all.

—Mark Anthony Stroman

On the afternoon of October 4, Tom Boston was driving home to pick up a refrigerator to bring back to A Paint and Body Shop. This was the name of the paint and body shop he owned up on Presidential Drive in northern Dallas, surrounded by a great many other businesses likewise dedicated to the repair and primping of vehicles. The shop's straight-shooting name somehow spoke to Tom's self-conception. He thought of himself with pride as a sober, boring, married isle of a man in a sea of "loopty-loops": meth heads and coke fiends; guys who couldn't keep a job longer than a couple of months; guys who made the mistake of dating strippers instead of just watching them strip; guys who became so familiar with the Texas Department of Criminal Justice that they took to calling it TDC, the way you call a buddy by his initials. Tom liked being better than these men, truth be told, but he also enjoyed using his body shop to reform them.

"I'm the first guy to take a guy that's had a past that nobody else will give a break," he said. It was charity-cum-hobby: "I take personal enjoyment in bringing someone in who's a real fuckup and trying to turn them around. And I've done that with so many people over the years, and there's been a small handful—a *small* handful— who have come and been real fuckups, and I can look back and say, 'Wow. The fucker really turned out to be somebody.' "

The reality, as Tom figured it, was that if you ran a body shop in the Dallas metroplex in this precarious new time—after the globalization came in and sucked jobs down the rat hole to China; after the affirmative action and political correctness took hold and you basically had to be a minority or woman to get ahead; after the wives and mothers went off to school and work and left the boys in the dust; after homes without fathers became the new normal for all Americans, not just one color or community—then the reality was that these were the kind of up-and-down, fate-battered men available to you. "I keep them around me because they make me look good," Tom joked.

While driving home that afternoon for his refrigerator, Tom noticed a hurricane of activity around the Shell station at John West and Big Town in the suburb of Mesquite. It was the last pump on his regular route home and where he invariably stocked up on gas and Pall Malls. He knew the couple that ran the place—the Patels, from India, who had run it since the early 1990s—and he even recognized their children. He wondered what the squad cars and yellow tape and camera crews were about.

He was ruggedly handsome, with a face coated by gold stubble and a hard, athletic body that was slowly melting into middle age. A chunky three-stone ring fortified his left pinky. He had an inbuilt thousand-yard stare. He was a former pro race car driver; a door from one of his old cars hung in the body shop. He had come to Texas from Ohio in the 1980s. He liked to remind people that, unlike the screwballs who worked for him, he had gone to college—studied theology there. He was doing this work out of choice. It was part of his heroic self-conception. He also didn't hesitate to tell people that his friends often flattered him by saying he should run for some kind of public office.

Crossing the station again on his return trip, refrigerator in tow, Tom pulled over. It was just before three in the afternoon. He asked a Channel 23 reporter on the scene what was going on. A shooting, the reporter said. The owner's dead.

The copper-wrapped bullet entered Vasudev Patel just above his left collarbone. It tore through the left side of his body—through his three uppermost ribs, then through his lung, then through three lower ribs, stopping just under the skin of his lower back. This suggests that he was crouching when it happened, bowing to his taker. It had happened earlier on that morning of October 4, around 7:30. The police found him lying on the floor in his own blood, perfectly still, beside the black pistol that hadn't saved him and an off-the-hook phone receiver. He was forty-nine, short, and mustachioed, with black-and-white stubble and a single umbrella of a brow. The last words he heard, according to the surveillance tape, were "Open the register now, or I will blow your brains out."

Tom was dazed: "I was like, 'Oh my God, can't believe that.' Hopped back in my truck, went on." A strange thought crept into his head shortly thereafter, though, and he couldn't shake it. It wasn't based on anything he knew firsthand, just some things he had heard . . . but really, what were the odds that one guy he randomly knew from one part of his life would kill another guy he randomly knew from another part of his life, even though he was sure they wouldn't know each other? "I said, 'No fucking way. Not even possible. It'd be a billion to one, zillion to one—who the hell? No way,'" Boston said. "Didn't even fathom the connection. About an hour and a half had gone by, and I couldn't get it out of my head. That's when I called a buddy of mine who I had raced with."

The buddy was a big-shot prosecutor downtown named Paul Macaluso. Tom told him that he was calling about the Shell station murder. He didn't have a formal tip or anything like that. Just a hunch that he wanted to get out of the way. It was more that he wanted to make sure it wasn't his friend Mark Stroman than to suggest that it was. He and Mark didn't keep in touch as much as before, but in recent weeks and months, he had heard second- and third-hand about Mark's saying some things about Arabs and fooling with guns; Mo Phillips had said something about a string of robberies that Mark was maybe involved with. It hadn't been all that alarming to Boston, since he had known Stroman to blabber about the darker peoples ever since they met in the mid-1990s. Boston had long ago convinced himself that Stroman was a wannabe and didn't mean much by it, but now he wanted to make sure. It was the duty of the kind of responsible citizen he fancied himself to be.

The Shell murder wasn't in Paul's jurisdiction, but he offered to make some calls. Eventually he found out that they were processing a surveillance tape from the store.

Tom told his friend to call back if by chance the tape showed a guy with two hog thighs for arms, decorated all over with tattoos.

*

WHEN TOM BOSTON hired Mark Stroman in '94 and took him under his wing, he offered the job with a condition: "If you're going to be in a position where you've got to meet with people on a daily basis in the front office, you're going to have to cover those up." The "those" were Stroman's rambling tattoos.

The body shop was in the sparse northern margins of the city, in a building typical of the neighborhood: a low, wide matchbox that clutched the ground and avoided having too many windows. Tom remembered Mark coming in off the street one day and filling out an application. He said he'd been working over at a body shop named The Body Shop. He'd started as a detailer over there and rose to the rank of manager. But he and a bunch of the guys weren't happy with the place. There was no room for expansion, he said. He wanted to run his own crew, but he'd take anything at this point. He was straightforward with Tom about his prison record, which he perhaps didn't realize was a bonus for a boss who fancied himself a reformer. Mark was bubbly and energetic, with a drive that Tom had always found missing from the industry. He had smoldering red hair and energetic eyes and ruddy, protruding cheeks and an easy, goofy charisma, and those sprawling tattoos.

Although they ranked not far apart in the layers of Dallas society, Tom and Mark thought of themselves in starkly different terms. Tom saw himself as better than his surroundings—an educated man who owned a body shop by choice. Mark, by contrast, had few of Tom's pretensions. Unlike Tom, he took pride in being a run-of-the-mill guy with run-of-the-mill ideas and tastes. There was a widely circulated manifesto of sorts, sometimes called the "Bikers Creed," that Stroman liked and sent around to friends. He gave it the alternative title "American Me," and it gave a flavor of his red-blooded self-conception.

The "proud American" described by the creed was a patriot who liked his cars, motorcycles, and ladies domestic. He relished a burger and fries like everyone else and drank regular coffee, not the fancy stuff that tasted like pancakes or fruit. He enjoyed the smell of rain, of bacon, and of auto fumes. He made no apologies for his love of naked women, in print or in person, and thought Hugh Hefner more of a revolutionary than Washington, Jefferson, or Lincoln. He liked country music and hated child molesters. He continued to say "Yes, sir" and "No, sir," no matter how old he got. He confessed to being confused about sex at times but was far from sexually confused. He believed that most of us do the best we can with what we're given and usually get what we deserve, and that just holding on could be as important as winning. He tended to trust his country more than his government. He thought America—its blood and culture and soul—ought to be preserved as it was, not perennially remade. He believed that if you didn't like America, you were free to leave it.

As it happened, this bleeding heart of an ex-con called Stroman had come to Tom Boston at the right time. "Managers in body shops are usually good for about a year, and then they either get comfortable or burn out, or they want to go someplace else," Tom said. "So I was getting rid of one at the time that was in that situation and was looking for guys—somebody to run underneath me." What he needed in particular was a good estimator: a guy who could be personable when customers came in, who could type the estimate into the software form they used, who didn't need it explained that insurance will reimburse one hour of labor for a dent the size of a quarter and four hours for something as big as your palm. When Stroman turned up, Tom sensed that he had found his guy. Mark was hungry and wanted to learn. Tom hired him and quickly discovered him to be "one of the most ambitious individuals that I have ever met," a climber in a pit of screwy laterals.

Tom trained his new protégé by taking him on sales missions, which meant wining and dining guys at Thrifty and Alamo and the other rental agencies, so that they'd think of A Paint and Body Shop when customers brought back banged-up vehicles. It might be lunch or dinner at the Sheraton by the airport or after-hours at the titty bar. Tom would manage the selling while his twenty-five-year-old apprentice, dressed in a white shirt and slacks, sat beside him in silence. Soon Mark had the handle of it, though, and he began making sales calls on his own. He took over the rental business, driving out to the airport most days to do estimates and then, via walkie-talkie, coordinating pickup and delivery of the vehicles by his colleagues. It wasn't simple work; you had to keep a lot of moving parts in your head at once. Stroman was making $500, $600 a week. Aside from a few red flags that Tom Boston somehow minimized at the time—like the time they lost the Dollar rental account because a company hotshot happened to be visiting Dallas, he happened to be black, and Mark happened to call him a "fucking nigger"—the boss was thrilled with his new hire.

Mark proved himself a natural leader of the shop's ordinarily anarchic men. In the cavernous garage, the guys listened to shrieking guitar orgies all day while spray-painting and forklifting and undenting the exteriors of cars, pickups, and semis. They either lunched out or ordered in to the back room, which was routinely thick with cigarette smoke. Mark had, as promised, brought guys over from The Body Shop. He ran the front office for a while and coordinated separate day and night shifts, which allowed the shop to start running around the clock. Over time, Tom gathered that Mark had wanted to leave the other place because he was trying to shake his old heat-seeking ways. The life of boozing and girls and fine powders was OK for the screwup he'd been when he surfaced from prison in '91, all of twenty-one and utterly alone; it was sustained by knowing the wrong guys at the last job. But now Mark had a wife and a daughter whom he bragged about to Tom. He wanted to show them that things could be different.

For a year or so, Mark earned steady checks, led a squad of men, and rose in Tom's esteem. Then somehow he reverted. "Mark started going off in the other direction again," Tom said. "He had money, and he was going out and partying with the guys—kind of leaving the old lady at home." Tom observed that Mark handled his work fine during the day but was running with what he called "radical" people or "druggy troublemakers" after hours. Tom claimed to be shocked to learn that Stroman's change of heart had been contagious among the staff, turning his body shop into a kind of drug den: "At that time, I didn't really know. I was kind of green when it came to all that. I felt stupid after a while, because then I found out what everyone was doing at my place of employment. I was like, 'What the hell?' I didn't know that shit was going on. There was ecstasy, there was acid, there was cocaine, there was meth. There was everything.

"Here I'm a fricking race car driver, so I'm lean and clean, and I didn't stay into that loop," Tom said. His emphasis could sound a bit like protesting too much: "I mean, smoking dope is one thing. At noon, employees would smoke dope. It's like cigarettes to me. I never really considered that a problem drug, so to speak."

Tom remembered a turning point in Stroman's tenure: the time one of his radical friends, a guy named Phillip with long red hair, shot himself or got shot—one way or another, the guy ended up slumped in a bathtub. With Phillip gone, Mark felt hollow and lost. Tom remembered him getting a new tattoo to commemorate his friend. He and some guys went down to the grave site, drank some beers and made memories. The incident stuck in Tom's mind. "I guess that was the time that I really saw that he just started going off on a different path," Tom said.

It was around this period, '96 or so, that Mark's wife, Shawna, walked out with their young daughter. It was said that she took much of the apartment with her. She'd been threatening it for a while and had warned him to straighten up. At the start, she hadn't known what a drug head she'd taken on.

Mark couldn't hide his devastation from Tom: he was "broke up about his wife, losing his kid—pretty broke up. Very depressed. Sad and depressed. Seemed like he didn't give a shit about anything anymore." Mark fell down a manhole of depression. At times, his sadness exploded into untamable anger. Like the time that restaurant cook came in with his truck. "Mark had brought the guy in, that's how I met him," Tom said. "Did the custom paint job. But apparently he was one of Mark's drug connects at the time, and they got crossways." Two weeks after Tom finished the job, he heard that Mark, still reeling from the breakup, had stuffed a fuel-soaked rag in the truck and "burned it to the ground."

Tom also remembered Mark starting to work out at a nearby gym known for its performance-enhancing expertise, and the boss suspected that his employee's growing temper and the tension in his face were related to that: "He was really short and just real pissy and real aggressive. I guess that's when he was starting to do the working out. He was going to pump iron, but he was doing steroids."

One of Tom Boston's other reform projects, also at the body shop, was a guy named Mitch Fayette—ponytailed, except for the long strings of blond hair dangling down to frame his face, and with a penchant for T-shirts cut off at the shoulders. He was about the same age as Mark and partied with him through the '90s. They had been together through all of it. But after Shawna left, Mark's behavior started scaring Mitch, who was no pansy. He remembered Mark doing lots of drugs, staying up till tomorrow night after night, hanging with the lowlifes and the bikers and people of that nature. Mark had long dabbled in chemicals, but this was more extreme. "He was hurting on the inside, and because he was hurting on the inside, he looked for a way to escape. And he started doing drugs, dating titty dancers, and that leads you down a vicious life of staying up till two o'clock in the morning and picking them up and partying with them all night and going right back to work the next morning. And then it became a vicious cycle like that. Life began to get out of control," Mitch said.

A propensity for fighting that Stroman was trying to shake when he came to Tom Boston—a tendency he had battled since childhood and then managed to suppress—now seemed to return. "If he liked you, you were golden," Mitch said. "But he was a rude, aggressive person. He would fight at the drop of a hat. Didn't even matter—didn't care how big they were, who they were, or what was going on. And he told me the same way out of his mouth, he said, 'You can't do anything worse to me than's already been done to me. They locked me up; they kicked me in the corner like a bad dog—you know, with people getting raped and killed all around. So I ain't going back there,' he said, 'no matter what.' " The "there" that Stroman spoke of was prison.

Sometimes, Mitch said, Mark supplemented this vow with a pledge to die in what he called "suicide by police officer." Were he ever to do something worthy of arrest—and it was not an unreasonable assumption that he would someday—Mark wouldn't go back to prison. He had planned it all out: he would shoot at the officers, forcing them to shoot him. And it would be over.

Tom was sympathetic to TDC alumni like Stroman, as perhaps he had to be in this line of work: "They are a convicted felon, and they're screwed up for life. They can't get a job. They can't do anything to better themselves. How do they expect them to do that when they've got a brand on them permanently for the rest of their life?"

Stroman was never direct with Mitch or with Tom about what had happened in prison. But this talk of suicide by police officer and other offhand assertions made clear that Mark's two stints inside—each a matter of months on sentences that were supposed to last years, until luck and prison overcrowding spared him—had scarred him in unknowable ways. They had, depending on whom you asked, either turned him into a racist or amplified a preexisting hostility—although Tom always knew it was just talk. Suspected, at least. "That's where he really got his racist stuff, because if you're a Mexican in there, you better be with Mexicans," Tom said. "If you're black, you better be with blacks. It gets real gangy."

Mitch, having known the same prisons, described it this way: "You could be the nicest white person in the world, not ever hate, not ever have any racial hate at all, and if you're thrown in that environment, you're gonna learn to hate." He told a story he had heard about a black man who goes to prison: a great athlete who talked like the "whitest guy you'll ever meet." When he arrived in prison, he got to talking with a white man. A black inmate kicked the chair out from under him and warned him: "You need to get in where you fit in." When the riots and fighting start, he told the newbie, you will understand. Mitch said, "It's a different world in there, and it's all politics."

So maybe it started in prison, or maybe it predated prison—Tom Boston only got to know Mark in his twenties. Whatever its origins, Stroman developed a propensity to call people he didn't enjoy things like "nigger-loving Jew," whatever that was. Some of Stroman's relatives refused to drive around with him because he would roll down his window and bark things like that. When Tom asked about Mark's weekend plans, he would sometimes answer, "Oh, nigger hunting in Oak Cliff. Wanna come?" Somehow Tom convinced himself that Mark never acted on such talk. It was just sad, mostly—a blustery hankering for relevance by a man deserted by love, fortune, and history.

Besides, a part of Tom—though, as a college man and a family man and a business owner, his situation was different from Mark's—understood at least a piece of it, understood that feeling of history's leaving you behind. Tom wasn't the type to harm anyone, and he had friends of different colors. For all his advantages in life, though, if he were to be honest, he sometimes felt himself faced with the same racial anxiety, the same sense of embattlement, confronting white-guy drifters like Mark Stroman in these changing times: a feeling that the old equations that had made it mean something to be white and a man, no matter how trifling a white man you were, no longer really computed.

"Well, nowadays, can you go out and qualify for government assistance? Can you get government-assisted houses? Can you get government loans? Can you get state contracts, federal contracts?" Tom said. "No. So much of it has to be black. The company has to be woman- or black-owned to qualify for all this stuff. The tables have turned to where the white community's now the minority. You've got all kinds of differences out there, all kinds of things to contend with. Most of them use excuses saying they can't get ahead."

Tom went on, "Everybody's supposed to have equal everything, but that's not the case. You've got the black community, reaching back a hundred years: 'Oh, we were slaves; we're owed this.' And if you look at—I'm now generalizing—the stereotype of the black community, you've got Oak Cliff: They've got big wheels and tires on their fancy cars, but they live in a shack. They're crack smokers; they don't work; they're out there all in prisons—they're full of them. You know, they're just trashy-type people. Well, that's not the case, but that's the stereotype. The Mexican community—well, you got Mexican communities that are legal. They came over to our country, they've got families, they've done everything legal, but they get put in with people that are swimming across, jumping the border and living in the backs of trucks, coming over here and causing problems. They're taking our money from jobs and sending them back to Mexico, and you've got a conflict there. And then you've got Arabs—Arabs come over. Well, you walk into a gas station and you're wondering something, and they don't speak English and you can't understand them. Well, that difference right there pisses people off—I don't care who it is. Or the Oriental community: If they can't speak English and you can't understand them, then that breeds a distance. That breeds some type of hatred."

So it wasn't that Tom didn't get where his protégé was coming from when he mouthed off with that race talk. But he, unlike Mark, knew to keep those feelings in check—and to keep his mind on family and work so that it didn't dwell in those darker places. One day Tom made a decision long in coming: he was better off as Mark's friend than as his boss. However much he liked the guy, however much they got along, he couldn't have a worker costing him accounts and burning down trucks he'd just painted.

"I brought him in and said, 'Hey, dude, we're friends. I don't want to get crossways. It's just come time that you're going off a different path,'" Tom said. He told Stroman to take his time; he didn't have to leave this second. Still, it was best that they part: "He wasn't on the right track for what I had going at the time." This was sometime in 1997. Stroman had worked there three-plus years.

Looking back, Tom wondered if he could have prevented the separation. He remembered warning Stroman, before the unraveling, "'Dude, you can straighten your act up. You got your wife, you got your daughter, you got your stuff. You can stop hanging around all these people.' I remember I told him, 'You could follow the people in the limousine, or you could follow the people with the shopping cart. It's your choice.' "

✳

Now, SITTING AT work, with that nagging thought swelling within, Tom tried to assemble what he'd heard of Mark lately: the news he had received from mutual friends, the glimpses he'd had himself. He knew Mark had found a job over at the body shop with the IRS issues near Cabaret Royale, and he knew it didn't last because Mark was caught road-tripping with customer cars. He had heard about Mark's trying to brand himself as some kind of gun runner. He knew about the .357 Magnum someone sold Mark and the AK-47 that Mark was peddling around town through an intermediary. The two men saw each other in passing from time to time and were still friendly. Tom had helped to set Mark up with a new trade, installing granite counters in rich people's kitchens, and had secured him a good job at a fancy house earlier that summer. He knew Mark felt terrible about accidentally breaking $3,000 worth of granite on that job, and that the mishap piled onto a series of other stresses that summer—everything from a string of parking tickets to the discovery of a lady friend of his in bed with a buddy.

The more Tom chewed it over, the more pungent the thought tasted. He remembered Mo Phillips, another ex-employee, coming by the shop just a few weeks earlier, saying some stuff about Mark being out to shoot Arabs. "I was like, 'Whatever,' " Tom said. Not because such a thing wouldn't concern him, but because he didn't believe it. He thought to himself: There Mark goes again, "flapping his gums"; what a "wannabe." Tom said, "He was always trying to get attention—always. He was always starved for attention, and he put on this persona like he was a rough, tough guy."

Maybe it was stupid to have dismissed news like that. A lot of things felt stupid now. Tom thought of seeing Mark at the car wash some days after Mo's visit. It would've been right in the middle of everything. Tom was shooting the breeze with an off-duty cop when Mark came over for a wash. Mark knew the cop, too, and when Tom saw Mark pull in, he made a meaningless joke. "He's the guy that did it," Tom hammed to the cop, pointing at Mark. Tom obviously wasn't referring to the shootings, since he didn't know a thing about them. He wasn't referring to anything. Mark didn't take it like that. He froze upon hearing those words. "Mark had this look on his face—it's hard to put it into words—just like stark terror," Tom said. "It was just, stop in his tracks. And Mark didn't want to associate or talk at that point. He was like, 'See you later,' got back in the car and took off."

Now the phone rang at Tom's office. It was about the call he'd made to his prosecutor friend. They needed him down at the station at once. He explained that he was not involved, had nothing to do with it. Within minutes, several police cars showed up at the body shop. Who did this? We need to know. You need to come with us.

The next thing Tom knew, at about 6:15 p.m., he was at the Mesquite police station. "They hauled me up there," he said, "and pretty much gave me the fucking tough guy fucking routine, and I'm like, 'I have nothing to do with any of this shit, and I don't want anything to do with any of this shit,' and they were like, 'Oh there's a reward and this-that.' And I don't even care about any reward, don't want to be involved, and I don't have anything to do with it and don't even want to mess with it. They locked me in a fucking room, did not come back, sat me with a paper and a pen." They made Tom draft a statement without having seen the video the prosecutor had mentioned. He could draft a second, updated statement after watching it, they said. When he finished, they led him into a room and showed it to him.

There Mark was, holding a gun, shrieking at that nice Mr. Patel to open the register, wearing a fake beard and those tattoos that Tom had once told him to cover. If you listened carefully, you could hear the lisp that had tripped him up since Plano days.

"Oh, God," Tom thought to himself. "Oh, God."

*

For as long as Tom knew him, Mark spoke only of his daughter Cassandra—the one he'd had with Shawna in the good years. Though Tom was convinced that he knew and understood Mark Stroman better than most, he didn't even know about his buddy's three other children, raised in his absence by a woman named Tena, whom Stroman had married—he sixteen, she fifteen—during his third attempt at eighth grade, about a year after getting her pregnant. There was a certain elusiveness to Stroman that would haunt many of those who claimed to have a handle on the man.

If Tom saw Stroman as a gum-flapping wannabe, the three children Tom didn't know about (who likely didn't know about Tom) saw Stroman in their own way, based on an equally limited set of interactions: as a father who couldn't bring himself to play father but flooded you with love when he came around; as a man who derided blacks and minorities and seemed to know a lot of the Aryan Brotherhood guys, but who never had trouble with their half-Mexican mother and quarter-Mexican selves. So it jolted them when, one day in early October, they were in Stephenville, Texas, staying at their aunt's, fixing to eat, when the TV announced some news about to be broken.

Amber, who had just turned sixteen and looked almost like a female facsimile of her father, had been trying to call him for a few weeks but hadn't been able to get through. Because he'd always gusted in and out of their lives, she never thought much of it. She had no interest in the TV that day and was heading to the porch to eat her pizza in peace. But as she crossed the living room, Channel 4 went into the breaking story. A Dallas-area male had walked into three convenience stores and opened fire on three Middle Easterners. They put up a picture of her father, followed by a video of him, wearing a cutoff shirt and jeans, walking into a store, shooting the clerk, peering into the camera for a lingering moment—right at Amber, it seemed—and walking away.

Amber stood there staring at the screen. Erica and Robert, her younger siblings, started to cry. Robert ran out of the house and down the road, sobbing. He was a giant of a boy, thick like his father, a school football player whom rival teams made plans about. He bolted down to the train tracks, to some abandoned old cars. He took shelter inside one and wept.

Tena Stroman—the children's mother and Mark's first wife— heard the news while traveling. Her sister, the aunt with whom the children were staying, called her when they saw it on TV. Tena wasn't regularly in touch with Mark, but she still thought of him as the great love of her life, and the news knocked her over: "My sister called me and told me that Mark Stroman has killed somebody. About that time, the phone started cutting out real bad. I heard my kids in the background crying, and I started, 'Where are my kids? Where are my kids?' I couldn't tell if she said Mark Stroman killed somebody or Mark Stroman got killed. I just went to ask where my kids were because I heard them crying, and she said that Erica was in the living room crying, pulling her hair; my son, Robert, took off down the road, on the railroad tracks, crying, and wouldn't let nobody mess with him or talk to him."

To Tena, it just didn't sound right. Mark was hardly a stranger to trouble, but she knew he'd never kill anyone. He was the kind of man who might slam an ashtray into a guy's forehead if he got fresh with his woman, as he had once. He might toss a man into the wall after a few too many at the Texas Trap. But not this. She called around to the local jails she knew and gave Mark's birth date—October 13, 1969—because she was sure it was some other Mark Stroman who had gotten himself into this mess.

No, ma'am, they told her. That's the guy. Same name, same DOB. There appears to be only one Mark Stroman.

✳

I⊤ BEGAN WITH running what he gathered to be Arabs off the road. As Stroman cruised Dallas in the days after his country was attacked, his victims would have seen a white 1972 Chevy Suburban pulling up beside them, with a rolled-up American flag in the windshield, maps of Texas on the plastic cases of his side mirrors, and resentful stickers on the rear window. "If I had known this," one said, "I would have picked my own cotton."

Like other vigilantes in the feverish days after 9/11, Stroman was not entirely sure what an Arab looked like. But he felt "anger and the hate towards an unknown force," as he later put it, and he knew enough to direct it at people with "shawls on their face." He was stuffed full of images of the attacks from watching TV, and entranced by a mood of vengeance in the country that was making even the limpest liberals perk up to his way of seeing things. "Everybody was saying, 'Let's get 'em. Let's get the dirty bastards. Let's bomb 'em,' " Mark said. "Who? We didn't know, but as Americans we was wanting justice." He claimed to have company in his dark pursuit: "I wasn't the only one in Dallas doing that. There was a lot of us out there hunting Arabs."

What began as harassment on the roads—presumably, pushing cars into emergency lanes and ditches, though Stroman wasn't specific—soon escalated. Stroman was seething over what those men had done to his country. He became certain that he had a sister working at Windows of the World, in the trade center's North Tower, and that she had been killed. Time would show this conviction to be without basis, though in general Stroman was lucid and in control of his mind, not given to such fantasies. He somehow convinced himself, nonetheless, that his government would prove too timid, weak, and sympathetic to the enemy to avenge his sister's death and the deaths of all the American innocents. Not long afterward, still fueled by the language of rage all around him, he explained his motivation thus, in words that would become an exhibit in his trial:

> I began to feel a great sense of rage, hatred, lost, bitterness and utter degradation. Although revenge wasn't my motive, I did want to exact a measure of equaility. I wanted those Arab's to feel the same sense of insecurity about their immediate surroundings. I wanted them to feel the same sense of vulnerability and uncertainty on American soil much like the mindset of chaos and bedlam that they was already accustomed to in there home country. How dare they come to America and be at peace and find comfort in country, our country, my country America, and here we are under siege at home, because we are the land of freedom.
>
> My sense of anger surged when I reflected upon the past that I'm a tax paying citizen whose hard earned dollar has been sent to those countries as a means of humanitarian aid. There homeland was a place our country feed when they were starving, medicated when sick, clothed when naked or cold, educated when in error and gave willing assistance and defended when they was under attack.
>
> I looked at the fact that over 5,000 innocent Americans lost their lives because some foriegner felt a need to make a statement at the expense of innocent people. Well I felt as Americans we needed to exact some sort of retribution and also make a statement here at home and abroad. That if we as American's was going to be under siege here at home then certainly they would have need to feel our pain. My sense of security and my right to live in peace and sanctity was all but shattered.
>
> As I began to reflect upon what I could do, would do or better yet should do in the wake of the World Trade Center atrocity, I looked at the situation and took an assessment. I then found myself going to the store to make a purchase, and there perched behind the counter, here in the land of the free, home of the brave, the land of the pilgrims pride, land for which my

forefathers died, the bell of life, liberty and pursuit of happiness had all been silenced by those people.

He was there perched behind the counter, here in the land of milk and honey living the freedom of liberty of the thousand's of victims of Sept 11, and here he is in this country at our expense was this foriegner who's own people had now sought to bring the exact same chaos and bewilderment upon our people and society as they lived in themselves at home and abroad.

It left me with this sense of just having had someone spit in my face. After all our country has done to help build, educate, and liberate their country and to see that those people thought so little of America and consequently the American way of life with such contemp and utter disregard.

In closing this was not a crime of hate but an act of passion and patriotism, a act of country and commitment, an act of retribution and recompense. This was not done during peace time but at war time. I, Mark Anthony Stroman, felt a need to exact some measure of equality and fairness for the thousands of victims of September 11 2001, for the United States of America and it's people, the people of this great country.

At half past noon on October 5, the day after the Patel killing, Dallas police made their way to Cayuga Drive, looking for Stroman, on the strength of Tom Boston's identification. Shortly after two, the cops saw a Thunderbird pull up. Stroman got out and seemed to remove something from his trunk. Fearing a news-helicopter-worthy standoff if they let him go inside what might have been an armed fortress, officers in raid jackets emerged and swarmed their man. Stroman tried to flee to the back of the house, removing a chrome Smith and Wesson from his waistband as he ran and dropping it to the ground. But the hiding was over. Stroman was arrested and read his Miranda rights. In the ensuing questioning, officers reported him laughing and crying at the same time.

The police soon came upon evidence suggesting that shooting three immigrant clerks was perhaps just the beginning of a much grander—and never consummated—plan. Mark Stroman, who thought of himself as an "allied combatant" going up against "enemy combatants," as he'd heard them called on the news, may have been contemplating a gruesome attack on a Dallas-area mosque—a kind of 9/11 counterstrike.

In Stroman's car the police found a loaded semiautomatic rifle with at least 150 matching cartridges; an Uzi knockoff with 29 cartridges; a .44 Magnum; a .45 Colt; a Top Line bulletproof vest; a pill bottle with a little cocaine; bottles of Effexor, an antidepressant, and Carisoprodol, a muscle relaxant; 2.5 grams of marijuana and rolling paper; and a hat that said, "Show me your tits." Long afterward, Stroman addressed what he called the "rumor" of his planned attack on worshippers at the Richardson mosque. It had crossed his mind, he confessed. He would become the patriotic American inverse of "Mohammed Atta and all them fanatics" from 9/11. After all, what a statement they had made. "In my mind, if I'd walked in that mosque and leveled about a hundred or so people, that would've made a statement, too," Stroman said.

Outpatient

"Where am I?" he remembers asking. Rais figured the voices belonged to the angels at the gates. He had always wondered about the Afterward. The voices sounded warbled and far away, as in the movies. They were beautiful voices—perfect women's voices. They seemed to be above him now. Were the angels holding his hand? Yes, he sensed that they were. Was this heaven or earth?

"Am I still alive?" He gargled the question through what tasted like a doubly salted ocean in his mouth. He resolved to try to open his eyes. He pulled at them hard. No movement, only feverish pain.

"Yes, you are still alive," the nurse said in that perfect voice. "Good morning!"

He was still down here.

Night had fallen and lifted. It was morning now, the first full day living with fresh realities. Memories of the incident started trickling back. Joyful tears poured over his bulging face. His jaw seemed under someone else's control; he had barely managed the few words he had uttered and sensed that more would be difficult. He couldn't swallow.

After a time, he understood that his two eyes were no longer on the same schedule. The right refused to bargain. The left hinted at being slightly more reasonable. Once again he pulled. And this time the left opened, glazed with its own saltwater. It was definitely not heaven, just a floodlit, sterile room, and he was on an adjustable bed, a woman gently clutching his hand.

It wasn't long before he asked to see himself. The nurse handed him a mirror.

"I looked at myself with my left eye open," Rais said. He saw stitches. Heavily seasoning the puffed right hemisphere were little blood-hued dots. These were where three dozen or so burning-hot pellets—designed to escape the cartridge and form a metallic spray to bring down erratic birds—had entered: they flew into his mouth and broke a tooth, flew into his cheek, his nose, his ear, his forehead. "That face was swelling like this big, and this area"—around the eye—"was a big bruise, like somebody punched you a hundred times," Rais said. "All those dots, all those gunshots. And I said, 'Wow, I look terrible.' Though I was happy that time that I was alive, once I see my face, I was in a shock. Will I live with my face like this for the rest of my life?"

It didn't take him long to wonder, "What will Abida think?"

The nurses informed him that, despite contrary appearances, he had been mightily fortunate. The pellets had flirted with entering his brain and, at the last second, held back. They were millimeters away when they stopped.

As Rais tells it, though he was sickened by his condition, even in this moment, another part of him—the part that always kept him in check—tried to spare him from a descent into self-pity: "I was thinking that, well, why should I complain? I got my life, so let's not worry about that right now." He remembers feeling a strange, immense gratitude. "I could feel the happiness—that how beautiful, how precious is just to live," he said. "How life is so precious. I got my life back, and I'm still alive." He could speak to his family again. See his mother, his father, Abida. That was the greatest blessing. If he felt other, darker things, he refused to confess them.

"That is the moment I think about every single day," Rais said much later. "And it also helps me to check and balance—that why should I complain, why should I think about small-small things, why shouldn't I do something better and bigger not only for myself, for others as well? Because if I enjoy life, if I control life, if I feel how life is important, then I should spread the message to others—those who don't see it the same way; those who spoil their life behind drugs, behind this and that. Tell them how beautiful is that, just to live."

Later that afternoon, on the same day he heard the angels, the hospital let Rais go. Because he was unfamiliar with the American health care system, he assumed this was a good thing. If they didn't need to do anything further, then he would probably, with God's blessing, recover quickly. On the other hand, his jaw wasn't moving, he could not speak, his right eye remained closed, and the right half of his head looked like ostrich leather. All this even a devout optimist had to acknowledge.

✻

IN THAT MOURNING house in Dhaka, the phone rang. It had been nearly a week since the mysterious call from Texas. Rais did not know his family had received that first call and so figured they knew nothing. He wanted to be able to move his jaw properly when he explained that, on a rainy afternoon, some man had fired dozens of scalding pellets into the right side of his face with a double-barreled Derringer pistol, and that he had nearly made it to heaven.

The family, with no news to go on, had seen its shock yield to grief, and grief begin to make way for transcendence. Now Rais's mother picked up the phone. This time, only silence. Then a hint of a grunt zipped through the undersea cables and into her ear. It wasn't much. It was enough. "This is me, Ripon," his shattered jaw mumbled, using a nickname from an earlier, happier time. "Amma, I am OK," he managed to add.

He cried, and she cried, and everyone in the house cried. For the longest time, no one spoke. They just held their phones to their ears and listened.

Amma asked about the injury, about his course of treatment, about whether Rais could eat. Come home as soon as you can, she begged. Mightily she praised God.

✳

WHEN THEY ASKED him to leave the hospital, the day after admitting him, Rais had mumbled some concerns. He would be fine, they said. He needed to return very soon for something called Outpatient Treatment. This was some kind of hard-to-understand American invention where you leave injured so that you can return and have done to you what they could also just do right now. Somehow, the act of leaving emergency care and returning as this so-called Outpatient made life easier—for somebody, though for whom wasn't obvious. It was not unlike the maddening rules of bureaucratic classification that gummed up every little thing back home. Apparently, becoming an outpatient changed whose problem you were, which in America mattered greatly.

Still, Rais wondered: If there was more to do, why not just finish it off? He was right here. Why would they release him if he wasn't whole? It would take time to understand that when an American hospital says you're free to go, it may mean that they're done with your insurance, not your problem.

In Rais's case, there was no insurance of any kind. Rais didn't have it, and Salim said the station didn't have it because he liked to keep costs down. It was part of his business model—that as well as

recruiting old schoolmates as workers and mortgage-splitting house-
mates, by persuading them that toiling behind the counter of someone else's convenience store was a swift path to owning your own.

The hospital assessors saw Rais's bills mounting. They were
already in the thousands of dollars: not only the ER care but also
the hospital filing fee, the ambulance fee, the 911 call fee. They saw a
fledgling immigrant and gas station clerk, and they had their ways of
predicting that he wouldn't be good for the money. He was out of the
hospital that afternoon. He returned to Salim's place with instructions to see an eye specialist by the name of Dr. Rand Spencer.

As it happened, Dr. Spencer was a fellow pilot who understood
how the prospect of losing an eye might especially frighten an ex–Air
Force man, for whom sight was a source of power and distinction. "If
that's part of your identity, then you've lost that part of yourself,"
he said. "From a psychological standpoint, it probably makes you
feel like you're less of a man than you used to be." The doctor was a
tall, solid oak of a man who wore tweed blazers over his scrubs. He
was one of the leading eye surgeons in the city, and not cheap. The
first appointment alone would be $500. Salim was generous enough
to pay that bill himself. During the first consult, the doctor peered
into Rais's uncooperative right eye. It was full of blood—in the deep
aspects of the socket and under the retina, where it risked destroy-
ing the rods and cones. The lens had been pierced by the pellets, and
a cataract was forming. Yet the eye could faintly perceive light. It
could, for example, tell if you were shining a flashlight into it. Without such light perception, there would have been no hope of saving it.
But this was modestly good news. A surgery was scheduled.

On the day of the shooting, Dallas police officers had come to
Rais's hospital bedside to show him images of known criminals.
Hundreds of pictures. They all kind of looked the same to him, but
he gamely picked four. They came to him again and again, and by
early October he had narrowed his choice to two. Now, on the day of
Rais's first surgery, he saw on television the news that yet another

mini-mart clerk had been shot. This one was at a Shell station in Mesquite. First Hasan, then him, and now an Indian named Patel. The first and the third had died at once. Rais was aware of being the lone survivor of the three: a strange, bittersweet stroke of luck. In the recent case, the store camera wasn't a fake, and the TV showed a video of the crime. The man in the video, raving furiously at the clerk, was the same man who had barged in and wanted to know where Rais was from. He matched one of the two photographs Rais had picked.

Rais went into the operating room. They put him to sleep with general anesthesia and pulled back his eyelids. Dr. Spencer saw now that two of the shotgun pellets, as best he could tell, had fully perforated the eye—gone in the front and come out of the back to settle somewhere behind it, where they would have to live forever. In that brief journey through the eyeball, much of the injury to Rais's sight had been achieved. The doctor removed the bloodstained vitreous gel behind the lens, which had developed into a cataract. He removed the lens as well to avoid the need for further surgeries. He applied laser to the retinal tears near the exit wounds, to prevent the retina from detaching, and inserted some silicone oil to hold it in place. Rais went home and was told to take his eye drops regularly and to hope for the best. If he kept praying, the eye might well see.

Dr. Spencer, who had a flourishing private practice, was willing to cut Rais some slack on the payments. "I was certainly willing to work with him from a financial standpoint and do whatever it took to not send him to the poorhouse because of my bills," he said. Still, the bills kept coming to Rais—from Spencer's office, from that initial ER visit. The outstanding dues swelled by the day, and Rais began to hear from all manner of people employed in the collection of debt.

Less than a week after the first surgery, he received a letter from a company that called itself a reimbursement specialist, signed by a so-called Financial Assistance Representative who didn't seem all that interested in assisting:

Dear RAIS BHUIYAN

We have attempted contacting you by mail and telephone but our efforts have proven unsuccessful. We understand that your time is valuable, and, therefore; will take only a moment to ask you to consider your hospital bill and the advantages of resolving it.

We feel certain you will be greatly relieved when this financial obligation is behind you. Also, taking care of these charges will prevent your account from being submitted to collections.

We hope you will take a moment of your time to respond to this letter. Your efforts could bring you financial assistance for your medical bill which is $12611.02.

I would appreciate a call as soon as possible at 972——. Thank you in advance for your cooperation.

Twelve thousand six hundred eleven dollars and two cents was close to $12,611.02 more than Rais possessed. He had a tiny reservoir of savings—barely enough for medicine, groceries, and calling cards—and no other assets. He wondered what happened in America to patients like him. Maybe the bills were somewhat for show, and the doctors kept treating you regardless—sending the bills as a formality, as Dr. Spencer did, but caring for you whether or not you could pay. Or maybe they did just cut you off. What in God's name would he do if they did that? What if, worse, they came after him? It was not a good time to be Muslim. Imagine being a Muslim who lived in Texas and refused to pay his debts to a Christian hospital.

✳

To RAIS IT was evident that the man who shot him was not a crazed loner, because inscribed across his body were the symbols of some sad, deranged tribe. He had to belong to something to do this—had to have some cause. Indeed, if an untrained newcomer went looking for fellow members of this tribe, they could seem to be everywhere in Dallas: bald heads, big arms and thick fingers, tattoos, sleeveless shirts, sports team jackets.

Rais decided to confine himself to Salim's three-bedroom house as much as possible. There whole days passed in worry and self-questioning. Should he leave home? Was it safe? Were they, whoever they were, still after him? They could strike at any time. Rais figured, "If I go outside, somebody from Mark Stroman's association will try to kill me, because I'm the only survivor."

Nightmares devoured his sleep. They made the attack happen to him again and again—that man with those searing eyes walking in, pointing the twin-barreled gun, asking where he was from, and then the stings. The days weren't much better, filled with flashbacks. He sank into an abysmal depression and knew he needed what the Americans called "help," even though he came from a place where people could be suspicious of such things. And yet help would cost so much. He was no longer simply an invalid; he was becoming a debtor. Bank of America, when it got wind of his situation, would close his account, compelling him to borrow money from friends and open an account in a community institution called Inwood National Bank. No therapy for Rais, then: "I said, 'Forget about that, going to a psychiatric, going to a psychological evaluation. Pray to the biggest psychiatrist in the world, which is God. Keep on praying to God.' He is my psychologist."

It must have crossed his mind from time to time how different it would be back in Dhaka. People spoke less of needing "help" there, because it was taboo, of course, but also because you had people. Rais grew up in that vast quarter of the world where you can ask friends you haven't seen in years to do some giant task for you, and they will be offended if you cheapen the situation by thanking them. In Dallas it wasn't like that. Even the fellow immigrants and Muslims whom Rais had met before the incident lived on their own one-bedroom, two-bath islands, at once in the community and apart from it. "They had their own lives," Rais said. They came to visit him occasionally, but it was not like it would have been back in Dhaka, where his wounds would be numbed, his mind stilled, by the sheer volume of people around him. It was not hard to picture it: He would lie in bed, and they would come—uncles with overwrought opinions about the war days and aunties with dishes he once claimed to enjoy and old schoolmates with evergreen dorm-room memories. All the while, he would be in the care of his parents and siblings—and, if she still would have him, his Abida.

He was reminded of what he was missing out on again and again by his family, who could not understand what was keeping him in Texas. His parents, who had been heroically patient with Rais's refresh-button dreaming, now regularly commanded him home. And Rais couldn't deny that he needed what family alone can give.

But he couldn't and wouldn't go home. Couldn't because the doctor said so—at least for now. As Rais understood it, there was some kind of gas bubble in his eye, and it could expand and wreak havoc when gaining altitude. Flying risked the total loss of sight in his right eye. However, the truth was also that Rais didn't want to go home, even after the doctor's orders eventually lifted—and didn't even want his family flying to America to care for him. This was a harder thing to explain over the phone.

His mother might have been more important to him than the rest of the world, but in this moment it was even more vital to Rais that she not see him or his face. He had to be strong for them. His father was weak from the stroke. Neither parent spoke good English. How would they manage to get around, let alone tend to him? He had no home of his own, being at Salim's still, and thus no place for his parents to stay. He didn't want them standing in line repeatedly at the embassy, as he had. Abida couldn't come because they weren't yet married, and she couldn't just hop on a plane and live with him in sin. If any of them did come, their welcome gift, Rais knew, would be vicarious despair: "They would have gone through the same suffering and pain—even worse than that."

It was especially difficult to tell Abida that he couldn't come home. But he had gone to America with a mission. He had worked so single-mindedly for his goals; he couldn't quit now.

The more they pressed him, the more he stood his ground: "I said that, 'No, I wanted to give it the fight, and maybe by the mercy of God things will change one day. I will make you proud. Let me stay there, and I will do my best.'" Rais was sure he would wither if he returned to Dhaka: "It will be haunting me for the rest of my life that I went to U.S.A. and I was shot and now I'm back home—and a loser. The background I had, that doesn't allow me to be a loser. I was a fighter, and I was a soldier, and I learned how not to give up. And now if I go back with this medical condition, with this fear and phobia, it will be always there in my mind."

※

For the longest time after the attack, Rais felt terrified of strangers. Who knew what agendas lurked in the hearts of men? Rais confined himself to Salim's house and made an exception only for regular visits to Dr. Spencer.

When Rais went for his next eye checkup, he found that while God still wasn't answering his prayers, He was at least receiving the messages. Wonderful news, at last: the petulant right eye could now detect and count fingers, could see Rais's shadow on the ground, could perceive his image in the mirror. It was a huge improvement over merely sensing light. "We still have a chance to save some vision," the doctor said triumphantly. That day, for the first time, Rais said, "I became very hopeful about getting my vision back."

A remaining complication was that Rais's retina had detached again because of the growth of scar tissue, which is not uncommon after severe trauma. In November, Rais had to return for a second operation to reattach it. The retina was refastened and the scar tissue removed. The doctor left the silicone oil in for the time being, though you didn't want to leave that in forever.

The bills kept coming. The postal service started to feel like a subsidiary of the debt hunters. Rais's barely established credit was soon shot.

"I was getting medical bills from every direction," he said. "The collection agents are bugging on me, they're calling, they're sending bills. And I didn't know from where I would have got this money— $60,000-plus. And I was thinking that, God, will I ever be able to get my life back in this country?"

Yet he felt grateful that it wasn't even higher: "If I'd be staying in the hospital, the bill would be who knows how many hundreds of thousands of dollars. So now no wonder they let me go from the hospital, because they saved their back, instead of sending more bills and not getting paid."

It was only the beginning of his experience with this essentially American institution of debt. In time, he would discover how debt contradicted those attributes of the republic for which he had left home: how it bound you to history, and kept you who you were, and replaced the metaphor of the frontier with that of a treadmill.

Sitting in Salim's house, still healing, Rais pleaded over the phone with the collection people. He tried to tell them his story. "We feel sorry for you," he remembers them saying in essence, "but this is our duty." He was incredulous: "You cannot even excuse me even after knowing all these things? So where's the humanity we talk about? That's what I told many of the collection people."

Immigrant friends stopped by from time to time, sometimes bringing food or a "few bucks" to help with bills. But Rais knew that their lives weren't easy, either, that they had dreams and hurdles of their own. He believed strongly that he should seek help only from big institutions: "I was feeling extremely bad that I should not be expecting this money from individual persons. It was my thought that a lot of organizations, they help people. And they're helping people in September 11." Rais believed that he had suffered on the Texan front of the same dismal war: "This incident happened because of September 11. At least can they come take care of my medical part?"

He called United Way and the Red Cross and told them he was one of the 9/11 victims in Texas: "They said that no, I don't deserve. I'm not eligible for any help because I'm in Texas. I'm not in New York City. And a victim of hate crimes of September 11 doesn't fall in their category in their rules and their regulations to be helped."

Still, they visited Rais a few times with small amounts of food and cash. They were sorry that they couldn't do more.

For the first few weeks at Salim's, Rais spent most of his time resting, praying, reading the Koran, and, twice a week or so, calling his family and Abida. Now, with his right eye slowly improving, Rais found himself looking toward the future. He started to tire of merely healing: "I thought, what I can do now, since I'm not going out? I'm wasting my time. So I thought about: learn something by staying home. That will pay me off later on." This was no kind of life: lounging at home, praying, fearing the outdoors and the tattooed men who prowled there. "If I just stay home, get the medical treatment, I'll be wasting time," he said. "So I invested my time learning." He couldn't take classes outside, because Stroman's associates could easily find him there, and he was reluctant to venture as far as a bookstore. What if he ordered computer-programming textbooks online and just taught himself at Salim's? It would help him lay the groundwork for making money again. A computer stood at his disposal. He sought advice from his friends in the field and ordered *Visual Basic 6 Black Book* and *Beginning ASP Databases* and other titles.

When Salim had phoned him in New York all those months earlier, Rais sensed that his old schoolmate regarded him as an investment. Salim had spoken with an aged kaka's confidence: he and his brother had a business, they needed people, and they wanted to create opportunities for friends. When that angry man stormed into their market, it had interfered with everyone's plans. Still, Rais figured that he was in good hands, because he was living with the man who brought him to Dallas and put him behind that counter. He assumed, correctly at first, that Salim would care for him—and would understand that Rais could no longer pay his half of the $800-a-month mortgage. It was Salim, after all, who got him into this situation.

For the first several weeks, Salim—and his mother, who lived across the street with an older son—looked after Rais with genuine concern. Salim paid for that initial visit to Dr. Spencer and gamely drove Rais to and from his medical appointments. After a few weeks, however, there were changes in the boss's demeanor. He sometimes ignored Rais; he spoke to him less and less, or on occasion not at all; he inquired less often about the state of Rais's injuries, then stopped inquiring. The tone of the hospitality turned day by day. Honor slid into duty, then duty into obligation, obligation into burden, and burden into imposition. The care, when it started, was like what family would provide back home. When it ended, it had grown distant and calculated. "I could feel he didn't want to go through that, because he's a businessman and I'm pulling him down," Rais said. Rais was no longer a friend in Salim's eyes, and certainly not a fruitful investment: "I had no use. I was a dead horse for him."

One day, with an appointment looming, Rais was hoping for his usual ride. Salim claimed to be too busy; he didn't have the time. "If you need help, go to a nursing home," Rais remembers his friend saying. "I cannot do this kind of thing for you."

Rais was dazed. "I couldn't believe how a friendly, sweet-talking person could tell me to go to nursing home, whereas I moved to Dallas by depending on him," Rais said later.

He knew that he had to get out. And go where? He was out of money, burrowing deeper into debt, possibly going blind in one eye, many oceans from his family, and now being pushed out of his only home. He remembered what he once asked Salim: "If I move to Texas, what I have there?" The question felt prescient now. The answer was becoming plain.

*

WHEN RAIS SPOKE to Abida by phone, she asked what his face looked like. "I kept telling her that, 'Don't worry, things will get better. I'm getting another treatment, and things are getting better, and my face is already healing that time—slowly, slowly—though I had a lot of scars. But it's healing.' So she was asking me, 'How bad is it?' I said, 'It's not really that bad.' "

"Do you remember I told you not to go to Texas, and I didn't have good feelings?" she asked. "I was going to tell you at the time that something bad was going to happen, but . . ."

Yes, maybe he should have listened. After all, her cryptically voiced fears had come true. What he wanted her to understand was that he hadn't gone to Texas for himself. "She was the main reason behind coming to Texas," he said. "If I would not have a fiancée, someone back home—I'm not blaming her, but just to analyze the point—I could have lived by myself in the New York City."

Abida wanted him home. "She was getting lot of pressure from her family to move on, and almost every week people were coming to see her at their house," Rais said. "She was going through tremendous pressure to find someone other than me." He couldn't fly home, he explained. He asked her for patience, for understanding and trust. "As soon as my doctor clears me to fly, I am coming home," he told her.

Several weeks after the shooting, the phone rang. It was a friend of Salim's brother, but he was looking for Rais. He had heard what happened to him and wanted to help. Could he interest Rais in a job with his company? The pay was modest, just minimum wage. The job was in telemarketing—convincing motel and hotel owners, mostly from their own corner of the world, to refinance. Whether or not it was a plot by Salim to get mortgage money out of Rais by giving him an income again, it was a generous offer, and it was only sitting and making calls, so it wouldn't tax his health. Rais accepted.

On the job, Rais met a kindhearted Bengali who immediately took a liking to him. One day, unprompted, he offered that Rais could live with him in his modest one-bedroom. Rais slept on the sofa for the first several days, then on a mattress on the living room floor. "Pay whatever you can," his new friend said. "I'll take care of the rest."

So in December, at the tail end of a bitter year, Rais's luck hobbled back to life. He left Salim's for his friend's place, where he paid no rent and never felt like a burden. In time, they would move to a two-bedroom. They would live together for roughly a year, at which time Rais would, at last, fly home to visit his family and Abida.

✳

WHEN THE TRIAL of Mark Stroman began the following spring, Rais was awaiting his fourth eye operation. A few months earlier, around the time Rais moved out of Salim's, they had removed the silicone oil that was holding the retina in place. In a matter of weeks, that unruly retina drifted away once more. This wayward tendency was not typical and not good. Another surgery was scheduled for later in the year. The doctor's best guess at this point was that maybe a quarter of the eye's functionality could be saved.

Rais was terrified of the looming trial. Because prosecutors wanted the maximum sentence for Mark Stroman, the trial didn't involve the attempted murder of Rais, but rather the actual murder of Vasudev Patel. Still, the DA's office had subpoenaed Rais's testimony, and he wanted to do his duty, no matter how hard it would be. In the days before the trial, anxiety nibbled on him day and night. "I was very scared that somebody will shoot me, will try to kill me," he said. He felt convinced that to be there, in the same room as Mark Stroman, in a building likely crawling with members of his association, was dangerous. But he had no choice. On the first day of the trial, the authorities were kind enough to pick Rais up at home early in the morning and drop him off at night. When he confessed his fears, they allayed them by entering the Frank Crowley Courts Building through a back door and ensconcing him in a small office not far from the 292nd District courtroom, where the trial would occur. He could sit there in peace until it was his time to testify in the penalty phase—that is, assuming Mark Stroman was convicted.

On the trial's opening day, April 1, 2002, Rais sat tight in that office. He refused even to go to the bathroom. A soldier-cum-film-buff couldn't be tricked so easily. "You see many times in the movies that in the bathroom crimes take place," Rais said. "People just go and snatch that head or this kind of thing. So I was very scared that if I go to the bathroom, who knows? Maybe Stroman or someone is following me, and they will go to the bathroom with me, and then try to kill me."

187

Ladies and gentlemen, in this case the evidence will show the following. It will show that on the morning of October fourth, 2001, that Vasudev Patel awoke, he got ready for work, he left his wife and his two children at their Mesquite home, and he drove a few miles to the Shell station that he operated at John West Road and Big Town Boulevard in Mesquite. He opened that station at approximately 5:30 a.m. that morning and began waiting on customers. And the evidence will show that he was working by himself that morning.

The evidence will also show that approximately 6:45 a.m. a man drove up to that Shell station in a silver Ford Thunderbird. He was also alone. The evidence will show that he was not a customer; he had not come there to purchase anything. Instead, the evidence will show that he was armed with a .44 Magnum caliber revolver. This man pulled up a bandana over his face and exited that Ford Thunderbird with that weapon. The evidence will show that that man is this man right here, Mark Anthony Stroman.

The evidence will show that Mr. Stroman walked to the front door of that Shell station. That when he did so, he already had that revolver down by his side ready for use. He got to that front door, he opened the front door of that Shell station. Mr. Patel was behind the counter. This man over here, Mark Anthony Stroman, as he opened that door, yelled out to Mr. Patel to give him the money in that station.

Now Mr. Patel kept a .22 caliber pistol under the counter for his protection. The evidence will show that as he saw this man come in armed with that .44 caliber revolver, that he reached under the counter for his weapon. As he did so, this individual raised up that .44 and pointed it at him. And Mr. Patel then backed away from the counter with that gun. And as he did so, this individual, Mark Anthony Stroman, shot him once with the .44 Magnum.

He struck him up here in the left-upper portion of his torso. And that weapon then tore through his collarbone and broke it. It broke five ribs. It penetrated Mr. Patel's left lung, and it finally lodged in his lower back, and Mr. Patel fell to the floor behind the counter.

And as he did so, the evidence will show that this individual here, Mark Anthony Stroman, immediately reached over the counter for that cash register. He knocked over the keyboard in front of that cash register. He attempted to open the register but couldn't find the key. He then looked across and pointed the gun down at Mr. Patel and started threatening to shoot him again if he didn't open that register for him. Mr. Patel couldn't move by that time and he was down on the floor.

And so what Mr. Stroman did at that time was he took that .44, he put it into his waistband and reached over with both hands and attempted again to open that register. And again he was unsuccessful in his attempts. At this point then he leaned across and threatened to blow Mr. Patel's brains out if he didn't open that register for him. And the evidence will show that, actually, as he said that, he was reaching in his waistband for that .44 Magnum. And at that time he glanced slightly to the left to where the windows were in that station. He immediately took his hands away from that revolver and hurriedly left out the front door.

The prosecutor went on to describe the arrest and the ballistics tests, and then he brought his opening statement to its conclusion.

The evidence will show that that man's intent there on October fourth was one thing, and that was to go in there to rob Mr. Patel and to murder him in the process.

⋆

THE TRIAL OF Mark Stroman began on April Fool's Day 2002. For simplicity's sake, the state had charged him with just one of his attacks—the Shell station murder of Vasudev Patel. The trial was assigned to Judge Henry Wade Jr., of the city's 292nd Judicial District Court. The courtroom was in the Frank Crowley Courts Building, in that buzzing judicial hive on North Riverfront Boulevard. It was an imposing, eleven-story fortress—its lobby six sets of stairs above the street—that handled the whole spectrum of legal affairs in the city: indictments and arraignments, sentencings and paroles, divorces and speeding-ticket contestations.

It was a depressing old place, where the conveyor-belt operators at security seemed to exhale their boredom in the face of every entrant and workers in the cafeteria mumbled during one break about the next break and the clerks looked up only after you'd been talking awhile. In the basement, men in sleeveless undershirts sat waiting for a chapter of their record to be handed over, and they gave the impression of being regulars. On another floor, a woman sat before a receptionist, trying to explain that the complaint she wanted to make involved domestic violence and that she preferred to speak in private. On floor after floor, families sat hoping to learn the fate of fathers and brothers and sons and, on some occasions, of mothers and sisters and daughters. They moved through a building whose bones were steadily weakening with time: the local press called its elevators shaky and "cantankerous," disparaged its bathrooms for emitting sewer smells, its floors for their long cracks, its thermostat system for making it icy in some courtrooms while steamy in others.

Judge Wade, in the 292nd District courtroom, had the advantage of having worked every side of a criminal case. Once an officer and instructor pilot in the U.S. Air Force, he had worked as a trial lawyer after law school; then as a prosecutor, conducting a hundred jury trials; then as a criminal defense attorney; and, finally, since 1995, as a judge. Though his obligations in this case were potentially daunting, he gave Stroman a good feeling. Something about Wade fostered trust in an anxious defendant.

On that first day of the trial, many worlds collided. Rais Bhuiyan was hiding from Stroman's associates in that small office and avoiding the bathroom. The widows of Hasan and Patel were in the courtroom. Stroman was of course there. Tena, his estranged wife, and three of his four children were there. Tom Boston was there.

The trial they had come to witness would boil down to one overwhelming question: should Mark Stroman continue living? It had become the focal question by a strange, improbable path.

In the months between the shootings and the trial, Mark Stroman had widely advertised himself to the world as a hate criminal. There was a strange television interview he gave in February, by telephone from jail, in which he admitted to the shootings and reportedly justified them: "We're at war. I did what I had to do. I did it to retaliate against those who retaliated against us." That month, while being transferred between units at the Lew Sterrett county jail, Stroman was written up for saying to a guard, "You'd think it was illegal to kill Arabs around here." He had obviously mistaken his captor for a sympathizer. When the guard informed him that, yes, it is illegal, Stroman retorted, "If you had loved ones they killed, you'd kill 'em, too."

In the letters he wrote from prison, he was equally blunt—and not merely about Arabs. "I don't know how much longer I can stand all these fuckin 'niggers,' " he wrote to a friend soon after arriving.

Beneath these words, he drew a Confederate flag and scrawled "Forever free!!!" In another letter, a new living arrangement seemed to bring relief: "I got a new cellie, he is 'white.' That's good, but he beat some fag to death with a fuckin hammer, only 35 times in the head. Damn! I thought I had a few issues :) He don't like nager's at all, so now there are 3 of us in for murder, all white. The nager's are worried about us :) Hell I'm even worried about us. Haha." At times he traded in jokes he enjoyed: "What's the difference between a dead niger in the road or a dead dog in the road: dead dog gots skid marks in front of it."

As during his earlier stints in prison, Stroman's whiteness became even more salient to him in that setting. The way he saw it, to be white in a Texas prison was, in an inversion of the usual rules, to be a victim from the start. Mark, like many of his buddies who had done time, was obsessed by visions of how big and ruthless the black prisoners were. Tena remembered her husband's saying how "loud and obnoxious" he'd found the black inmates. If white guys like them didn't band together, didn't strike before they were struck, they stood no chance. This was part of the logic of an affiliation that Stroman claimed in prison—the "Peckerwood Warriors."

The term "peckerwood" was a long-standing epithet in the rural South for poor whites, in the same genus as "redneck" and "cracker"—sometimes slung derisively at them, sometimes embraced pridefully by them. It had become favored by the white-power movement more recently and had reportedly come into use as a label for aspiring associates of the Aryan Brotherhood, a white supremacist prison gang and meth-trading crime syndicate that Stroman was sometimes said, inconclusively, to have run with. News reports connected him to the highly secretive group. His daughter Amber said, "From the beginning, he's been a lieutenant. That's the highest rank you can get in Aryan Brothers." Stroman himself denied it, citing his half-Mexican ex-wife as proof: "Now if I was a member of the Aryan Brotherhood, me having a Spanish wife—that would kind of make me a hypocrite. You have to be—if being proud of who I am, my skin color, makes me a racist, then I'm a racist. But no, I'm not. I don't hate the blacks, the Spanish. I don't hate Jewish people. I don't hate—well, I was gonna say, I still have animosity towards the Arabs. Seeing people being hung from bridges and decapitated, that still infuriates me. But no, I'm not a racist. I believe in being proud of who I am. My mother's got a lot of Cherokee Indian in her, so I'm a mixture."

Stroman's tattoos, photographed in detail after his arrest and offered in the trial as state exhibit No. 125, seemed to tell a different story. A swastika graced his right pectoral, and an indecipherable figure of some import appeared to be hanging off the side of it. Adjacent to it, just under the cross hanging from his neck, was etched "187," presumably a reference to Section 187 of the California penal code, which begins, "Murder is the unlawful killing of a human being, or a fetus, with malice aforethought . . ." It was a common marker for men who claimed to have committed that act, in California or beyond. On his left pec was a rose, with "In Loving Memory" above it and "A Bro" below, which might or might not have referred to the Aryan Brotherhood. Between his pecs, a little way down toward the abdomen, were raging flames. Rather more moderately, the word "Harley" decorated a forearm.

The state's investigation also unearthed photos of Stroman horsing around in "SS" neo-Nazi T-shirts, calmly clutching a rifle and handgun in one snapshot, throwing his hands exuberantly skyward in another. A different picture showed two young children, apparently his own, standing before a neo-Nazi flag and giving their best little "Heil Hitler" salutes.

Now in prison, Stroman stayed true to this record, mailing a friend on the outside a poem he loved about the Peckerwoods. Different versions of the poem floated around American lock-ups, and prosecutors would use its words against Stroman at the trial. They spoke to ideas of white pride and white power, and to the way they could become, in the eyes of certain prisoners, the only way to protect yourself inside:

Peckerwood Warriors, down for a cause
Texas convicts and solid outlaws
The rules they live by are written in stone
Awesome—fearless they are bad to the bone
The unit they live on can't take their pride
They live in a warzone, they are ready to die
There bodies are solid + blasted with ink
To earn their bolts ⚡⚡ is how they think
The strength they possess as they go into war
Was passed down to them by the great mighty Thor
They go into battle with their head held high
Some will get hurt, others will die
None of this matter's, the battle is on
They'll fight to the finish, till their strength is all gone
In time they grow calloused, ruthless + hard
Small price to pay, to survive on the yard
They are Peckerwood Warriors down for a cause
Texas convicts and solid outlaws

Some of Stroman's correspondence rose above crude jokes and racist bluster to suggest something like a worldview. He claimed to be reading tons in prison, following the tentacular effects of 9/11 with particular interest: "I have never been on top of the news like I am now. It really sucks. This whole world is falling apart right before our eyes." The ideas he formed from his readings and observation were grounded in a profound sense of besiegement. He felt himself and people like him to be standing on a shrinking platform at which minorities and immigrants and public dependents were nibbling away. This worldview was distilled in an eleven-point manifesto that he loved and often circulated to friends. It was yet another document that did the rounds among men of his ilk, and on the Internet it was sometimes falsely attributed to prominent people, only to see those claims debunked on "urban legends" sites. Stroman gave the manifesto his own title: "True American." It declared:

1. I believe the money I make belongs to me and my family not some midlevel governmental functionary with a bad comb-over who wants to give it away to crack addicts squirting out babies.
2. I think playing with toy guns doesn't make you a killer. I believe ignoring your kids and giving them Prozac might.
3. I don't think being a minority makes you noble or victimized.
4. This is my life to live and not necessarily up to others expectations.
5. I believe that if you are selling me a Dairy Queen shake, a pack of cigarettes or hotel room, you do it in English. As a matter of fact, If you are an American citizen, you should speak English. My uncles and forefathers shouldn't have had to die in vain so you can leave the country you were born in to come here and disrespect ours and make us bend to your will.
6. I don't think just because you were not born in this country you qualify for any special loan programs, so you can open a hotel, a 7-Eleven, trinket shop or anything else.
7. I believe a self-righteous liberal democrat with a cause, is more dangerous than a Hells Angel with an attitude.
8. Our soldiers did not go to some foreign country and risk their lives in vain and defend our constitution so that decades later you can tell me it's a living document, ever-changing, and is open to interpretation. The dudes who wrote it are light years ahead of us. So leave it alone.
9. I never owned, or was a slave, and a large percentage of our forefathers weren't wealthy enough to own one either so stop blaming me because prior white folks owned slaves, and remember tons of white, Indian, Chinese and other races have been slaves too.
10. I don't believe in "HATE CRIME" legislation, even suggesting it pisses me off. You're telling me that someone who is

a minority, gay, disabled, another nationality, or otherwise different from the mainstream of this country, has more value as a human being than I do as a white male? If ya kill someone that's a hate-crime. We don't need more laws, we can't enforce the ones we got.

11. I will not be frowned upon or be looked down upon or be made to keep silent because I have these beliefs and opinions. I thought this country allowed me that right.

Like this manifesto, Stroman's worldview braided together a variety of ideologies and outlooks: Fox News talking-head talking points and Hells Angels fuck-the-worldism; Aryan Brotherhood racism and Texan exceptionalism; Cato Institute libertarianism and middle-aged white-guy bitterness; old-fashioned nativism and Focus on the Family–style concern about social decay; "True American" national pride and a post-9/11 clamoring for "moral clarity." Yet his ideas, as they emerged in his own writings, spoke of a man who had not grappled with them so much as heard things often enough to pick out what he liked and didn't. Stock phrases that affirmed his instincts stuck with him and became the basis of a philosophy.

What had probably never occurred to Mark Stroman was that his tendency to hate could ultimately save his life. In fact, in Texas at this moment in time, it was different from what he suspected: committing a hate crime could get you off easy. If the state ascribed his actions to simple hatred, Stroman might have received nothing more than a life sentence. To give him the Death, as they sometimes called it in Texas, they had to accuse him of a fancier thing called capital murder—murder committed during one of a handful of other crimes, like arson or robbery. If a man entered a parking lot, shot a black guy because he was black, and sped away, he might well be looking at life. If he walked into a store and stuck up the same guy for $300 and then, having taken it, murdered him, he could get the Death. Another quirk of Texas law complicated the situation. Texas did not begin giving sentences of life without parole until 2005.

Before that, recipients of life sentences were eligible for release, assuming good behavior, after forty years on the inside. In short, to accuse Stroman of a hate crime would be to risk his walking the streets someday.

The signature of Stroman's mini-mart visits had been that he took nothing. In the case of Hasan, he walked in and just shot him; the police report noted a stash of $100 bills left untouched. In the case of Bhuiyan, same thing. But there was a wrinkle in the murder of Patel. The surveillance tape showed Stroman barging into the store, yelling something to the effect of "Give me the money," shooting Patel, and then seeming to fumble with the register. Stroman took nothing in the end, but those words and that fumbling complicated things.

The dilemma for prosecutors was this: even a cursory glance at Stroman's history and statements, and at the details of the shootings, suggested that these were not really robberies. The man had taken no money. He had gone after an Indian, a Pakistani, and a Bangladeshi—the latter two Muslim, but none of them Arab—in the name of avenging attacks he and many others blamed on people who looked like them. "This whole September 11 thing has devastated everybody's life," Stroman said. "And then here I am—I step in and become an American terrorist." For prosecutors, however, trying Stroman for a one-man War on Terror meant forgoing the death penalty, which meant his possibly reentering the free world. That outcome the government was unwilling to brook. They had had Stroman in their custody many times—starting with arrests before his armpits sprang hair—and yet had failed to reform him or lock him safely away. They were determined not to repeat their mistakes. Whatever the law, there was only one thing to do with a man like Stroman. Bob Dark, the junior prosecutor on the case, described it plainly: "This man needs to die."

A decision was reached. The Bhuiyan and Hasan shootings, where Stroman had taken nothing and sought nothing, would be put to the side. Stroman would be tried solely for the murder of Patel, during which he had barked "Give me the money" and fiddled in vain with the cash register. His attempt at a counter-jihad would be repackaged for a jury, and for posterity, as a garden-variety robbery-murder, committed to raise money for paying child support and bills—perhaps with a twist of hate but nothing more than that. Mark Stroman would be charged with capital murder, for killing Vasudev Patel "in the course of committing or attempting to commit robbery."

Years later, Bob Dark could safely admit that it was the hatred more than the robbery that motivated prosecutors. They didn't seek the Death because of that "Give me the money." They sought it to get rid of a hateful, incorrigibly violent man, and "Give me the money" became a legal pretext. "Probably the main decision in seeking the Death on him was sort of the retaliation factor that he had—seeking out foreigners," Bob Dark said. As he talked further, he began to hedge: "I guess in his mind he thought he was retaliating on behalf of the country. At least that's what I think he thought. What he was trying to convey was that he was acting on behalf of the American people. But what he was probably doing was acting on behalf of himself, trying to rob some people."

✴

GREG DAVIS, THE lead prosecutor, stood before the jury and led off the opening statements. He framed the case as a simple robbery-murder centered on that utterance of "Give me the money." In its facts the case was uncomplicated, and Stroman's defense lawyer, an amiable man in his midforties by the name of Jim Oatman, made it simpler still. He decided not to give an opening statement, which was his chance to give the jury another frame for seeing the case. When the prosecution finished with many of its witnesses, Oatman declined to cross-examine them. "The defense has no questions," he got used to saying. He also called no witnesses on Stroman's behalf.

He seemed to know something about his client's chances that no one else did.

The stakes of the proceedings could barely be felt in the way they unfolded. Here, the death of a man—and now the possible killing of the killer in turn—became boring and routine. It droned on like a school-board hearing more than a capital-murder trial. There were just eleven witnesses in all. The prosecution called Alka Patel, the widow; a handful of police types to establish the basic, incontrovertible facts of the case; and a few of Stroman's buddies, to whom he had boasted about doing some robberies and killing some Arabs.

The prosecution rested. Then Oatman rose: "Your Honor, ladies and gentlemen of the jury, the defense will rest its case-in-chief." What should be noted is that its case had also just begun. The beginning of the defense of Mark Stroman was also its end, because his team called no witnesses. The court adjourned early that day, to give the judge time to prepare instructions for the jury.

The jury's duty wouldn't be easy. The Death is not often thought of as a philosophical affair. If the country as a whole seemed to be losing faith in capital punishment, Texas was the stubborn outlier. Its system was often labeled corrupt and racist and inept. But even in Texas, it wasn't effortless to get rid of a man. It remained a grave, complex endeavor, for it required the asking of big, nettlesome questions about the nature of a man's life. In the case of *Texas vs. Stroman*, No. 0140949V, stripping away the basics of where, when, and how, the ultimate decision—life versus death—depended on the jury's answer to three such questions:

Which was Mark Stroman's sin in the killing of Patel—hatred or greed?

Was Stroman irredeemably violent, or could he be changed?

Had life given Stroman any choice but to become what he was?

The first of the three questions—whether Stroman came to the Shell station as a robber or, in his telling, a counter-jihadist—belonged to this first phase of the trial, which was to decide his guilt or innocence. If Stroman was convicted, and convicted of capital murder rather than the generic kind, the latter two questions would come into play, as the jury considered how to dispose of his life.

The jurors reconvened the next morning. The judge explained to them the intricacies of the charge of capital murder: "Our law provides that a person commits capital murder if he commits murder, and he intentionally commits the murder in the course of committing or attempting to commit robbery." They were shown a surveillance video that showed the defendant doing that very thing, and then showed Vasudev Patel squirming and dying. During the presentation of the video, Alka Patel stepped outside the courtroom, wishing not to see it.

"Ladies and gentlemen," Bob Dark said in his closing, "this is a very dangerous, vicious man shown by the videotape. Mr. Patel didn't have a chance. I'm sure when Mr. Patel awoke that morning on October fourth of 2001, he had no idea what was awaiting him when he got to that store. He probably figured it was just another day at work. Said good-bye to his wife. Children were probably still asleep; thought he'd be seeing them later on in the day. But, lo and behold, he was about to meet Mark Stroman. Ladies and gentlemen, you can take back the videotape with you when you go back to deliberate and look at it again. I know it's a very shocking, very emotional thing to watch for the first time. But it just shows you what this man is capable of doing and what he did. The state will ask you to find this defendant guilty of capital murder, because that's the only just, honest, and fair verdict in this case. Thank you very much."

Jim Oatman then rose and gave his closing, which was also his first real statement to the jury. He suggested that they find his client guilty of murder but not capital murder, which could bring the death sentence: "No doubt there's a brutal crime, no doubt he deserves to pay, and I'm not asking you to acquit him. He is guilty of knowingly causing that man's murder. He is a murderer. There's no justification or excuse for that. When he fired that gun he was reasonably certain to have caused that result, which was that man's death. But he didn't have a specific intent. And as hard as that choice may be for you, if you watch that video and listen to yourself and stay true to your oath in this case to render a verdict based upon the law and the evidence, he is not guilty of capital murder. He is guilty of murder. I wish you well."

The jury departed for its deliberations and came back in less than an hour, around 11:15 a.m.

"Has the jury reached a verdict?" the judge asked.

"Yes, we have, Your Honor," the foreman said. He passed a sheet of paper up to the bench.

The judge read the verdict aloud: "We, the jury, find the defendant guilty of capital murder, as charged in the indictment."

The judge called a fifteen-minute break. At 11:30 a.m., the parties were to return to decide if Stroman deserved life or the Death.

✳

For the jury, the harder work now began. The set of facts in the case—the whodunit—was straightforward enough. The judge's instructions, in the phase just ended, asked the jurors if they believed, beyond a reasonable doubt, that the defendant was indeed the man who strode into that gas station, robbed, and killed. There was that complexity about specific intent to rob and capital murder. Still, by and large, a juror could feel fairly confident that Stroman was guilty as charged.

Now the court wanted something more demanding from the jurors. They had to decide if Stroman should continue living. "He's sealed his own fate," Bob Dark said. "He's walked himself to the death house. He's like a cancer on society. And you twelve jurors have to be impersonal, as a surgeon is with his knife, and remove that cancer. It's just like when you have gangrene of the body. You have to amputate that portion and save the person."

The jury would not make this decision in the way one might imagine. It had little to do with seeing crime-scene photos or watching lawyers bicker and witnesses sob. The jury had to decide if Stroman met certain conditions, and to do so by asking itself perhaps unanswerable questions about a man's life and making and character. The jury would have to mull over what shaped this Stroman, what made him what he was. It would have to consider whether he could have become anything else—and whether, if allowed to live, albeit in prison, he could still.

The court referred to these more speculative questions as "special issues." First came Special Issue No. 1: "whether there is a probability that the defendant, Mark Anthony Stroman, would commit criminal acts of violence that would constitute a continuing threat to society." To answer yes, the twelve jurors would have to be unanimous. To answer no, at least ten would have to agree. Saying yes kept open the possibility of the Death; no guaranteed a life sentence. It was not an easy question, in part because the jury had to decide whether a man can pose a threat to "society" when confined to prison for the ensuing decades.

If the first question yielded a yes, the jury would move on to Special Issue No. 2: "Do you find from the evidence, taking into consideration all of the evidence, including the circumstances of the offense, the defendant's character and background, and the personal moral culpability of the defendant, that there is a sufficient mitigating circumstance or circumstances to warrant that a sentence of life imprisonment rather than death sentence be imposed?" Here the jury had to be unanimous to say no, nothing mitigated the crime, which would then lead to a sentence of death; if ten jurors found something mitigating in Stroman's history, that would be enough to save him.

This had ceased to be a trial about a crime and instead become a trial about a man's nature—about whether there was any good reason to grant Mark Stroman the fortune of another act.

The grist for this second phase of the trial would be fragments from the story of Stroman's life. Like Tom Boston, who thought he knew Stroman intimately but didn't know about three of his four children; like Tena, who had always loved the man but had never been able to hold him; like their children, who thought about Stroman far more often than they actually saw him; like the parade of police officers who would testify about Stroman's arrests going back to boyhood in Plano—like all those who'd crossed his path, the jurors would come to know the defendant only in peeks. It hadn't been the sort of life that anyone could wholly comprehend.

It was hard for either side to turn the defendant into a fully realized character. Stroman was, in court as elsewhere, a screen for the visions of others. All that could be offered—one witness at a time, and in the accompanying documents submitted to the court—was a scattered portrait of where Mark Stroman had been and what he had known, and a panoply of theories about how a man like this is manufactured. For the juror, there was no clear way to separate verities from falsehood in this retelling. There was no straightforward guide to who was lying and who was telling it as it had been. Even so, the portrait might give a feeling for the man, and a feeling could perhaps grow into a verdict.

⋇

THE JURORS WERE asked to picture him, this little boy with a stutter ripe for teasing and wisps of red hair and ears as big as his cheeks. He comes into the world on October 13, 1969. His birth certificate contains a secret that would not be revealed to him for years: he was not Mark Baker, as he would long assume; he was, in fact, Mark Stroman. His father was not that sputtering old truck of a man called Wallace whom Mark would grow up with but some old consort of his mother's whom he would never truly know. In the corner of America he entered, it was more and more like that.

Tena Stroman, Mark's maternal aunt, and the defense's expert-witness psychologist all argued to the jury that the Bakers' home in Plano was not a good place to make the mistake of being young. Tena put it simply enough: "They didn't want nothing disturbing what was going on with their life."

Jurors heard story after story about Mark's early years on Latham Drive and later Kidwell Circle in Plano. Not long after Mark's birth, his mother, Sandra, ran off without explanation, leaving the three children with her mother. The family had supposedly gotten a call some months later from a hospital in Shreveport, Louisiana, saying that Sandra had been found pregnant and lying feebly in a gutter. Her own sister, Sue Carlson, testified that she returned, expecting twins, lived at their father's place until the delivery, gave the twins away for adoption, and finally returned home.

The jury heard from her sister that Sandra was a neat freak, with a "compulsive disorder on cleanliness," whose own children—Mark and his two sisters—were "never allowed to sit on the furniture." Carlson also described the heavy drinking whose air filled the household like turned milk: the "happy hour" that Sandra and Wallace regularly threw themselves around 4 or 5 p.m., which invariably led to fighting and calling each other "every name under the sun"; the requirement that when such drinking began, the children keep themselves to their bedrooms, because Wallace just wanted to have his drink, chew on his dinner, and be alone with his wife, however much they quarreled. Carlson even remembered a Christmas dinner at Wallace and Sandra's when Wallace insisted that the children eat in their bedrooms. She had heard Wallace calling Mark "stupid," "ignorant," "dumb," "worthless." She claimed that Wallace kicked Mark in the head and thumped him in the ear and forehead.

"Sandra and Wallace lived, and still live, in their own world. They have a confined life to where nothing is important to them except them," Carlson testified. Later she added of Mark Stroman:

"He didn't have a chance, sir. He didn't have a chance that most children have. He was put out from his own parents, not feeling welcomed or loved. He didn't have the nurturing that a child deserves."

Tena, who had married Mark when she was fifteen, seemed to share this idea of Stroman as a victim of fortune, a man who couldn't be expected to transcend his parentage. She told the jury of a principle by which Wallace had raised him: "If Mark would get into trouble, or if he had somebody was picking on him, he would tell Mark if he didn't go back and whip him, that he was going to get whipped—that Wallace was going to spank him." Tena also claimed that "they would put him in his room for days and make him read the dictionary." A psychiatric evaluation from 1983 noted another punishment used in that home: because Mark was allergic to grass, he was often required to cut it.

"Mark stayed grounded most of his life when he was there," Sue Carlson said.

The defense's psychologist, Mary Connell, testified that Mark's mother once said something to him about having been $50 short of the money required to abort the fetus that became him. She told him this story with regret at having been so broke. "She said she wished she had had a dog," the psychologist told the jury. "That it would have been better if she'd had dogs instead of children."

The jury also heard—from Tena and the psychologist and others—of an important escape hatch in Mark's boyhood days: his grandparents. They were his maternal grandmother and step-grandfather, to be precise, and they had a construction business of their own. They were somewhat more prosperous than Wallace and Sandra and lived on Old Seagoville Road, in an almost bucolic corner of southeastern Dallas. Their house was wide and low, set on a five-acre property where they kept horses that young Mark loved to feed. It was surrounded by quiet lanes, shaded by a canopy of trees, on which he loved to ride his bike. Several witnesses spoke about how Mark would bolt to Old Seagoville whenever he fled Plano on two wheels.

"Mr. Cox loved Mark," Tena Stroman said of the grandfather. "He always told him to be a good man, to grow up, take care of his family, work and be there for his family. He loved Mark. Mark loved his grandpa."

The facts of Mark Stroman's early life, dreary as they seemed, were not altogether unknown in his social milieu. It was a familiar cycle: a boy born to a tired, scattered father who wasn't really his father; passing through some combination of childhood misdemeanors, extra hours on school tests, special ed, visits by probation officers, stints in boys' homes and juvenile prison; and landing at last on the giving end of tired, scattered fatherhood.

Over the years, Stroman would develop a loathing of state interference in people's lives and of the idea of dependency. He believed that people and their families should be left to decide how to live and spend their money, and that they should take advantage of that opportunity and make no excuses. One of the things that Stroman's trial showed was how this attitude might have grown out of a concrete knowledge of government intervention: Stroman had been in and out of the state's supervision since before he shaved. For all his reverence for family and contempt for the state, the trial record also suggested that the state had tried at least as hard as, if not harder than, Stroman's family to fix what afflicted him as a boy.

Where he grew up, the family was a weakening institution. It struggled to teach young men like Mark the homespun virtues that still hung in cross-stitch on the walls. Imperfect as it was, it was the state, alone among the players in Stroman's life, that kept vigil over his growth. It chronicled him consistently through every little stunt or fight or crime that led to paperwork. The state came to know him through this paper: the angles of his fingerprints' turns, the loopy curls of his penmanship, the cadences of his writing, his strengths and weaknesses in school, the locations of his birthmarks (right forearm, right thigh, and right shoulder blade), the inching-up of his height and the swings of his weight (5'1"and 124 pounds in November 1981, at age twelve; 5'6" and 153 pounds in January 1983; 6' and 155 pounds in June 1985), the streets where he'd lived (Latham Drive, Kidwell Circle, Old Seagoville Road, East 15th Street, Clearfield Road). In this long witnessing, the state was the closest thing Stroman had to a father figure, with all the Oedipal ramifications. Stroman would come to loathe the government that tracked him so closely. And yet, for all the data it racked up on Stroman, there was so little connecting of dots—so little seeing.

The state knew, for instance, that he got mostly Cs in third grade at Weatherford Elementary in Plano but earned more Bs in the fourth. The next year, it knew that he could add and subtract whole numbers and solve word problems with those operations but struggled to multiply and divide; that he aced graphs but struggled with fractions. It knew that in the realm of reading he couldn't identify the main idea of things, couldn't recall facts and details, couldn't tell you the sequence of events in a story he'd heard, couldn't tell facts from nonfacts, couldn't draw conclusions—but that he could, against all the odds, write fluently. He spelled and punctuated and capitalized and structured sentences with a flair that seemed to reveal a fiery intelligence that his life situation was working to contain. He couldn't do the things that involved listening—taking voices in. His fifth-grade teacher gave him "needs improvement" ratings on obedience to school rules, respect for authority and for others, and self-discipline. But he could express himself.

The state also knew that one evening the following year, with Mark in the sixth grade, a young boy named Chad was riding his bike to a 7-Eleven in Plano. He came upon a pair of boys who struck him as mean-looking. He turned around and sped off the other way. The mean-looking boys started trailing him. Stroman was one of them, wearing a red windbreaker and jeans, holding nunchakus—two sixteen-inch-long chrome-colored pipes linked by a chain. Mark asked the terrified boy for his money. The boy replied that he had only a few cents. Mark's associate rapped the boy on his face with a closed fist, leaving a scratch, and then the two of them fled. Mark was caught and eventually sentenced to probation for the attack. He was ordered to avoid "injurious or vicious habits," to remain within the county limits, to submit to home visits by an officer, and to avoid places that sold alcohol.

What the state didn't know about was the unseen occurrences in Stroman's home life that fueled the things it could see. Thus the jury would get limited insight into why, for example, Stroman suddenly failed sixth grade and was made to repeat it: Ds in English, music, science and health, and social studies; Fs in math and reading; and, for a saving grace, an A in physical education.

During his second shot at sixth grade, in the spring of 1983, Stroman was riding around Plano on his bike, dressed in all red, white, and blue, when he came upon a silver Chevy pickup truck parked on the street. He came close enough to notice the keys lying in the truck bed. He decided to trade in his bike for this better ride. He opened the unlocked door, hoisted himself into the front seat, pushed the truck into neutral, and rolled backward down the inclined street. He was seasoned enough at thirteen years old to know that you don't rev up the engine of the truck you want to steal right in front of the guy who might shoot you if he heard.

Then Mark turned it on and took off. He drove over to the TTO Game Room, where he picked up a friend named Matthew Kirby, and went roaming around with him. After a half hour or so of cruising, Mark saw a police car and panicked. He hooked a sharp left down what turned out to be an alley and ran into a wooden fence, bringing down a perfectly good ten-foot stretch of it. He ran off northbound on foot; Matt Kirby grabbed his bike from the truck bed and vanished east. When the police caught Mark a short while later, he said he had run away from home a couple of days before taking the truck. He'd stayed in some vacant houses on Lakeshore Drive in Plano, and, according to the police reports, left his little thirteen-year-old crime signatures—a broken window here, Coke cans lazily adrift in the swimming pool there.

Some days after his arrest, a pair of psychologists named Sylvia Gearing and Dan Cox, of the Plano Child Guidance Clinic, evaluated Stroman. They ran a variety of tests—vocabulary, inkblot, thematic apperception, house-tree-person, Bender-Gestalt, and Minnesota Multiphasic Personality Inventory—and found that, while the thirteen-year-old was wild beyond measure and severely tormented, he was intellectually above average, far from insanity or being unable to control his own actions. The resulting report became part of the trial record, the better to help jurors decide Stroman's degree of responsibility for his deeds:

BACKGROUND INFORMATION

During the family interview with Mark and his parents, they reported that Mark has been in repeated trouble with the law for the last few years. Specifically, they stated that Mark's difficulties began when he was approximately nine years old. Past problems with this youngster have included stealing parts of bicycles, "car-hopping", [redacted], aggravated robbery, runaway, and disruptive behavior in the school. The Bakers asserted that they have tried numerous strategies to help their son but none have been successful. In December, the Plano school reportedly refused to let Mark attend classes and the Bakers placed him in a Christian Academy. However, three weeks prior to this psychological evaluation, he was refused admission by this particular school.

In discussing the family situation in general, the Bakers noted that they have had marked difficulties with Mark's older sisters, ages 19 and 16 years respectively. The oldest sibling presently is married and the second daughter lives with her grandmother. The Bakers admitted their confusion and concern about how to handle their son and stated that they "don't know what to do with him."

When Mark was interviewed individually he discussed his parent's reported marital problems and stated that they had had frequent separations. Additionally, he talked about his inability to relate to his father in a satisfying manner and noted that his father didn't know how to act around children. In general, this youngster does not appear to experience his parent's home as a stable and pleasant environment. [Redacted]. He reported that his parents are planning to move to Balch Springs in the future. When asked how he thought he would behave in this new environment, Mark replied that he had "these feelings that I'll get into trouble."

CLINICAL OBSERVATIONS

Mark presented as a pleasant youngster who was quite shy during the family interview. However, during the individual interview, he was quite self-disclosing and gave information even when it was not elicited. While he talked, at length, about his individual and family problems, this youngster evidenced little insight into his behavior or his feelings. His testing behavior was appropriate and extremely courteous. He seemed to be concerned about impressing the examiner with his sincere efforts.

ANALYSIS OF TEST RESULTS

On the Peabody Picture Vocabulary Test, Mark obtained an intelligence quotient of 106. This score falls within the average range, representing a percentile score of 71 and a mental age of 15.3. This data suggest that Mark's inadequate school performance may be caused by motivational and emotional factors.

Personality testing indicates that Mark is an individual with poor self-esteem who experiences little ability to control either his own actions or rewards and punishments from his environment. One of this youngster's central concerns is a wish to avoid any significant level of subjective distress. Thus, many of Mark's actions appear to represent an acting-out of negative feelings so he can feel less internal discomfort. This impulsive style suggests a lack of ability to delay gratification and a low tolerance for frustration of immediately experienced egocentric needs. As a result, he fails to aspire to ambitious goals which demand hard work and short-term sacrifice, instead preferring a more hedonistic "live for the moment" approach to life.

Mark generally views the world as a hostile and unpredictable place which demands constant scrutinization. He invests a great deal of energy constantly scanning his environment for clues of impending punishment, which he experiences as being largely arbitrary in nature. This tendency implies a lack of consistent parental rewards and punishments, which would shape socially desirable and conforming behaviors. Mark's sense of what is wrong seems to be dictated largely by externally imposed punishment rather than by internalized social norms. He does not seem to view interpersonal relationships as a major source of need gratification, and may have little, if any, conception of what emotionally meaningful and consistent relationships are. In general, Mark seems to live from moment to moment, seeking immediate hedonistic gratification while dodging environmental punishment as best he can.

These were the years before scientists amply understood the physiological, neurological, and psychological toll of childhood stress. It would later become commonplace to think of a youth like Stroman's as having been spent on something like a war footing, awaiting attacks that could strike at any time, from any direction. The war footing seemed capable of rewiring body and mind, resulting principally in inner torment for certain people and in lashing out for others. But the psychologists who looked at Stroman, for all the facts they uncovered, concluded that he needed no therapy or other individualized treatment. He was too unsophisticated, they found, to sit with a therapist and pick through his past. What he needed was the structure of the youth penal system:

> Given his general lack of empathy and mistrust of others, his lack of internalized social norms and his emphasis on impulsive pursuit of immediate gratification, he does not appear to

be an appropriate candidate for psychotherapy. In view of the chronicity of his acting out behaviors and the parent's lack of effective intervention with this youngster, placement outside the home is recommended. Such placement should provide him with a consistent stable environment with structured and clear limits placed to interact with stable and nurturing adult figures who would facilitate this youngster's learning of more appropriate ways in which to meet his emotional needs.

On May 2, 1983, on the strength of that recommendation, Mark entered the care of the Texas Youth Commission. It was a sprawling juvenile penal system that would serve a total of 6,081 children that year, according to its annual report, through five institutions for delinquents, a program for emotionally disturbed youth, seven halfway houses, two camping programs, parole supervision, and more. Older jurors might have remembered the TYC for causing the State of Texas a great deal of heartburn in the 1970s and '80s. A group of inmates, led by a plaintiff named Alicia Morales, had filed a class-action lawsuit against the TYC in 1971, alleging systemic mistreatment of juveniles. After surveys and interviews with hundreds of inmates, Judge William Wayne Justice issued a stern order in 1973, finding abuse, neglect, racial segregation, and much else in the TYC system and immediately forbidding many of its practices.

His "findings of fact" painted a dire picture of the youth penal world. Correctional officers regularly abused prisoners, "including slapping, punching, and kicking," as well as "racking"—"requiring the inmate to stand against the wall with his hands in his pockets while he is struck a number of times by blows from the fists." Officers had used tear gas, including in times of peace. Inmates were assigned "repetitive, make-work tasks, such as pulling up grass without bending their knees." Some were told they could not speak so long as they were inside, and a fear of reprisal had chilled the reporting of physical abuse. Educational offerings were minimal for many prisoners, despite their grade-school age.

Mark Stroman entered the TYC system ten years after these findings and the judge's ruling, well into a process of reform and monitoring that would continue for years. A month after Stroman's commitment, Judge Justice wrote a follow-up order praising the commission's progress in transforming itself. But he tempered his optimism "by the recognition that personnel will inevitably change, and that, just over a decade ago, many of the individuals who then comprised the officialdom of TYC, and at least one of the attorneys who represents them, unregenerately and callously endeavored to preserve and perpetuate debased, execrable institutions in which juveniles were tortured and terrorized."

On May 12, 1983, ten days after Stroman's commitment, his case-worker, Michael Harrison, reported that he had "adjusted well." He was mixing with peers and was polite. His daily living skills and social skills received high marks from "houseparents." Harrison wrote, "Mark can be a negative follower given the opportunity. To date, Mark has had seven restrictions, most of which have been for loudness and horseplaying, and has handled these restrictions well."

Stroman now had a number in addition to a name: he was 0603582.

✶

IT WAS TENA'S turn on the stand: "Mark treated me like—he was—he treated me like I was—he gave me everything. That's why—that's why I fell in love with him when I met him. He gave me everything. He made me—he made sure I didn't need nothing—no, sir." Fate and age had swollen her considerably from the woman that Mark had met in the streets of Pleasant Grove. She looked out at the jury from small, well-meaning eyes, set in a puffy, weather-beaten face. She was telling the jury about those long afternoons in the mid-1980s when Mark had entered her life. He was a refugee from Plano and from his parents, taken in by his grandparents. He and Tena and her sister would play in the streets. He was always getting the girls into trouble, always raising the stakes of play—whether smoking an illicit cigarette or racing riding mowers around and nearly running Tena over.

The jury would have gathered that the period of their courtship was a volatile time for Mark. After bouncing around the outfits of the TYC system—the Statewide Reception Center, the Gainesville State School, the Fairfield Camp—he had been released on parole. He returned home, and it quickly grew clear that the TYC's aspiration to reform children hadn't worked in this case. The old struggles resumed. At times, Mark showed progress; at times, he seemed destined for a life of trivial crimes and unprovoked bar fights. The paperwork told the story. If he wasn't at one school lunging at Mexican students with a chrome-plated chain and carrying a studded wristband in his back pocket, he might be at another school pulling a five-inch pocketknife on black kids and threatening them with a baseball bat. If his family wasn't reporting problems with spray paint, beer, and girls in his bedroom, the police would be finding him with a butterfly knife on the 400 block of South Buckner, a quarter mile from where he would many years later shoot a Bangladeshi clerk. If he wasn't getting suspended or expelled from a Christian school for making threats, he might be smashing a double-pane window to break into a guy's house. A juror could easily surmise that the true problems lay under the choppy surface of this young man's life, but these underlying currents remained invisible.

"I, Mark Anthony Baker, am relating this statement to Det. Leon Mace, as he writes it for me," began one of the many police reports, in which he relayed one of his crimes (and exotically renamed his mother).

> Today, Friday, 06/21/85, I decided to go to the house at 1816 Williamsburg to steal the guy's weed (marijuana) that lives there. I know this guy's name is Glenn. I went to the back part of this house and used my knife to unlock the kitchen window

and then I crawled through this window. I had only been inside a minute or two when the police arrived and caught me as I was trying to sneak out a front window. I knew this Glen guy had marijuana because I had broken into this same house a couple of weeks ago and stole his marijuana and $100.00 in coins. I had broken into this house the first time to steal marijuana also....

I did not know where Glen kept his marijuana so I had to search all over for it. I finally found it inside a box on a shelf in a closet in a room which must have been an office because there was a computor in this room. I also took the coins out of a large glass bottle which was holding the door open in the master bedroom. There was exactly $100.00 in coins, which I took. I have since then spent all of this money, and I have smoked all of the marijuana....

My mother, Guadalupe Baker, lives in Austin, TX, but I live with my aunt and uncle, Joe Garza in McKinney and have for about one year. However, I have not been at their home for about 1-2 weeks. I have been staying in the Plano area, with various friends. Last night, Thursday night, I had spent just wandering around Plano.

There were many such incidents. But the jury also discovered how, earlier that year, when Tena built up the courage to tell Mark that he'd gotten her pregnant, that a pea-sized Stroman lurked within her, Mark had seemed to step up. The details provided were sketchy, but a few months later, Mark's parole officer reported that he had agreed with his family to work full-time at his grandparents' construction company. Not long afterward, he was said to be doing "extremely well" there.

Amber Stroman entered the world on September 9, 1985. She favored Mark from the start, looked just like him. Tena and Mark were married the following January. She was fifteen; he was sixteen.

The three of them lived in a place of their own down the street from Tena's relatives. A portrait from the period shows them all dressed up, Mark in a dark jacket and red mullet, Tena looking older than her years in a sweater vest and a white shirt. They were young and in love, and she could tell Mark's devotion by how he acted anytime another man so much as laid an eye on her. They fought and cleaved, Mark and Tena, fought and cleaved—but always loved.

The jury learned of these things but also learned that, six weeks after their wedding, the police found Mark living alone and illegally in a vacant apartment in eastern Plano. His bicycle was propped up against the door to fend off people with guns and questions. A few months later, the cops caught him pointing a rifle at four boys and threatening them. On Christmas Day 1986, Mark was arrested for burglarizing a building. That crime was to steal food, according to one of his lawyers. Three weeks later, Tena gave birth to their second child, Robert. These facts were, again, easily available; the reasons behind the lurches remained for the jurors to interpret and explain.

A parole officer who visited the Stromans around this time was able to muster some hope. "Prior to his marriage this past year," the officer wrote, "he had a poor, negative attitude and seemed to have a chip on his shoulder. Since his marriage, he seems to have settled down and seems to realize his responsibilities of working and taking care of his wife and daughter, with another child on the way." The officer noted that, although Mark's education had not gone beyond middle school, he was now "seriously considering on getting his GED." He was working full-time for the Layfield Construction Company out of Kearns, operating a bridge machine, taking home $331.26 a week and spending less than a fifth of that on rent and utilities. (This left it unclear why Stroman would be caught living in vacant houses around the same time.) The Stromans' home on Clearfield Road was a "nicely furnished two bedroom frame house," the report said. Mark and Tena were "very close and supportive of each other. Communication is very good."

The parole officer added, "Mark admits that he has in the past been associated with negative peers. He admits to a rugged life but now he is married with a small child and another child on the way.

He works long hours and hopefully has settled down to a productive life."

Later that year, though, three days after Stroman's eighteenth birthday, he and a buddy began a string of burglaries—burglaries in which, again and again, the thieving paused and the thieves ate some of the food they had found. After being caught, Mark confessed:

> On Friday, Oct 16, 1987 in the morning Charles Kenney and I went to the back of the house. We jumped the fence knocked on the back door. No one answered so we broke out the window. I went in and let Charles in the sliding glass door. I hit a bedroom and Charles sacking food. We gathered up the jewelry, and things we wanted and left the back way. We jumped the brick wall and entered a vaccant building and ate some of the food. We seperated some of the jewelry and left going to the vaccant house. I used the credit card (a Mobil card) from 3441 Ave N at Hwy 5 and Parker Rd to buy a carton of cigerettes and a case of beer....
>
> On Monday Oct 19, 1987 during the morning Charles Kenney and I entered a vaccant house next to 1620 Armstrong. Open a window in vaccant house jumped out went into the back yard of the next house looked around and I broke the window. I entered and let Charles in the back door. Charles started taking the VCR. I started in the bedroom. We found coins, jewelery, knifes, camera, binos, jam box shirts, boots, hat, and a pillow case which we put everything into. We took everything to the vaccant house (next door) stashed VCR in the attic and we left with the jewelry and went to the vaccant house on Williamsburg. We seperated everything and we went to the Texas Pawn Shop and Charles pawned a pocket watch. In the vaccant house on Williamsburg we stashed the pillow case, the coin boxes and some of the jewelery. I took the coins from the collection to byuy food, that Charles and I ate....

It was around this time that Tena got the gash in her neck that she insists Mark didn't cut. The jury heard the story from her, which gave a flavor of their life together. "Me and Mark was down at my grandmother's," she started. "And we were kids, we were kids. And we were down at my grandmother's and we started off going to watch movies with my mom, and we winded up going getting beer. And we sat down there and we played quarters between the two of us with the case of beer, and we winded up getting drunk. And we walked home and left our car down there, and we got to arguing. And I got the knife and I acted—in my mind I knew I wasn't going to hurt myself, but I got to acting—I acted towards him like I was . . ."

She paused to find the right words.

". . . like I was going to cut my wrist. Because I didn't think that he loved me anymore and I wanted him—I wanted to see that he would stop me. And so I acted like I was going to cut my wrist. And he come in there, and he said, 'What are you doing?' I said—you know, it just went into an argument. And he said, 'Give me that knife.' And I said, 'No.' I said, you know, I said, because I felt like I was pregnant. And I said, 'I'm not—if we're not going to be together, then, you know, I've already had one baby by myself,' and I said, 'I'm not doing it again.' And he tried to take the knife away from me, and we had it, and he had his hands on it, and we were pulling at it like this. And he must have looked off or blinked or something, but it—I did like this, and when I did, it stabbed me right here."

The jury also heard how, on September 8, 1988, Tena gave birth to her third child, Erica. Mark, then eighteen, was on and off with Tena at this point, and it was one of his virtues that he treated Erica like his own daughter—though he and everyone else knew she wasn't. He even tried to convince the authorities to let him be there for the birth, but a felony was a felony. He had robbed again, stealing rifles and jewelry and checks; he had then gone on a spree with those checks. This time the reckoning was serious. They gave him five years in hard time at TDC. Then a strange thing happened. Some official came to interview him in the Dallas County jail, where he was awaiting his transfer. Because of overcrowding in Texas penal facilities, there was an order to grant "parole in absentia" to certain prisoners before they even made it to prison. Despite his intimate personal history with Texas law enforcement over the years, Stroman was deemed suitable for release.

On Election Day 1990, more than a year after he got out, Stroman was picked up, along with a buddy, at a Dillard's store on Preston Road in Dallas. He had in his shopping bags a pair of cross-training shoes, a London Fog jacket, a bottle of Yves St. Laurent cologne and another scent by Polo, a woman's purse, three men's sweaters, two pairs of men's pants, and three pairs of jeans. The $589 spree was the unintended courtesy of one Mrs. Terry Hanes, who was leaving a nearby Pep Boys a short while earlier when a man rushed up behind her, grabbed her neck, and jerked away her purse. This, too, was a felony—and now the second one. Mark pleaded guilty and received an eight-year sentence. But again he was paroled—perhaps for the same reasons as before, though the record isn't clear—and freed after a matter of months.

The jury heard how, during one of Mark's stints in jail, his grandfather came to visit him. He told his grandson that he would likely die while Mark was serving out his sentence—and that Mark would probably lose Tena. As it happened, both prophecies came true. When Stroman emerged from his considerably abbreviated sentence in the middle of 1991, Mr. Cox had gone to the next world, and Tena was more or less finished with Mark.

The defense lawyers presented no witnesses who could speak about Mark after this period. The people he'd known since boyhood mostly fell out of his life. New faces came into the picture. The expert-witness psychologist who was working for Mark's side and interviewed him extensively testified that he became involved with a waitress named Shawna. The psychologist also testified about his growing reliance on drugs in the 1990s—including meth. Stroman told the psychologist that sometimes he woke up early in the morning and saw trees out the window, and all he could think was that the narco police must be hiding in there. Mark told the psychologist that meth for him was like coffee for others—not some exotic drug, just the fuel he came to need to row himself through the days.

For the next several years, however, Stroman stayed clear of police reports and prison terms. He appeared to be enjoying some measure of domestic tranquility, which meant that the state's tracking of him mostly stopped. Then in the middle of 2001, not long after Rais Bhuiyan and Salim finished cleaning out the gas station and opened it for business, Stroman was out drinking one evening at the Texas Trap. He loved the joint, always had. Someone called 911 and reported that a man at the bar had a gun on him. One of the things Texas is strict about is keeping guns out of establishments where alcohol accounts for a majority of revenue. The police arrived around 6:15 p.m. and found a .45 caliber semiautomatic, with one round in the chamber and two in the magazine, tucked into Stroman's waistline, just above the family jewels. They took him straight to jail. Fortunately for Stroman, he had some friends called the Templetons, who were generous people. He was friends with Bob and had gotten to know the parents, too.

They bailed him out and brought him home. Soon he would be crashing on their living room sofa, not far from the gun cabinet that had grown fuller and fuller through the senior Mr. Templeton's long service with the Dallas Police Department. Far from Dallas, meanwhile, final preparations were under way for a series of airplane attacks on the country Stroman so professed to love.

⚹

As it turned out, Rais had been anguished about nothing. When they called him to the stand, they wanted only the barest details— where he lived at that time, the basic facts of his shooting, the identification of that man over there as the shooter. The purpose of bringing him up there was to remind the jury that in addition to the killing of Patel, who was the focus of the trial, Stroman had killed another man and shot a third. Most of the questions they asked Rais during his few minutes on the stand required monosyllabic confirmations more than answers.

The happy news that Rais could give the jurors was that he'd had three eye surgeries and was awaiting the fourth. He hoped it might restore as much as a quarter of his vision.

The judge thanked him and asked him to step down.

✳

THE LAST TWO witnesses for the defense during this punishment phase were its Hail Mary passes. As the evidence had mounted, it had grown harder to sustain the idea that Stroman would pose no continuing threat, that he would enter prison and somehow become a wallflower. What could be argued—though it might have offended every bone in Stroman's "True American" body and struck him as typical liberal Democrat hogwash psychobabble—was that his past prevented him from turning out otherwise, that he should be spared because he could only have become what he had.

Mary Connell, the defense's expert psychologist, took the jury through a PowerPoint presentation about Stroman's life: "As a baby enters the world, his chances for good development are best if he's wanted, if he's loved, if he's the product of a stable family and a healthy pregnancy, if there's been prenatal care that's good, if there hasn't been toxicity such as alcohol abuse on the part of the mother." Stroman, she said, knew few of those advantages. She speculated that he could have had fetal alcohol syndrome, given his mother's habits. She suggested that the back-and-forth between Plano and Seagoville would have disoriented Mark. The incessant needling by Wallace and the swipes about dogs and abortions by Sandra would have injured the boy's self-esteem and his "confidence that his parent's going to be there tomorrow and is going to love him and take care of him."

Dr. Connell sought to frame Stroman's drug use in a similar way, to push it out of the choice column in the jury's mind and into the column of predetermination. Once Mark got into meth, she said, he lost a great deal of control over himself. She attributed his rage and propensity to violence to the drug: "People who are using metham- phetamine don't lie around in a stupored state. They have lots of energy; they want to do things. They're also agitated and aggressive." She insisted, from her hours of interviewing Mark, that he believed someone was trying to kill him around the time that 9/11 came. She couldn't tell if this fear was delusional or real, but what mattered was that the fear, combined with the drugs, would have placed Mark on a perpetual battle footing: "He was experiencing paranoid ide- ation at times and was, in fact, predisposed to suspiciousness and guardedness, as are many people who are drawn to this drug. The drug allows you to stay up and stay hyper-vigilant and keep a watch over your shoulders."

So when word of 9/11 reached Stroman, Dr. Connell testified, it might have given a tripped-out man a kind of permission: "When he heard about these incidents, he was in a state of heightened agita- tion, aggression, crazy thinking. And it affected him, perhaps, much as it affected many other people. But I think in many respects it affected him even more, and became for him kind of a license for an outlet for a lot of his aggression. Guns had always been a part of his life. He had a significant arsenal, and he was by now heavily armed, in a highly agitated paranoid state, and he took action. And he rep- resented that he believed that anybody and everybody would have done the same thing if they'd had the nerve."

Dr. Connell was followed by a psychiatrist, Dr. Stonedale. She believed Stroman suffered from acute stress disorder, a precursor to the better-known post-traumatic stress disorder. Scans of Stro- man's brain, made after his incarceration, had found "generalized status slowing," which could be consistent with epilepsy. There seemed to be swelling and damage to the brain, perhaps caused by drugs or by epilepsy. An MRI had found a wedge-shaped section of the brain, in the right frontal lobe, where the blood flow had all but stopped—again, a possible consequence of drug use or of injury. That area of the brain happened, Dr. Stonedale said, to be the area that governs emotion and impulsivity and acting-out. The doctor also noted that Mark was receiving Seroquel in prison—an antipsychotic drug used to treat depression, bipolar disorder, and schizophrenia. But Stroman was getting a "sub-therapeutic" dosage of 200 milligrams a day, in Dr. Stonedale's view, when in fact he needed 600 to 800.

As she closed, the doctor suddenly spoke more bluntly. It happened when Stroman's lawyer asked if there were adequate programs in the prison system, and from the state more generally, for the addicted and otherwise troubled.

"There's very few programs, unfortunately," Dr. Stonedale said. "I work at the Parkland psychiatric emergency room, and we have probably a dozen drug abusers a day coming in looking for programs. Some of them don't really want to be helped, but a significant number of them do. And there aren't any programs. There's nowhere for them to go; there's no funding. They'll sit in our emergency room sometimes for twenty-four hours while we're on the phone begging people to take them in. The system is broken. People doing drugs— you know, yes, no one is making them do it, understandably. But we're not helping. We're not doing anything to help them. We wait until they commit a heinous crime, and then put them to death."

For the jury, it might have been a jarring idea: that Texas didn't necessarily execute people because they were irredeemable, bone-rotten murderers, but because it didn't know what to do with them earlier in their lives, as they built up to that crime. It was a simple algorithm to kill people who had killed. But to unravel the knotted problem that Stroman had been for the government over the years—that took time and programs and subtle understanding.

✳

Stroman may not have enjoyed the defense offered on his behalf. He believed in the right to make choices, as his manifesto and prison letters showed, and in the sovereignty of those choices in governing a life. He believed that casting a man as helpless robbed him of his dignity. He liked a quote he had clipped: "We don't rise to the level of our abilities; we fall to the level of our excuses."

Tom Boston, who attended the trial and who shared many of Mark's intuitions about these things, wrestled long afterward with whether his buddy could or couldn't have been otherwise.

"Everybody's always got a choice, at any point, no matter what part of their life," he said. "They've always got a choice. And they may have a lot more obstacles than the normal person; they may have drawbacks, no matter what their situation. There are people that are quadriplegics, and they think the world's against them because they don't have arms and legs. But there is always something they can do. You can't use excuses. A lot of our society uses excuses, and that's what probably breeds a lot of the hate."

As he watched the trial, Tom felt himself swinging between excuses and condemnation in his own assessment of Mark. "I know that he wasn't in his right mind," Tom said. "Whether it was drug-induced, whether it was his childhood, or whether it was stress he was going through in life—whatever the reason was, the bottom line was, he wasn't there. He wasn't. It wasn't something a normal person would do. So obviously I knew at that point it was a combination of drugs and stress and all the things he was going through, and he just hit rock-bottom."

Tom wasn't sure if this was what they called mitigation in the court, but he also believed that execution was no solution. Maybe a life sentence would work, or maybe a mental hospital. But that belief also wavered the more he thought about it: "When you go back and you're like, he's just a piece of shit trash, do you just get rid of trash or do you keep them around?"

The trouble with the excuses theory was that Tom's life seemed to contradict its premises. "I was brought up in a dysfunctional family. I was beaten to shit as a child," he said. His mother was a "pill popper" and merciless in her abuse. Tom thought of himself as a perfect candidate for an Oprah confessional or a Jerry Springer confrontation. "I don't look back and say, 'Well, I'm going to do this because I had this as a child.' I mean, everybody's got something in their childhood. Nobody has a storybook-perfect deal. And everybody's got things that set them back. No matter whether it be alcoholism or finance problems or educational problems, whatever, you can come up with a million-zillion excuses. But you've gotta overcome that. It's up to you as an individual."

However, Tom also sensed the country changing in ways that he figured would nourish more Mark Stromans than Tom Bostons, in those cases where it could tip either way.

"You look back years and years ago, and a family used to be this dad, the mom stayed at home, took care of the children, nurtured the kids, took care of the house—everything," he said. "Then you start having a bad economy. Bills up, inflation's up, more cost of food. So then you start breaking up the family unit. Mom's at work, the dad's out working, then who's with the kids? Then the schools. If you got a good school, your kid may turn out all right. That's the private sector. If you go to public schools, it's like a war zone, so that's like a mini-type prison." He had managed to place his own children in private school.

Though Tom had suffered abuse and knew its toll, a part of him even wondered if modern taboos against hitting one's children were hurting the young: "I look today now, where kids aren't getting spanked with a belt, they aren't getting reprimanded, and our whole society's going to shit because of things like that. And I'm not saying beat your freaking kids. Your dad would say, 'I'm gonna get out the belt.' And he wouldn't get it out, but you had to have the threat."

Tom went on, "You've got trouble-makers as kids that don't have any respect for their parents or people, and they're off on the wrong track already. So then you can't discipline the children; the schools can't discipline children; they're not getting it at home. They're little hellions. They're spoiled." It begins with rebellions like Mark's long years earlier, he said, and no one knows how to nip them in the bud: "They get in trouble, they go through the system, and it just snowballs."

Everybody's always got a choice, Tom had said at first. The more he talked, the muddier it got.

✳

B︎OB DARK, THE junior prosecutor, stood before the jury and began the first of the closing statements of the penalty phase: "You're not responsible for the defendant being in the position he is, facing the death sentence. So don't for a moment think that you are. Don't go off on any guilt trip like the defense will probably have you do. The defendant got himself in this jam by his own conscious, deliberate choices. For the past twenty years, he's left a trail of crimes and victims. His criminal history is a road map that leads directly to the death house."

Dark told the jury that rehabilitation wasn't possible for a man like Stroman. He couldn't, and wouldn't, change. Then the prosecutor turned to the mitigation question. Had the defense given satisfactory reasons for why Stroman's past somehow excused his deeds? "Oh sure, we heard from some professionals from the defense," Dark said. "It's that same stuff. When all else fails, blame your parents for not giving you enough love or because they disciplined you. That's what they fall back on for you to feel some mitigation, some sympathy for this man. The sympathy should be for victims in this case."

Dark said the real choice facing the jurors was whether or not to spare Stroman's future victims, because this defendant would surely strike again: "He will never learn. He is the way he is. No one is going to change him. He's a consumer of life, not a contributor to it."

Jim Oatman rose and, with Stroman beside him, tried to cast his client as a kind of all-American terrorist. Here was a man life had given no shot and who, like so many errant young boys in unpronounceable republics, was given renewed purpose by the notion of jihad.

"Ask yourself, did this man over here choose his parents? Did he choose that she might abuse drugs or alcohol? Did he choose that she would not even come when he's facing execution? Did he choose that he would flunk in school? Did he choose to have that stuttering problem that he had? No, he didn't choose those things. Things happened to him in his life." Of course, Oatman conceded, Stroman made bad choices, too. But the combination of the choices he never had and his poor selection among the ones he did have left him coldly alone, convinced that no one loved him. This isolation, Oatman argued, fertilized his client's mind for the idea of waging a reverse jihad.

"Terrorism and racism reaches out for those people," Oatman said. "Says, 'We'll love you. Come in to us. And because of what you believe about Muslims, what you believe about religion, we'll give you life everlasting. And if you'll strap a bomb to your body or fly an airplane into a building, you will have done for the glory of God.'"

Finally, it was the lead prosecutor's turn. Greg Davis began by apologizing to the victims of Mark Stroman's crimes and their families, because Texas "has made several mistakes with him," he said. All those years ago, the state had put him on probation instead of jailing him, sent him home to give him another chance, told him to do better, try harder. Those days of leniency, that "horrible deadly mistake we made with him"—it was all over now.

Davis's approach in closing was to present Mark Stroman as a false prophet of the American dream who got in the way of people actually living it.

He spoke of the Hasans, the Patels, Rais Bhuiyan—of how they had left their certainties and come to America in pursuit of hazy dreams. "You see, if there's any true Americans here in this courtroom, this isn't one of them here," Davis said, speaking of Stroman. "These people back here who actually believed in the ideals enough to leave their homeland to come here—why? Because they believed that this was the country where you could pursue your life, liberty, and happiness. That it was that great of a country.

"And it is a great country. It's a great enough country that even a cold-blooded murderer like this sitting over here can be given full due process. And it is a wonderful country we live in. But those dreams were wiped out. And they become nightmares now. Why? Because this man over here had another dream." Davis quoted Stroman's own words: "His dream was to kill them all. To kill them all."

※

IT WAS IMPORTANT to Stroman that he be wearing a Harley T-shirt when the decision came. He asked Tena to buy it and bring it to him. His lawyers wanted him more formal, but he figured it was best to be himself. He was sitting there in that T-shirt, with a little American flag on his table, when the jurors came back. It hadn't taken them long.

The jury foreman, Lloyd Roberts, addressed the judge. On Special Issue No. 1, they found unanimously in the affirmative. Yes, Stroman would be a continuing threat. On Special Issue No. 2, they found unanimously in the negative. No, there was nothing in Stroman's past to mitigate what he had done.

So the Death it would be.

Judge Wade officially informed Stroman of his sentence. An order would be sent to the executioners "to carry out this sentence of death by intravenous injection of a substance or substances, in a lethal quantity sufficient to cause your death, until you are dead."

Judge Wade looked over to the defense table. "Mr. Stroman, good luck to you," he said.

"Have a good one," Stroman said. "Thank you, sir."

Hospitaliano!

Would Abida remember the magnets they hung? Would she remember when they would speak on the phone after midnight, in the earliest days, slamming the phone down when a snooping relative picked up? Would she remember giving him recipes when he lived in that house in Queens, long before the day of the bee stings?

Even if she did, would it matter?

There was no way to know but to return. It was the end of 2002, and Rais was at last taking off from Dallas for a trip to Dhaka. It had been more than a year. The doctors had cleared him to fly. He left, bound for a woman who had waited long enough to become a wife.

✳

THEY MET AT a relative's home. When Abida saw his face, she told Rais it looked good; she was surprised not to see scars. Aside from this comment, though, it was instantly clear to Rais that something was wrong—something that hadn't been communicated to him (or, just as likely, hadn't been heard) over the phone: "She was a different person, no emotion or feelings in her voice or face. Seems like she did not know me and we're there to have a formal conversation." She needed to give Rais some news: "She told me she has changed and was going to marry according to her family's choice." Her family had already chosen someone, in fact, and she would respect their decision. "She can't come back, it's too late, and I should move on with my own life" was the message a stunned suitor took away.

"She said that she couldn't wait for me anymore, and it was too much pressure from the family," Rais said. "She had to move on. And I did not blame her, because I know that she was always under pressure. So this shooting incident expedited her mom's efforts to push her more: 'Now this guy's shot, and he's stuck there; he cannot come back, so how long you gonna wait? Blah, blah, blah.' If you hear same thing every single day, how long you can go with the same bullying?"

Rais knew he could win Abida back. He just needed time; she just needed to see him in person some more, to reconnect and remember. It needed to be less abstract. He went over to her house in the ensuing days to talk further, to dig out what sentiments could be saved. But Abida was cool and seemed to have "changed mentally," Rais felt: "She didn't show any sign of feelings or love towards me." It was like a different soul in the same body.

In one of their conversations, Abida brought up a delicate subject, on which she needed Rais's cooperation. A few weeks before Rais left Bangladesh in 1999, he and Abida, without telling anyone, had quietly secured a marriage certificate from the government. They intended it, Rais said, "as a last resort to save her from marrying someone else as per her mother's choice." They didn't consider themselves married, as there had been no ceremony before God. Now Abida asked Rais to sign some paperwork to annul that union. Rais sensed that he had some leverage: "I did not agree with that because I wanted her to come back." It wasn't long before a letter seeking a divorce arrived by post.

"The relation ended like an *Unsolved Mysteries* case," Rais said. They hadn't even formally said good-bye: "There was no hug or touching, or any angry conversation."

History—big or small, national or personal—is little more than the story of the collision of perceptions, as a wise historian once wrote. So it was with Rais and Abida. For as long as they'd been together, Abida had been at once awed and frightened by Rais's ever-swerving dreams; her persistent questioning about Texas had betrayed a recurring anxiety that he was always elevating something—his ambitions, perhaps his friends, who knows what— above his commitment to her. In Rais's mind, it had been precisely the other way around. He loved the rhythms of New York. He had gone to Texas to make money and save up and get a big house and be able to pay for a proper wedding, all so he could take Abida away from that obstructionist mother and that hard country and into a life worthy of her virtue and beauty.

Rais thought of all he'd done to keep that dream alive. The planning, scheming, and waiting; the paperwork, applications, and visas. In weaker moments, Rais added to that list: being shot. If it weren't for Abida, he would have happily taken his Diversity Visa, stayed in New York, and gotten along fine. "I felt betrayed at that point," he said. "That after doing all these things, all the hardship I went through, I came back home, and now you're leaving. I felt really extreme pain in my heart, and I wanted to give up."

It felt at times like another shot full of burning pellets. The effects, at least, were similar. Rais couldn't find sleep many nights. He couldn't get himself to eat and watched his body slowly wither by the day. He spent most of the time in his bedroom and didn't want to talk to anyone. He taunted himself by playing his and Abida's favorite songs. He recognized in himself the depressed characters he'd known from movie screens—he sensed particular resonances with Shahrukh Khan's character in the hit Bollywood film *Devdas*, although without the alcoholism. His mother, meanwhile, was crying every day, wondering why God would doubly betray her sunshine boy.

Days grew into weeks. Rais's sadness began to disgust him. It was dragging the family down. His depression had become everyone else's, too. One day, he was managing to eat some breakfast around noon. His mother wanted to talk to him. She hugged him and, crying, delivered a simple message: enough.

"Just forgive her in the name of God," Amma said of Abida. "Maybe it's good for you and her that she moved on with her life. Think positively that God gave your life back not to destroy with someone who failed to keep her promise."

Rais clutched her and cried and knew that she was right: "I could not go with the pain anymore, and I didn't want my mother to cry anymore. I said to her, 'I am back to you. I won't think about her anymore.'"

It took time for that aspiration to come true, but slowly the pain and shock within Rais began to yield to something more like transcendence: "I was thinking every single day, that is it really worth it to give up life for a woman, for someone I loved so much?" Maybe his error hadn't been in selecting Abida, but more generally in devoting himself to the bounties of the below-world. Instead of replacing her, he would turn his attention toward more godly things, eternal and changeless things. He sometimes managed to convince himself that he was better off without her. "Is it my loss or her loss that we're going apart?" he asked himself. "It's not my loss—I thought about this. She is losing me. I'm not losing her."

As he convinced himself of so many things, he tried to convince himself that his pain had to stop. How could he abandon his cause? How could he forget that he was marked, was bound for other, greater destinies?

"I cannot lose all these goals just for this one incident," Rais told himself. And thus in April 2003, as an American president from Texas launched his second war in the Muslim world, Rais flew back from that world and resumed the Texan life that he'd launched because of Abida—now without her, and determined all the same.

✳

THE OLIVE GARDEN was just off 635 in Mesquite, on a stretch of Americana where the restaurants were little manors, each with its own parking lot, theme, and breed of systematized friendliness. It hung just below the highway, surrounded by a variety of establishments peddling that special American blend of casual, corporate-efficient, and faux-subversive: an Outback Steakhouse ("No rules, just right"), a Hooters ("Delightfully tacky, yet unrefined"), a McDonald's ("I'm lovin' it"), and a TGI Friday's ("In here, it's always Friday").

Phil Amlong was a manager at this particular Olive Garden. He was silver-haired, a little pudgy, a man who lived by the corporate mantra of "Hospitaliano!" Amlong never forgot that customers were to be called "guests" and that you couldn't tell if a man was a cocktail guy or wine guy just by looking at him. He remembered how one day a nice young man from Bangladesh walked into the restaurant and applied for a job. Rais came recommended by his friend and compatriot Malik, who already worked there. Rais had no experience serving food, it was true, but the young man was good at turning personal needs into more general-sounding imperatives. He told the management that he needed a break and that he would make them proud one day. He got two weeks to prove himself. Before long, he was working double shifts on the weekends.

The new job allowed Rais to move out of his friend's apartment and get his own one-bedroom place, on Milton Street in Dallas, for $570 a month. It was a big step to live on his own. Even without the use of a right eye, he had grown comfortable leaving the house, making his way around the city, visiting the Richardson mosque or friends'

homes. But a part of him still trembled at what Mark Stroman's associates might do if they finally tracked him down. He had contracted a
phobia without its own prefix—of these tattooed people, skinheads,
maybe white people; he wasn't even sure whom to fear—but time
had convinced him that dodging them wasn't sustainable. He had to
put himself back out there, and he calculated that a restaurant, filled
with people throughout the day, would be safer than a gas station. "I
need to go and start doing something that will help me to overcome
the fear," he figured. "Then I thought about going to restaurants and
working, because it's a safe environment. You get to meet a lot of people, so I'll be able to get a chance to talk to people and overcome my
fear." And it was true that if a man wished to face and transcend his
fears of white people, the Olive Garden was an excellent choice.

To work at the Olive Garden is no joke. You have to know what
you're doing and bear the company spirit, lest your guests ever feel
like customers. At the outset, there are menus and protocols to
memorize, exams to take, and a mini-apprenticeship with a seasoned server. "You go through a classroom, basically, is what you're
doing," Phil Amlong said. You must learn to converse with your
guests as though they've walked into your home and you want to
impress them. You need to be able to rattle off names like Ravioli
di Portobello as though they were your grandma's recipes, to know
your Mezzaluna from your Vesuvio, to remember without fail which
wineglass goes with which grape. Every manager adds to the stan-
dard indoctrination some personal touches. Amlong, for instance,
makes sure to teach new staff that there is a first time for every wine
drinker, that it often happens at an Olive Garden, and that fruity
reds are the tenderest way to lose that particular virginity. He taught
recruits like Rais that prejudice was the greatest enemy of tips: "If
you want to be a good waiter, take off the blinders. Don't judge people by the way they look, what religion, their sexual preference, the
way they dress. You don't judge them, you treat them like the same
way, and at the end of the day you make 25–30 percent."

At first, Rais made nowhere near that much in tips. It was partly because he shied away from conversation, skipping the customary "So, what brings you out tonight?" or "Heading to the rodeo after dinner?"—which, at this particular branch, people often were. It was also because Rais knew nothing about what he was serving, especially the alcohol. The only time in his life that his friends had experienced him drunk was on graduation night at the military academy, when he stumbled about and teased a guy in the bathroom. But his stupor had been fake: he pretended to take a gulp, then furtively dumped the wine into a friend's glass. ("By the mercy of God, I avoided.") He had never touched a drink in his life. But he now realized that if he wanted to make any money at the Olive Garden, he had not only to serve alcohol but also to promote it like a connoisseur.

First, he had to persuade himself that it was religiously acceptable to sell what was haram, forbidden, to drink. It required him to argue to himself that his economic survival was at stake and that God would be amenable so long as Rais planned to live better down the road. "You shouldn't die to keep a religion" was how Rais rationalized it. He also had to learn the art of small talk, of chitchat, of local political griping. "Anybody can drop the food on the table," he said. "It's also, like, make them comfortable, talk to them, see what they need, communicate with them, join with their conversation. Those are the good serving techniques." To refill his stash of utterances, he sidled up to his fellow servers whenever he saw them talking: "You have to understand the football game. You have to understand the baseball game a little bit. You have to understand what is going on in the city." He would press them for help: "How can I do good? What I'm lagging behind? Tell me because I never served before, so I have to learn. So what I'm supposed to do?" He also picked up that, here more than back home, humor was acceptable in almost any situation. The purpose of life seemed to be the pursuit of an elusive quantity called fun. As a server, being able to make light of things could prove even more important than bringing the food.

Learning these things was not unlike learning to fly a plane or unload server memory. It was a skill set, and Rais felt most at home when coating himself with skills—and moving forward rather than hunkering down, as he had been of late.

Amlong liked to give Rais and Malik their own section of the restaurant on weekends. They worked well together: Malik the playboy, flirting and hamming; Rais the good soldier, able and earnest. They each could pull in five or six hundred a day on weekends. A few times a month, on their days off, the two of them would come in and dine together, availing themselves of their 50 percent employee discount. They served the motley parade of humanity that passes through a Dallas-area Olive Garden—local big shots, unknown to the world, who could throw down $100 for a special bottle of Amarone; the fifteen-minute celebrities of *So You Think You Can Dance?*; guests at a three-hundred-person rehearsal dinner; a foursome of elderly ladies who introduced themselves as widows, prompting Malik, who heard "weirdos," to laugh inappropriately; a guest who interrogated Rais about what he sucked at night to get his teeth so white; a customer on whose head Malik accidentally dropped a bowl of salad; people who they discovered tipped white waiters more; a football player who wouldn't remove his sunglasses in the restaurant and made Rais read the menu out loud, before leaving a trifling tip, which one of his friends returned later to supplement.

For Rais, the greatest challenge remained alcohol. On a good night, it could account for most of a server's tips. Rais, devout to the bone, was also pragmatic and driven enough to decide that if one was going to sell alcohol to the godless, one might as well be good at it. He was mostly blind in one eye, but his other senses stepped up to help him get around. He saw his promotion of alcohol in much the same way: to succeed, he had to lean on abilities other than his sense of taste.

"You have to talk in such a way that you really drink that, and you know the taste," he said. "You can tell the details—like a car seller.

Like all the ingredients, how it tastes, the flavor, if it is crispy, choc-olaty, spicy—the wines, the cocktail drinks, everything. You have to memorize the description, where it came from, and what kind of body structure of the wine, what are the ingredients in the cock-tail drinks. And also you have to understand the guest—what kind of mood they are in. So should you offer them a cocktail drink, or should you just offer them a glass of wine? You have to read the guest as well, according to their appearance. And if they're not knowledge-able, if they have no idea about wine and alcohol, then you have to give them some education. Then they will feel comfortable."

He was relying on Amlong's advice but was also growing confident enough to write some of his own rules. And his new talent at sizing people up and schmoozing and educating folks about drinks he'd never tasted began to pay off. In some months, the mimic became the highest-grossing alcohol seller. Years later, Amlong still couldn't believe that Rais had achieved these things while all but blind in one eye. "I never knew," he said. "He never conveyed that."

Two castes of people, broadly speaking, work at the Olive Gar-den: those passing through, maybe while in college or on the side of a more prestigious but low-paying job, on the way to bigger things; and those bound to stay there, or places like it, forever. If you look closely, you will notice that the two castes are physically distinct—in haircuts and weight classes and textures of skin. It didn't take long for Phil Amlong and the others to realize that Rais, though he came to them needy, belonged to the former caste: he was one of those onward people who sometimes blew through their lives. Amlong knew that he would turn up every weekend in that uniform that was always so nicely starched and pressed, until the inevitable day when he would outgrow it, as he had so much else.

Rais's contact with the more rooted underclass was an education. What struck him at the Olive Garden, making these new friends, was that the Americans he worked with didn't share his ability to reimagine and remake himself. They seemed not to know how to take advantage of their own, fortunate country. And they were often left to themselves, without anyone to cushion their falls or witness their triumphs.

Little things stood out to him. A fellow server wanted to lease a car but complained of having no one to cosign the agreement. Rais couldn't understand that: "I feel that, how come they have no one in their family—their dad, their uncle?" If he had only recently settled in America and already had friends who would sign on a lease for him, how could people who had been here for donkey's years lack such connections? Rais saw his colleagues having to beg for rides or commute by foot on major roads in the searing heat, and he wondered why their family members weren't picking them up—especially the young women. He felt offended on their behalf.

Nor could he make sense of the draining dating lives his colleagues led, cycling through one fling after another. "Once you go through multiple partners," he said, "then you always think that maybe the next one will be good; maybe the next one will be good. And that's why you keep dating people to find out."

He inquired about the family backgrounds of his colleagues. He often couldn't believe what he heard. "Why family is not really together?" he wondered. "Yes, they come together for Thanksgiving or maybe Christmastime, but rest of the year, I don't see the strong bonds. People ask me, 'When is the Mother's Day in your country?' It's every day. I don't just call my mom or send some gift for them once in a year. I call them every day. And whenever I call them, I say, 'What do you need? Do you need some money? Do you need anything? What I can do for you from here?' Because as their son, as in the Islamic teaching, I'm supposed to wipe my parents' feet every single day, just to show them how thankful, how grateful I am to my parents, just to give me birth and brought me this world."

The parent-child relationship seemed very different in his colleagues' lives. He sensed that many of them had been damaged, long before they got to the Olive Garden, by the chaos of their childhoods.

"Most of them said that there is no peace at home," he said. "Whenever they go home, they feel no love, no affection at home. Parents are busy with their own lives. Other siblings, they're with their own world. So they will come out on the street and hang out with their buddies, do stupid things that make them feel happy. And few of them, they said that's why they end up doing drugs; that's why they even end up selling drugs."

He sometimes referred to the resulting style of existence as the "SAD life"—his acronym for a life beholden to sex, alcohol, and drugs.

A part of him wondered if it was some kind of commercial conspiracy—getting all these young people to quit school, unskilled, to create a labor force for unpalatable jobs: "There have to be some kids that drop out from college, from high school. Otherwise, some jobs, they wouldn't get people. If everybody becomes successful, then who will populate the strip clubs or the nude bars? Somebody has to go and work there. Somebody has to go and promote the alcohol business."

Conspiracies aside, what Rais was perhaps discovering was that the liberty and selfhood that America gave, that had called to him from across the oceans, could, if carried to their extremes, fail people as much as the strictures of a society like Bangladesh. The failures looked different, but they both exacted the toll of wasted human potential. To be, on one hand, a woman in Bangladesh locked at home in purdah, unable to work or choose a husband, voiceless against her father; and to be, on the other, a poor, overworked, drug-taking woman in Dallas, walking alone in the heat on the highway's edge, unable to make her children's fathers commit, too estranged from her parents to ask for help—maybe these situations were less different than they seemed. What Rais was coming to see, through his Olive Garden immersion, was the limits of the freedom for which he had come to America—how chaos and hedonism and social corrosion could complicate its lived experience.

Rais had come from where the self was given too little, and now he lived where at times it seemed to take too much. "Here we think freedom means whatever I wanna do, whatever I wanna say—that is freedom," he said. "But that's the wrong definition. That's why people end up making more mistakes. Freedom is not whatever you want to do, whatever you want to say." Freedom, by Rais's lights, was "nothing but a responsibility."

He compared these observations he made about America to how, years ago at the cadet college, his nose had almost burned off at the extraordinary stench of his classmates' dorm room, while they, who had grown accustomed to it, no longer detected it. "There is something good here, something bad here; something good over in our place, something bad there," he said. "We can see these kind of things, like how I used to feel the smell in those rooms. As an immigrant, we see what these people are missing here. But if they live here, they got used to it."

He did, though, share one burden with the Americans: debt. By the middle of 2003, he still had $60,000 in unpaid medical bills. The surgeries were complete and had failed to restore anything near a quarter of his vision, as once hoped; he was resigning himself to a life with one good eye. The good eye—a superb eye, in fact, with 20/10 vision—would have to compensate for the bad one, which could perceive only the barest hints of light. He had to give up whatever hope he had of seeing three-dimensionally, or of being aware of what was coming at him from the right side. He had to accept not being good at things he was good at before. There would be headaches, surely, and a need to focus fiercely where others cruised. All of that he could handle. He had even, at last, found an affordable clinic called Pathways to treat his depression. He went for a series of therapy sessions and was prescribed some mood-enhancing medications.

But the debt hounds still haunted Rais. Above and beyond the problems he observed with sex, alcohol, and drugs, Rais was jarred by the American relationship to money. "Is everything all about business and money?" he would ask the collectors—for whom, understandably, it was.

✳

As rais struggled through the rebuilding of a life, the Hasan family had their own troubles. It was Waqar Hasan, in the midst of grilling a burger, who had been the first victim of Stroman's war. Not long afterward, his widow, Durreshahwar, learned that his death was only the beginning.

She and her four daughters had been in the country since 1994 on temporary visas. In 1996, Waqar applied for a green card, which would allow the family to stay indefinitely. His petition approved, he filed for Durreshahwar and his daughters to be converted to permanent residency, too. Their applications were pending when Stroman went out Arab-hunting.

Durreshahwar now learned that because her husband was the sponsor of the application, and because he no longer existed, she and her four adolescent daughters could not remain in the country. Her brother, Nadeem Akhtar, said the family understood that they had just weeks or months before having to leave.

They hadn't come to the United States for the obvious reason and in the obvious way; their story didn't fit what a visitor might have imagined seeing Waqar working the grill where he would one day die.

Waqar was, as his brother-in-law tells it, a quiet man—a slogger at work, a Muslim who tried to get in his five prayers but was not very religious, the kind of guy who receded and listened when the conversation turned to knotty subjects like God or politics. When working at the store, he would phone his mother—who lived with his wife and daughters back in New Jersey—and linger on the line with her for two or three hours each day.

A few years earlier, Waqar had been a successful businessman in

Karachi, the dense and maddening port metropolis on Pakistan's western coast. Nadeem described the family as living in a house with more bedrooms than they had use for; they employed a chauffeur, a gardener, domestic servants. The money came from rent on properties they owned, some gas stations, and a business importing infant chicks from Holland and growing them into curry-bound chickens.

It was a good life, but it was also a lawless period in Karachi and in Pakistan generally, and the Hasans found themselves a target. Nadeem said Waqar's father was kidnapped and held for ransom twice: they got him back for around $100,000 on one occasion and double that on another. Waqar's office had apparently been plundered by armed men. The family's home had been robbed of much of its gold. It was not entirely clear if their money alone, or also some political connection, was responsible for these incidents. Waqar and Durreshahwar began to wonder every time they sent the girls to school whether they'd get them back. It was time to go.

Waqar Hasan ended up in New Jersey, where his brother was running a business of his own—an Exxon station. Within a year or so, his wife and daughters joined him from Pakistan.

Like Rais, Waqar eventually found himself talked into Texas. He hated the cold in New Jersey, hated shoveling all that snow. Nadeem, his brother-in-law, was already in Dallas and spoke reverently of it. The weather was like Pakistan's. It was easy to start a business. Houses were cheap. Once again, Waqar left his family behind and flew away to establish a suitable life. Once it was ready, he would bring them to Texas. He started working at a mini-mart called Mom's Grocery and soon bought it out. He worked at the store himself, along with a few employees, sometimes putting in more than twelve-hour days. He could see the horizon drawing closer: this new peaceful life with his mother, wife, and daughters around him, his brother-in-law close by, a fine house in a neighborhood with good schools.

Then the bullet entered his right cheek and swam through his jaw and halted in the muscles of his neck.

That was mid-September. Durreshahwar and the kids had planned to leave New Jersey and join him in December or January. Now she would have to leave America.

In Washington, a Democratic congressman from New Jersey heard about the Hasans' situation from a staffer. Rush Holt's district had a sizable immigrant population, and he considered himself a special friend of South Asians; at election time, he hoped they would consider themselves special friends of his. Because of the demographics of the 12th District—which spread across four counties and included Princeton as well as various towns containing the word "Brunswick"—constituents' visa problems were nothing unusual. Still, something about the Hasan matter stood out to Holt when it came to his attention. Somehow the thought of those young daughters, their father recently murdered, being booted out of the country seemed so manifestly unjust. Holt was among those politicians who in the aftermath of 9/11 were vocal not only about thwarting further attacks but also about preventing an American turn toward intolerance.

"All across the country America reacted in dismay when they heard in September 2001 the news of the hate crime that took the life of Pakistan-born Waqar Hasan," Holt later wrote. "When they learned that the murderer committed his brutality as a perverse retaliation for the attacks of September 11, as an act of twisted patriotism, they knew this was a blot on our country. And all Americans felt the pangs even more deeply when they learned that Waqar Hasan left behind a struggling widow and four little girls. For most Americans that was the end of the story, as they went back to their busy lives. The wheels of justice will turn and take care of this, they thought. What they did not think about was that the United States had already incurred an obligation to the Hasan family."

Holt visited the Hasans in New Jersey. He paid his condolences and offered to help. He promised to take on the deportation issue as a personal challenge. His devotion was not easily explained. For more than a year, his staff called around to the relevant agencies to ask what might be done. The answer came back again and again: nothing. Waqar's application wasn't transferable. "When he died, their right to stay in the United States ended," the congressman said.

The silver lining, for now, was that the flurry of inquiries from a congressman's office froze the Hasans' situation and kept them from having to leave immediately.

Their conventional options exhausted, Holt and his staff began to ask what else they might do to create an exception for the Hasans. Someone on the staff had a wild idea. "It required a new law to create a place for this family," as Holt later put it.

The idea involved something called a private bill. It was a rarely used tool in Congress: pieces of legislation, approved by both House and Senate and signed by the president, that named a person or group and specified a change in the law that applied just to them. Among the reasons private bills were uncommon was the obvious possibility of corruption. "If you're making a law for one person," Congressman Holt said, "the committee has to ask—everyone should ask—'Is this a quid pro quo for special interests or special favors? Is this blatantly unfair to the people who are not covered by the private bill?'"

Undeterred by all this, on February 13, 2003, Holt introduced his private bill, HR 867, in Congress. The proposed legislation was titled: "For the relief of Durreshahwar Durreshahwar, Nida Hasan, Asna Hasan, Anum Hasan, and Iqra Hasan." (Whatever happened with the legislation, it once again protected the Hasans from deportation for the time being, pending the bill's fate.)

Holt, still junior in his second term, called, wrote letters, and sent packets of clippings to his colleagues, trying to overcome the inevitable skepticism and inertia. He lobbied influential members, including Jim Sensenbrenner, a Republican from the Milwaukee suburbs and chairman of the House Judiciary Committee, and Sheila Jackson Lee, a Democrat from Houston also on that committee and the ranking member on its Subcommittee on Immigration,

Border Security, and Claims—which had oversight over private bills of this kind.

At last, fifteen months after introducing it, Holt got the bill through the Judiciary Committee. It took another two months to pass the House, and another four for the Senate. Finally, on October 30, 2004, as a group of U.S. Marines died in an attack by Muslim extremists in a far-off place called Fallujah, President George W. Bush signed HR 867 into law and gave five bereft Muslim immigrants a renewed chance at an American life.

"The people of the United States and our government have an odd attitude toward immigration and immigrants," Holt said later. "Often forgetting our own origins, and even our own best interests, we resist diversity and even lash out against others like ourselves, because we mistakenly think they are not like ourselves."

America, he said, "strives to give hope, fairness, and compassion. But these are not automatic. Cruel fate or happenstance often threatens to crush hope and opportunity. Irrational human passions and prejudices can thwart justice and fairness. The demands of life in a busy, complicated society and the exigencies of a complicated legal code can crowd out compassion."

Yet sometimes, Holt said, "we see hope coming out of tragedy, a fair result out of an insane injustice, and compassionate concern out of impersonal laws and regulations."

✳

Rais's FORTUNES WERE also turning. Not long after returning from Bangladesh, he had gone for Friday prayers to the mosque in Richardson. It was one of those strip-mall suburbs of Dallas where far more acreage is dedicated to parking than to doing the things you parked to do. Richardson was full of immigrants, including a fair number of Muslims. Its halal restaurants offered stacks of a publication called the Muslim Yellow Pages (A to Z Printing & Promotion:

"We Welcome the Islamic Community"; A Plus Automotive Repair: "Ask for Hasan"; Texas King, a meat purveyor: "Eat of the things which Allah hath provided for you, Lawfull and good"). At the Richardson mosque that evening, Rais saw a man he thought he recognized. He walked over, apologized for interrupting, and asked if he was a Bangladeshi and a graduate of the Sylhet Cadet College.

The man was a little stunned. Well, yes, he was.

It was an old schoolmate who now lived in Dallas and worked in technology, for Texas Instruments. He invited Rais to his home to catch up properly. When he heard Rais's story, he felt an urge to assist him. Though Rais was happy working as a restaurant server for now, his dream remained to get into IT. His schoolmate offered to help. Come to think of it, he knew the perfect guy for Rais to meet.

So Rais went to see Ahsan Mohammed, who was an important man in the community—a database administrator at an esteemed company, a board member of the mosque, and, in his spare time, the founder of a small IT training academy called Safa Soft. Mohammed would begin by asking students about themselves, where they had worked, what they already knew, before suggesting a course of study. In Rais's case, he recommended that he train himself in Microsoft's SQL Server platform. It was a database system that companies used to store data and retrieve it as customers, say, bought books online or returned shoes or renewed subscriptions. It was like Microsoft Excel on steroids, built to handle thousands of simultaneous queries. The work of administrators like Mohammed was to keep the database humming: allocating more space when needed, debugging, diagnosing blockages. Getting such work now became Rais's next mission.

Mohammed couldn't recall if he charged Rais the usual $600. Rais remembers getting the course for free, and Mohammed's giving him free textbooks as well. The teacher was taken with the seriousness of his student, the intensity of his monocular focus, the tragedy that he stoically bore. Rais completed the course, while working at the Olive Garden on weekends, and continued to pop in to Safa Soft from time to time after finishing to greet his teacher. One of the things that distressed Rais about America was how little respect teachers received: "Back home, if the teacher comes across, we stand up. We do the same thing here, but in the court. Because the judge is there to punish us or to give us freedom, we have to respect. How come we can't do the same thing for the teachers—those who make us a human being?"

Around this time, in the middle of 2003, Rais caught another break. After his long battle with debt, he won a $50,000 grant from the Texas Crime Victims' Compensation Program. Dr. Spencer's office had helped him apply. It was a boon, and yet it still fell $10,000 short of his bills. He contacted the program to ask for a little more but was turned down. They said something about it having to be a "catastrophic disaster" to go up to the $100,000 tier.

If the grant wouldn't grow, the bills would have to shrink. Rais enlisted the state program in his cause, faxing them bills and asking them to lobby his creditors for discounts. He reached out to those creditors directly, too, and tried to cut deals.

"I had to go back and forth, negotiating with all the creditors— the hospital, the ambulance service," Rais said. "Going back and forth, back and forth, back and forth, for several weeks. Finally, Dr. Spencer gave me a break; hospital gave me a little break. Finally, the medical bill came down to $42,000. So now the victims fund, they were asking me to give them back the $8,000. And I was saying that, 'It's not $8 million; it's not $800,000. It's just $8,000, which is not even your monthly salary.' " How could this rich country be so stingy? "I was just shocked," Rais said. "How could you ask that $8,000 back?"

He wrote back pleading his case: he needed the money to help with rent, get a car, maybe see a psychologist. He had been able to get his eye treated because Dr. Spencer was kind. Many other needs remained on hold.

The program relented and let him keep the money.

All this while, he had been working at the Olive Garden. Toward the end of 2004, he found a job applying his SQL Server skills during the week while continuing to wait tables on weekends. Phil Amlong remembered Rais having left only one time, for a better opportunity at a Cheesecake Factory. But his protégé had returned within maybe six weeks, because they put new staff out on the patio, where in a city of air-conditioning junkies there were few tips to be had. Rais remained at the Olive Garden for more than three years, until the moment that Amlong always knew would come.

Rais approached him one day to say that he was leaving. He was grateful to his boss for the chance he'd received, but now a new opportunity awaited. It was some job involving computers. Soon Rais was gone.

[Please Write Back]

Stroman still remembered the day they brought him down to the Polunsky Unit in Livingston, Texas: "I come here with three squad cars from Dallas Sheriff. When I left Dallas County coming to Death Row, there was four officers in each car. And coming down here we drove like a hundred miles an hour. They had the lights on and blocked all entrances. It was like I killed the president. When I got here that was—I don't know—that was like a shock of the world, shock of my life, coming to Texas Death Row. And then when I seen the big emblem of the State of Texas and it said 'Death Row,' it made my heart jump to my stomach."

As he became prisoner No. 999-409, Stroman struggled with the rhythms of this long-stay hotel for the doomed. His letters and other writings offer a detailed portrait of his life inside. The days began around 3 a.m. with the ardent banging and slamming of Death Row's steel gates and doors, and then of the food slot of each inmate's bathroom-sized cell. Even in deep sleep, Stroman claimed to feel the

metallic vibrations in his body. "Chow Time! Chow Time! Lights on
if you are eating," the guard would bark; sometimes Stroman could
tell that the man on duty was really just a boy, his voice cracking into
a squeal. There wasn't much time to snap out of bed and secure your
breakfast: if you didn't flip your light on and stand at the door by the
time they passed, you might get VR'd—recorded in their logbooks as
a "verbal refuse."

If you made it in time, you could count on some permutation of
these things: a stack of pancakes (which Stroman found "cold raw
doughy"); "a spoonful of eggs that wouldn't fill up a small baby";
"sour" applesauce (which he thought not even an infant could tolerate); biscuits, jelly, and butter; cereal or "watery oatmeal"; coffee
(which he routinely felt was either too cold or too diluted).

The jolt of the breakfast service often rattled and angered Stroman. He found a certain comfort afterward in his solitary morning
rites—washing his "old weathered face"; brushing his teeth, sometimes with only water and sometimes, when friends mailed commissary money, with toothpaste; heating water to make his own,
better coffee; crossing off one more day on a calendar that for him
had no firm end date as yet. He paid special attention to which of his
neighbors was next in line for the Death. Ordinarily, the guys gave
each other hell. But a man nearing the end deserved sympathy and
respect at recreation time.

Sometimes Stroman would exercise—maybe eight sets of fifty
push-ups, a few hundred knee-bends. Sometimes, on a radio bought
at the commissary, he would listen to the lone Dallas station he
could pick up down in Livingston, three and a half hours by car from
home. The traffic bulletins made him especially nostalgic—hearing
the names of the streets that had made him, of the expressways and
satellite towns of his scattered youth.

He would stare out the window for long stretches with the faint
hope of witnessing the unusual. One day he fixated on the wild
cats that roamed the Polunsky grounds. He was jealous of their

fatness—proof of their being better fed than the prisoners. He also noticed that the rats near Visitation were unfairly corpulent. In the letters he wrote and journals he kept, he recorded the quotidian miseries of the Row, the little brutalities that evoked the great brutality to come. Like his sighting of one of the wild cats, around 10 p.m. on a Saturday, caught in the razor wire above the fencing that enclosed the sidewalk leading to Visitation. He seemed, when he later wrote of the incident, to identify with that cat, "yelping in pain, blood dripping from its wound and as we walk by not one word was said."

When money was working in his favor, Stroman could shop at the commissary, which sold stamps and typewriters, radios and toothpaste, and all manner of food. Once a week, the inmates could fill out slips, which one of the guards would pick up, later bringing around their purchases on a cart. One of the crucial items the commissary stocked was petroleum jelly—crucial if you didn't want to wake up wet in the middle of the night, first thinking you'd dreamed yourself into peeing, before realizing it was rain transpiring from the free world. Stroman learned to take a fistful of jelly and smear it into the slender cracks on the walls and ceiling.

Polunsky also turned Stroman into an exacting, concerned, vigilant eater. A good deal of his writing dwelled on food. Food was the way the free world came into life on the Row, and it was a reliable barometer of political conditions in the building: when the prisoners misbehaved and the unit went into lockdown mode, there was a likelihood of crudely smashed-together sandwiches (noodle/tuna/mustard, or cheese, or peanut butter); when important holidays came, barring some recreation-hour melee, things could get fleetingly awesome. It was not unheard of on such occasions to get through your slot a full apple and full orange with breakfast, or, later in the day, chicken-fried steak with mashed taters awash in gravy, or a pork chop and brisket with pie and cake, or some fresh bread or red beans or mixed veggies. Sometimes it wasn't obvious why such a meal had arrived—it wasn't Christmas, wasn't Thanksgiving, wasn't the

Fourth of July. On those days you had to figure, as you delved into the deliciousness, that one of your buddies was about to get the poison, and that you were benefiting from the flurry of visitors and the need of the guards to maintain appearances of tending prisoners well.

The telltale sign of a special-reasons meal was silence, when men who otherwise couldn't stop talking dwelled silently and wholly on their plates.

On most days, assuming the unit wasn't on lockdown and an individual prisoner wasn't in solitary, the men had an hour or two for recreation. "Our outside recreation is a cage surrounded by four very high concrete walls with bars and screen on top," Stroman wrote. "Its like a cage at a zoo, all we can see is the sky. For example, it's the size of a garage and you would be able to park two cars inside this area." In theory, it was a relief to get out of a tiny cell and out of your own head and into the company of others. But Stroman, whom no one ever called an introvert, found himself less and less drawn to others: "I've noticed I've pulled back from this little society I live in."

Out in the free world, Stroman had always been at the lower end of whatever ranking one wanted to go by—money, education, occupation. Many of his ideas seemed to develop as a means of emphasizing what lay beneath him: ungrateful immigrants, breeding drug addicts, minorities making it where he hadn't because they convinced the government to shaft guys like him and give them the spoils. Out there, feeling superior to those around him was a constant—and perhaps exhausting—effort, whose reward was maintaining some of what a more honest man might have called self-esteem.

Here at Polunsky, it was different. For the first time in a long time, Stroman could feel himself to be one of the more respectable and less screwed-up people around him: "There's some sickos in this place and tons of child molesters. Makes my stomach flip. I'm no angel by far, but I do have respect for women, children and our elderly." In here, as in few other places, he didn't need to invent much to be able to imagine himself as someone's better. He could engage in a commonplace, and somewhat tenuous, prison sanctimony: the prisoner who was at least not one of *those* prisoners.

The hierarchies of Death Row were as intricate as those of a bee colony. The starkest line, in Stroman's eyes, was between ordinary murderers like him and the rapists and killers of the most vulnerable, whom he didn't even deign to speak with or refer to as "men" in his writings: "the grandma killers and baby rapist pedophiles who are down in the hole because they can't keep their private parts out of their hands and tend to show all the female guards every chance they get, so those sicko's are excluded from my talks and from the word 'men.' " Nor did he admire those who raped grown women. Turning women into widows was, apparently, not in the same league of cruelty in his mind.

There were other lines, too—for example, between the guys who could afford stuff at the commissary and the guys who couldn't. Or between the guys who had backers out there in the free world, fighting their case or posting their letters on a blog, and the guys whose sphere of influence went no further than the unit. There were lines dividing the guys whose women stayed with them, the guys who had no women, and, most improbably, the guys who had managed to get with new women while incarcerated, through visits and letters. There were lines between the black guys, the Anglos, and the "Spanish" guys. A line between those who got visitors and those who didn't. A line between the guys in solitary and the guys in regular. There were subtler divides that Stroman perceived, too, like the one between the inmates who maintained the energy to complain about spoiled beans and such and the ones who were already apprenticing for the passivity of death. Stroman called the latter "death waiters who have just gave up and don't care what is tossed in their cages."

It was the crazies, though, who most haunted Stroman. It offended his sense of honor to be lumped together with them, and yet they, in the fullness of their craziness, rendered forgettable the mere wildness he had struggled with all his life. Here were real-life people who lent him the dignity-by-comparison he had always sought from others, especially the dark and foreign. He really could feel himself to be superior to the one guy, convicted of sex offenses, who insisted that his cell was being gassed and that the CIA had planted a tracking device within him. He felt superior to the guy who he claimed "pulled out their eye and ate it." As Stroman wrote, "This is NOT normal behavior at all." He felt better, too, than the guy who stashed three squirt bottles of his own shit and launched a fecal fusillade against three guards, who left "chocking and gagin' as they ran." Or the guy a few cells down from him, who barked like a dog: "His mind is vanishing fast and he gets no help from the medical staff. They all just laugh and shake their heads as they walk away from his cell. They do not care if one has mental issues and are in complete denial that these isolation cells are having any effects on people going insane." Or the bearded guy who would sit on the cell floor, enclosed by a bedsheet, with "that glazed over look of someone who is not home," as Stroman put it. "He would sit there all day and mumble to himself and would hold conversations with some invisible force. The guards would even ask me about him. That's all this dude did . . . mumble and sit on the floor medicated to the max."

From time to time, one of the inmates would kill himself. On occasion, a guard would do the same. These deaths, and of course the scheduled ones for which the Polunsky Unit existed, knocked Stroman in the head every time. It never got easier.

"I believe death lies dormant in all of us, just waiting to bloom," he said.

*

AFTER THE INITIAL shock of Polunsky, what got to Stroman was the solitude. Prison nibbles at a man, especially when twenty-three hours a day of it pass in total isolation. That nibbling can reveal unseen qualities—can show what kind of a man he really is, when his prior circumstances and lifelong relationships are stolen from him and he confronts the fact of having only himself. In Stroman's case, prison revealed him to be, among other things, an avid and caring correspondent, dashing off letters every day, waiting on the replies, managing a complex weave of transactions by which he solicited and gathered money, received photographs from some for forwarding to others, enlisted support for his appeals, and attempted to burn off his sins with compensatory kindnesses.

From the moment of his arrest in 2001, he reached out with particular fervor to his buddy Bob Templeton and his parents. He had met Bob through another guy who had hired Stroman to do a marble job. Bob's mother, Marge, said her son was easygoing and simple and wary of confrontation, especially compared to his new friend Mark. But Bob came home and glowed to his mother about Mark. "Even though Bobby was older by a year, Bobby looked at Mark as big brother, because Mark defended him and protected him whenever they went out," Marge Templeton said. The first time Mark took Bob to the Texas Trap, for instance, Bob told his mother this story about an interaction with a stranger: "He sat on a stool and the guy said, 'That's my stool.' Bobby said, 'Oh, OK. I'll move over.' Bobby moved over. The guy said, 'That's my stool, too.' Bobby said, 'Oh, OK.' About that time, Mark walked in and said, 'Hey Bob!' and the guy turned around, said, 'Oh, you're friends with Mark? Then you can have the stool,' and moved all the way to the other end of the bar."

Bob's father, Billy, was a retired Dallas police officer who now was head of security for a company downtown. Marge worked for the same company, as an auditor in the accounting department. Bob worked underground in the company's garage. His parents liked Stroman and felt grateful for his love of their son. Which is why they agreed to bail Mark out of jail and take him into their home when he was caught wielding that gun at the Trap in July 2001. He had been sleeping in their den during the nights of his Arab-hunting spree—he on the couch, Bob nearby on the bed.

Stroman was good to the Templetons, bringing leftover marble from his stone-cutting job to spruce up their kitchen. They were good to him, too, enough so that he'd taken to calling Bob's parents Mom and Dad. It sure didn't feel like cheating on anyone to do that. They trusted him with their house and their boy and their over-grown collection of guns—including Billy's prized *Dirty Harry* gun, of the very kind used in the movie, which Mark eventually borrowed for his war. "That one was under the mattress in our room," Marge Templeton said, "and we didn't realize he'd figured that out."

STROMAN BEGAN WRITING to the Templetons as soon as he got inside. Five days after the arrest, he confessed to Bob of being "in a world of shit and I caused it all." He thanked Bob and his parents for their support. He was truly sorry for all he had done. The only recompense he could offer for the chaos he'd brought into their lives was his Chevy Suburban. Stroman told Bob that he'd confirmed with a police officer that the truck would be released to his buddy before long; he said he knew he owed more. He asked Bob to send him old photographs from his album, for some two-dimensional compan-ionship. It wouldn't hurt, he hastened to add, to have twenty or thirty bucks put into his commissary account. The letter ended with this bracketed plea: "[Please write back]".

Two months later, on December 3, Stroman wrote to Bob of not knowing what to feel anymore. He was sure Bob wouldn't under-stand what he was facing. Though he didn't want to sound like some crybaby, he wrote that "when you didn't show up for the visit last weekend, it broke me up inside." But he did appreciate that Bob sent those three photographs. Bob had always been there no matter what, had never let him down before. Bob was his best friend of all time, and Stroman was determined to invest in him. He enclosed a tattoo pattern. He had gotten that particular tat already, and hoped Bob would join him so as to match. Of course, Stroman would understand if he didn't.

Stroman swelled with gratitude when reply letters arrived—especially when they contained money: "You just don't realize how much you help me by showing me so much love & compassion—I even bought a pint of ice cream & and a 'cold' Coca Cola—I was in heaven for a few moments." He asked for various other things, too—photos, of course, but also addresses of his friends and death penalty opponents, a Xerox of some handkerchief of his, a picture of his old cat.

When replies from the Templetons were slower in coming, Stroman was filled with despair. To Bob's mother, he wrote: "I know you are busy, and have a million things to do, but I am pleadin with you to please send those pictures I have been asking you this for a full year now, and all of you keep ignoring my request! ?? Why mom ??" He didn't have stamps or paper to waste on a one-way correspondence. On another occasion, he begged again for photographs: "Stop ignoring me Mom. Please, please, please, please, please, please, please, please, please, please, please, please." Bob's silence, in particular, kicked Stroman in the gut: "Your exact words were you'd be my Bro til the bitter end—Bob everyone who counts in my life has turned and walked away from me and thats the coldest and lonliest feeling I have ever encountered." Why had Bob pulled away? He pleaded to his old friend to stop treating him like a "nobody."

"A DAY WITHOUT human contact," Stroman wrote in one letter to the family, "makes the mind wander and run scenerio after scenerio through the mind." Because in his case those scenarios were universally unpleasant, letters formed a bridge to an isle of sanity. In that new place, he could leave his life behind and lose himself in mastering the conventions of the form. Thank you for your last letter. Did you receive my last letter? I hope your health is well and your spirits, too. Did you look for the photos I asked about? Maybe look in the other album. How is the cat doing? Have you gotten the picture I sent of me with the big-breasted lady, back in the good ol' days—and, more pressingly, could you send it back, please? Please.

Stroman's letters to the Templetons often came adorned with stickers. He loved stickers. Stickers of the American flag (regularly proportioned in some cases, in others heart-shaped), of the Dallas Cowboys, of Harley-Davidsons. A lot of kitten stickers. A Garfield sticker here and there. A run-of-the-mill green smiley face, presumably when his correspondents—the Templetons and a handful of others—had sent him nothing better in a while.

At times, he sounded in his letters like a little boy begging for attention. The letters also showed him to be obtuse—unable or unwilling to come to grips with his deeds, ever focused on the failures of others.

The correspondence revealed how prison challenged Stroman's deepest nature. If he had believed anything on the outside, it was that he needed no one and owed the world nothing. But at Polunsky the open sweeping prairies of time, the intense solitude, the floor-pacing waits for something as simple as a two-line letter from another being, who could choose to write it or choose not to—these things left it plainer than ever to Stroman that his fate in this world was inextricably bound up with others'. Altered circumstances made it harder to sustain the fantasy of his self-containment. The evidence to the contrary was overwhelming and growing. The letters made his position very clear: he now—let's just say it—depended. Depended on kindnesses for which he had little to offer in exchange. Depended on people electing, out of sheer goodness, to devote five minutes of their lives to jotting a letter that, with the leverage of solitude, would furnish hours' worth of reading, rereading, and remembering on Stroman's end.

With time, he learned what those who knew him recognized as a new style of talk, the barest hint of a new way of being—asking for what he needed, admitting when he lacked, urging others to imagine being him.

"Sure do wish you'd write me back little brother," he wrote to Bob. "This is a lonely freaking hell hole and I need a bro—Bob, put your self in my shoes or sandles :)—I wait every single day at my door praying, I get a letter and pictures from you or Mom. That's a bad feeling when the mail man just passes my cell by."

The Templetons could be excused for their hesitation, because at times it seemed that their old friend was making amends and advancing as a man, and at times not. "There is not a single day or minute that passes by that I don't regret my actions or wish it was over," Stroman wrote on one occasion. On another occasion he might descend into complaints about being surrounded by "child molestors, niga's and sicko's," or asides like "How is the Wetback across the street doing?" or gimmicks like encasing a letter in an envelope decorated with an image of the Pink Panther penetrating a panty-less Pink Pantherette. He sent Tena and his daughters old pictures of himself that others had sent him: Mark in the mid-1990s, strung out late at night and staring at a camera as though it were a freshly landed alien ship; Mark at home in front of a Confederate flag on his wall; Mark wearing a skull-graced "I'm proud to be white" hat; Mark holding one gun while wearing another in his waistband, pointed toward his genitals; Mark sporting a "Rebel to the End" T-shirt. To some of the pictures he added special Nazi stickers; he scribbled messages on the back of others, like "Fuck them Arabs. Your bro on the Row, Mark."

He was particularly proud of his connection to some VIPs on the Row—the men who had gotten to Polunsky by dragging a black man named James Byrd Jr., chained to the back of their truck, over asphalt until his body hit a culvert and his head, shoulder, and arm separated from the rest of him. Stroman sent the Templetons pictures and other paraphernalia related to the "Jasper dudes," as he called them, projecting that they might soon be "worth something."

He helpfully captioned one of the photos: "This one drove the truck when the monkey was on the chain—niga was hitchhiking :)" And he added to the pictures' bona fides by including on the back of one a note from an actual Jasper dude: "Welcome to the Row, Slayer! It's not that I don't care for coloreds—fact is, I simply love white folk better." It was made out to "Slayer" because Stroman had introduced himself as the "Arab Slayer." The envelope containing one of the Jasper photos featured Mark's own artwork: a sketch of him in a big black convertible, bald and with a goatee, an unheld gun floating above him, and the Templetons' address ringed by chains.

Then the very next day he might be in a wholly different state, wanting to know how his little cat was doing or confessing to Bob that he would be "lost and so suicidle with out you and Mom/Pop." Or he might send a mildly misquoted Bible verse that he hoped would soothe the recipient as it had him: "For God did not send His Son into the world, but that the world through Him might be saved." Or a Monet still-life postcard, or the lyrics to a Johnny Cash song, or an image of a fetching woman: "I'm sending a picture of a big tit bombshell—wow—look at them jugs :). Send back with next letter—I wanted to share that with you :) Sluts are cool."

In December 2003, Mark tucked in a legal update. One of his appeals had been turned down, and the news reminded him that he wanted the Templetons in the room if and when the execution came. In the spring of 2004, one of Stroman's neighbors was executed, and he wrote of the man's eyes catching his as he walked past for the last time, said it truly had an effect on his soul. Though an execution date had yet to be set and there was still the possibility of further appeals, he felt the ticking grow louder and louder. He asked Bob and his brother to carry the casket at his funeral: "You know I want both of you assholes as pallbearers when I'm buried—if not I'll fucking haunt y'all both!"

In the middle of 2004, Stroman posted to the Templetons a

printout from the Web of the room where he expected to die: the very same gurney, same beige straps, same buckles, same lily-white pillow, same little viewing window, same green-painted brick walls, same protruding rod for his right arm. He sent Bob that particular photo, which someone else had presumably mailed to him, because he wanted him to imagine his old Bro on the gurney and to picture himself loyally bearing witness through that window.

Around that time, Stroman also mentioned that an Israeli film-maker named Ilan was making some kind of documentary about him, and that he would love the Templetons to contribute: "Its safe to say Id be honored to have y'all do the enterview—I need some good words from yall—because they will probably portray me as a evil racist pig :) and not show the human side of me—the compassion Mark that y'all know." He wrote shortly thereafter to inform them that he'd confirmed with the filmmaker that the movie would humanize, not villainize, him. He was excited about his upcoming meeting with the guy.

Bob Templeton, young as he was, had long suffered from heart trouble, and his health updates filled Mark with gloom: "Say, Bob, I'm so sorry to here about you being so sick and if I could give you my heart and body parts—I'd do it today to save your life—I'd do it for anyone in the Templeton family." In the fall of 2004, Stroman received word that Bob's dad now had health troubles of his own—his kidneys. The compassionate Mark he'd written of seemed to surge forward at this news, inspired as well by the anxiety of awaiting an execution date that seemed never to come. He made Mr. Templeton an offer: "I swear this on all my children souls—if Id be able to and the state would allow it—I would give you my kidneys and take my execution ASAP. And I mean that and the offer stands—I'm not sure what the laws are—but I am more than willing to do this for you—if it's possible—I am serious Pops—I love you that much and owe you more than that."

✳

WEEK AFTER WEEK, Stroman wondered if Tena, his ex-wife, would visit. He occasionally wrote her letters or sent pictures: "Tena," he scribbled on a Polaroid once. "Happy Birthday . . . I wish I could spank ya." Sometimes Tena wished that, too. Sometimes not.

By the time Mark launched his war, they'd been separated for many years, but the way Tena talked about him you'd think she was still his woman. "Man, I loved me some Mark Stroman," she said many years later. "I loved me some Mark Stroman. I'd lay down in a mud puddle just to keep his Tony Lama boots from getting wet. I loved me some Mark Stroman."

She was fourteen when it happened. She was living with her parents in Pleasant Grove, where Mark's grandparents also lived. The first time she met him, he nearly ran her over with a riding mower just for fun. She was together at the time with a slightly built Mexican boy named Pablo. She was part Mexican herself, into the whole low-rider thing, and drawn to a boy whose Mexican blood came even more purely distilled than her own.

All she knew about Mark was that his grandparents lived at the end of their street and that they were people with "money and horses." Their five-acre property was surrounded by quarter-acre plots like her own. Mark, who didn't live with these grandparents all the time, "didn't know nobody and nobody talked to him," Tena said. The little rat—and she called him that with love—always wanted attention, though. Tena, Pablo, and Mark would sit together eating pizza and talking. "When that little boy I called myself going with would go home, Mark would start coming over, and we would talk," Tena said. "I was fourteen, and we just talked and talked. He would let me brag on my clothes, he'd bring me over rings and jewelry, and paper dominos, and he made me feel really important—you know, pretty. He made me feel like I was the shit. I know that's hard to understand being fifteen and me fourteen, and if you would have told me that I would have had his three kids and his grandbaby in the end, I would have said you're nuts."

She had liked the Mexican, but now she fell for contrast. Mark was a rambunctious but silent redhead cowboy of what she figured to be good breeding; she was a simple girl from a working family. She felt herself falling for him. A few months after he almost ran her over with that mower, they got together. She would sneak over to the main road from her quiet, leafy street and into his grandparents' house, and they would talk and talk, and do that thing, "and then, you know, I got pregnant with Amber."

Mark responded in the way that boys of that age will: by professing to be too young for the effect of a cause for which he seemed altogether ready. Tena fired back, "Well, you weren't too young to turn off the security code to let me in!" He disappeared for the duration of her pregnancy. She had Amber, by cesarean, on a Monday, and came home that Friday. Mark called that night, as Tena remembered it:

"I was fixing Amber a bottle, and I was walking through the kitchen, and the phone rang, and I said hello, and he said, 'Tena?' and I said, 'Who's this?' and he said, 'It's me. I heard you had the baby, and blah blah blah,' and I said, 'Yeah.' He said, 'Is she pretty?' I was trying to act tough, this bitch mode, and I said, 'Yeah, she's pretty—she's mine.' And he said, 'Well, can I come and see her?' " Tena invited him to come over on the following Monday. Though it was only a moment's walk from his grandparents' place, the red-headed cowboy showed up two hours early.

The fleshy reality of that baby affected Mark. Two weeks after the birth, he came around to Tena's house full of mission: "It was outside, and I was sitting on a swing, and he got down on his knees and asked me to marry him." At first, she swatted him away like the housefly he was. "I told him he was just trying to get in my pants again: 'I already found out who you were.' " Not for the last time, Mark would convince her that the bad him wasn't the real him. They married less than four months later—on January 8, 1986.

By that time, Amber was no longer with Tena. Right after the birth, Tena's mother had behaved as though unperturbed, even relaxed, about her fifteen-year-old daughter's destiny. Tena remembers her saying, "Go out. You're a kid. Do what you do. I'll take care of the baby." Tena accepted the deal and went out a few times. She returned one night to discover her mother gone. She had taken Amber with her, to a town a few hours' drive away called Stephenville. Amber would spend the rest of her childhood there, away from Tena. Years later, Tena would explain it to Amber like this: "I was a kid. I was chasing your dad, and I couldn't just jump in a car and go to Stephenville and get you."

Tena's idea of Mark was different from her own children's, or from Tom Boston's, or from that of the psychologists who had testified at his trial. Her struggles colored her vision of him—and could be clarifying or occlusive, depending on your own. She thought of him less as a man divided against himself, ricocheting between states of rage and levity, and more as a man whose good traits were also his bad ones.

Mark was sweet, Tena said; was homey; was a rebel; was a fighter: "He'd go through spurts. He'd be at home and then get a 'wild pair,' like my grandmother called it, and he'd wanna take off." He wouldn't have appealed to every woman, but he might have to a woman raised on honor-culture ideas of a man's love as being fundamentally about protection, about the cultivation of a fearsome reputation that kept trouble at bay.

"He was that type that if he loved you, if he cared about you and loved you, then you didn't want to mess with this" was how Tena put it. If her sister came home telling of a stolen purse or busted eye, Mark took care of that. If someone looked at Tena at the wrong angle, Mark took care of it. It became possible for Tena to think of his violence and love and sociability and life-lust as being cut from a single cloth: "He always said his two favorite things in life was fighting and F-ing—but not in that order. Everybody loved to be around him. If the party was boring or whatever, as soon as he got there, it would lighten up. Everyone would start laughing, having a good time. People thought they were cool to be around him."

When more children came along, Mark showed little interest in fatherhood. Tena, instead of condemning him, became a master of making excuses for him even more articulate than those he made for himself: "I think Mark loved as much as he knew how to love. Part of the reason that I don't think he wanted to settle down and be a family man after we got married and stuff was because he didn't know; he'd never seen it. You can't be something that you don't know about. I cook hamburgers and work at a hamburger joint. You couldn't put me in an office and expect me to do any secretary work. If I don't know nothing about it, I can't do it, and Mark never had that. He never had a dad to learn to be a dad."

There had always been harbingers of his fate. Tena saw much of it. Most of the time, it didn't rise above the level of drinking and fighting. But there were instances when he just evaporated for days, and she knew he was up to something, and she'd find out all about it only when he returned. There was, obviously, the drug use. It started, as it so often does, with pot. Then it evolved, as it was starting to do in these parts, into meth. Mark had already done it but was angry when Tena told him she tried it. The drug blew her away: "Just gives you this euphoria, this energy, makes you think everything's OK, makes you feel good about yourself, gives you lots of energy. And it's like that for a while, until—I guess, after using it for a while, it becomes to where you have to have it."

Meth conquered Tena more fully than it did Mark. "It's not a good life," she said. "It makes people live a hard life. A lot harder than their lives were supposed to be." In Tena's case, the meth stripped her of basic functionality and left her no better than a vagrant at times. Mark's problem was always his resilience. No matter how much he did, how much he drank and smoked, he never became a helpless junkie. Everyone who knew him said they couldn't remember him

without work, which in his milieu was a trait more commonly associated with rich people.

Tena's pride over this latter attribute of Mark's was still palpable:
"Always worked. Always had money. Always had cigarettes. Always
had beer." (It was a defining line where they lived—who had ready
stocks of such things, and who bought as they went.) "Always had
nice apartments in Garland-Mesquite area. You know, he never
lived in any slum. Or one time he had an apartment at Lake White
Rock that had a fence around it—so it was, you know, a security gate.
Always had nice apartments with nice furniture."

These were the things that made Tena feel safe and valued, and
that somehow distracted her from everything else—including the
things, like stealing and living in other people's property, that contradicted the nice things. Mark knew how to play a woman like this,
knew how to be doting in the ways that would satisfy Tena. Like when
he convinced the court, in the autumn of 1988, to delay the start date
of his prison term so that he could see his baby Erica being born.
That she wasn't, purely speaking, his baby didn't curb his desire to
be there—nor cause him to treat the child any differently thereafter.
The court delayed the term as long as it could, and then at last he
turned himself in. Erica was born shortly after he surrendered.

Tena, in bearing another man's baby, was violating the letter, but
hardly the spirit, of their marriage. Mark was, as she tells it, a worse
offender: "There was no problem with mine and Mark's sex life. He
just wasn't always getting sex with me—that was the only problem."
She was from a world where women often accepted that the talents
by which men won them were portable—that what worked on them
would naturally work on others. "He charmed them women," Tena
said. "He could talk to them and make them feel like they were pretty."

When he came out of prison the first time, after a matter of months
inside, they were still together. But between then and returning for
a second stint, Mark's runaway "F-ing," as Tena called it, which she
had tolerated, graduated into that other thing that women like her

mortally fear, and the fear of which makes them tolerant of mere F-ing: love. He fell for a waitress named Shawna, whom he would eventually marry and have a daughter with. "It was out of nowhere," Tena said. "I thought that we had worked on us, and I just had Erica and everything." They drifted asunder. By the time he returned from prison the second time, his beloved grandfather had died—and Tena had finally gone.

All these years later, it wasn't lost on Tena that—as far as she heard, at least—Mark Stroman proved a stabler father and husband to the next woman, despite all they'd gone through together. She heard that with Shawna he was regularly at home, that he changed diapers and made bottles—that he became, unhesitatingly, a dad. But Tena heard that eventually he also ran around on Shawna, and he didn't stop with the drugs, and one day she just left. ("Karma's a bitch," as his daughter Amber said.) Tena and Mark spoke from time to time after that. She knew how broken up he was about the split, about Shawna's not wanting her daughter to grow up around his lifestyle and friends and antics. "I think Mark thought that everything he cared about and loved left, whether he had anything to do with it or not," Tena said. Betrayal was something Mark had struggled with since boyhood, and now it flared again: "He just put on that 'screw-it' mode—either I'll hurt you first, or I get hurt. Life's all about hurt or get hurt."

Yes, Tena loved Mark Stroman. Yes, she would lie down in a puddle to keep his boots dry. But when she got that phone call from her sister, telling her that Mark Stroman had killed someone, it was as though she finally got it. So Mark waited year after year to be called to Visitation to see his Tena. His Tena never came.

∗

"No, MAN—DON'T WORRY about your tears. Don't worry about the tears. Few tears makes you very human. We're going to start with some very simple questions." The camera was behind Ilan Ziv, rolling, pointed at the prisoner on the other side of the glass. Stroman, with little else to occupy him, had prepared for this encounter for a long while. "Believe it or not, I had a good speech planned for you when I come out here," he told the filmmaker. But his tears were betraying him.

"Just be yourself—that's fine. So you really feel remorse," Ziv said, his words more calming than his appearance. He looked like a well-aged version of the Israeli paratrooper he once was: bald-headed, thick-chested, with an intense, skeptical stare. He was naturally combative—the kind of man who begins many of his thoughts with "No, no, no," even when he's about to agree with you, just to make sure you hear what he's about to say.

Ziv—the son of a Holocaust survivor, a veteran of the Israel Defense Forces, now a documentary filmmaker consumed by questions about why people hate—had ambled into Stroman's life almost by accident. He had been commissioned to make a film about grassroots peacemaking initiatives. As he did the research, he grew convinced that his subjects were "wonderful people with zero impact on society." In his discouragement he cast around for alternative projects and became interested in the string of hate crimes committed after 9/11 around the United States. He encountered a woman in Chicago who was connected to the family of Vasudev Patel, which led him to write a letter to Mark Stroman sometime in 2004, asking if he might interview him. Stroman turned him down, saying that he was in the middle of his appeals and had been advised to stay away from the media.

They continued to correspond, though, and Ziv's description of the project began to change Stroman's mind. He wrote to Bob Templeton that he had had Ziv "figured all wrong." The filmmaker had convinced Stroman that the project's aim was to "show the complexities of the situation, to create an anatomy of the events and to humanize it." It wasn't long before Ziv received a second letter from Stroman. The appeal in question had failed. Stroman wanted to tell his story. "He put a condition," Ziv said. "The condition was, could I help him to buy a typewriter?"

One hundred or so dollars later, Ziv was sitting across from Stroman at Visitation. Though inches apart, they were separated by glass and were speaking to each other through black phones attached to metallic cables.

Stroman was a sea of red skin, green ink, and white cloth. He still wore the cross above his "187" tattoo. He sat opposite Ziv, bouncing with nerves. He explained that he had been waiting for a while and was "real hyperactive." The guards had asked him to remove his crucifix for some reason, which unsettled him. After a minute, he decided he wanted it on and refastened it.

Stroman was full of concern at the beginning. "You look very different from your picture," he said to Ziv. A friend had sent him a printout about Ziv from a website. He asked his visitor to repeat his name, to make sure it wasn't some impostor. "I like your barber," he said a moment later, bald man to bald man, to ease the tension.

Stroman began by confessing how suspicious he'd been of Ziv at first. He was expecting the usual portrait of him as a racist hater. "My wife's Spanish. I'm not a racist. That wouldn't make me a very good racist, now would it?" Stroman said.

Stroman wanted Ziv to know that he had lived well, that this present situation was the exception, not the rule. "I've got four awesome kids," he said. "I've always worked my whole life." His jail terms before this had been minimal: "My whole life, I was locked up six months at one stretch for an eight-year sentence and then three months. So nine months before 2001, September, have I been incarcerated. I've had a good life."

Ziv asked about the chaos of Stroman's childhood and how it had affected his life.

"No, I know what affected my life," Stroman said. "It was September 11." He asked if Ziv had been in New York on that day.

"Oh, absolutely," Ziv said. "I saw it from the roof of my building."

"Then you'll never—then you know what I felt," Stroman said, gesturing toward Ilan, hoping not to be left hanging.

"I know what I feel," Ziv said. "You tell me what you feel."

His voice cracking and preparing for a cry, Stroman explained how it had "trickled down all the way over here." His eyes were wet. They searched Ziv's face for any evidence of agreement, or at least understanding. Stroman said he still couldn't forget those days: the hatred he felt toward the Arab world, the sight of people jumping from the towers, the stories of people trapped in Flight 93. "I'm very patriotic, and my country was attacked, so I kinda . . ." He snapped his fingers. "I took it personal." He was sobbing now, and almost whispering.

Ziv tried to focus him. What actually made him leap up on September 15 and begin his attacks?

He blamed it on the looping reruns on television. "It's just boiling up and boiling up, and I just snapped," Stroman said. He acknowledged that, like so many other vigilantes, he had failed to target the people he thought he was going after. "I guess I'm that dumb Texan redneck where everybody from the Middle East is an Arab to me," Stroman said, his face now brightening, a smile breaking open. "In my view, that was my stupidity. Even the man from India, I thought he was an Arab."

He told Ziv that he'd never killed before, and that he'd felt almost possessed at the time of the shootings. He wasn't in his own body, wasn't in his own mind, he insisted.

Whenever Ziv tried to get more specific, to ask what Stroman was thinking during each shooting, he stared back blankly. He seemed vague on the details of his own deeds, and appeared unable to go beyond generalities and television-derived platitudes.

It was the shock of "the worse atrocity in American history," he said. He recited again the tale, make-believe or imagined, of a half-sister who worked at Windows on the World: "Last thing I heard was that she still worked there. Well, I'm watching the bodies jump. I'm watching people hold hands jumping off the buildings. I'm traumatized. I can't get ahold of anybody and"—he shook his head for a moment—"I just snapped."

That no such woman had actually died in the World Trade Center no longer much mattered.

Talking with Ziv, Stroman lurched back and forth between self-justification and shame. He said it still haunted him, everything he'd done. Even when he closed his eyes, he couldn't escape. "My whole life, I've kind of been full of—I'm more on the wild side," he said. "You can tell by looking at me. I've enjoyed life. But I've never killed anybody. And that's something that's hard to explain." As he spoke, he was thumping the table in front of him every few seconds for emphasis.

Ziv asked how he explained it to himself.

Stroman said that he was only just now coming to terms with it. He was coming to terms with his own looming end as well. He had been on the Row a little more than two years—long enough to know he wasn't getting out.

"My appeal?" he said. "I got about as much chance as a snowball in a hot skillet." This line he hammed up for Ziv, putting on his best incredulous face. Ziv obliged with a gush of laughter and a table slap of his own. That laughter made Stroman smile.

He said he was trying to have a good outlook on things. He knew, without a doubt, that he would die by the state's hand. Just today, his neighbor had gotten his date and broken down in sobs next door.

The deaths of neighbors were the bluntest kind of foreshadowing. "I seen a lot of people walk that final walk and not come back," Stroman said. "I've seen people drugged outta here, being pepper-sprayed, gassed, kicking and fighting on their way to their execution."

Ziv asked if Stroman believed in God.

"Oh, yes I do. This is kinda weird to say, but if I wouldn't've come to Death Row, my eternity would've been lost," Stroman said.

It was one kind of solace Stroman could take. In his understand-ing of Christianity, his long trail of sins could be washed away if he got his heart right with Jesus before the end. In fact, Stroman was persuaded that but for the commission of these murders, he would not be heaven-bound: that it required his utter bottoming-out, which prompted these years of isolation and undistracted one-on-one time with God, to earn salvation.

Ziv didn't entirely follow this logic, and asked Stroman to explain.

"If I'da died out there on the streets, and my lack of faith—I'd have been screwed for real, for an eternity," Stroman said. The crimes that he claimed to regret had bent his trajectory toward paradise.

Frequent-Flyer Miles

In the America of the aughts, nothing said you belonged like buying a car you couldn't afford. A year before quitting the Olive Garden in 2007, Rais treated himself to a Nissan. The burnt-orange 350Z, at close to $40,000, was a splurge, even to lease. But those curves that gave it the look of a high-tech, Japanese-made egg; those vast, road-devouring wheels; those prowling, vicious headlight-eyes . . . It had won the Most Sex Appeal Award from *Road and Travel* as well as the more buttoned-up Most Significant Vehicle of the Year honor from *Edmunds*. Rais was the farthest thing from flashy, wearing simple clothes and living in a modest home. But if he could manage the lease of $500 or so a month—and, with debt out of his life and his software career taking off, he thought he could—it might remind him each time he drove that he was safe, that all was well.

He drove his little rocket around for two years. He quit the Olive Garden in that period and began to work full-time in IT—as a database administrator for a local energy company called Crosstex. He stayed a few months, then moved on to similar work at the University of Texas at Dallas, and then, the following year, found a gig at the Zale Corporation. To the outside world it was a diamond store. But it needed people like Rais because on the inside, like just about every other business in America, it had become a technology company, maintaining large and growing libraries of data that had to be constantly updated and instantly retrievable, so that when a dumped man in Phoenix returned a ring, the next minute an agent in Boston could tell a customer yes, that one is still available. Rais loved the work, loved the firefighting and problem-solving: a server outage here—hop on the conference-call bridge to fix it; a slowdown there—allocate some more memory. In material things, at least, all was well with the world, except for that car, which was a financial drag. "My eyes were bigger than my pocket that time," Rais said. It had been a rare mistake for him, and a very American one. He was assimilating. After twenty-four months, he was free of the car, and relieved.

It took another year—until late 2009, with a new, declaredly antiwar president in office, and this era of conflict seemingly on the wane—for Rais to feel settled enough to fulfill a pledge. Now thirty-six, he had promised years earlier to take his mother to Mecca on the Hajj pilgrimage. Until now it had been close to impossible, given their distance apart, the expense, and Rais's injuries and dedication to work. His mother knew that Rais couldn't find the time to eat well or sleep enough or find a wife, let alone organize a pilgrimage to Mecca. For his part, Rais had been unwilling to go while in debt: among the faithful, there were divergent views on whether debtors could go on Hajj, and Rais, as was often the case, found himself on the conservative side of the argument. His view was that a person had to settle his liabilities before taking off for a faraway kingdom, lest piety become the refuge of deadbeats. Now debt was behind Rais, and he was financially sound.

Late in 2009, Rais flew to Dhaka. He stayed there a few days and caught up with the family. Then he and his mother boarded a plane, bound for Jeddah, Saudi Arabia. It was the first time for both of them. They were going a few weeks before the official Hajj dates, so the place wouldn't be "fully loaded" with visitors, as Rais put it, borrowing the language of the American car dealerships he had come to know. Theirs was one of the special Hajj flights, and already packed with pilgrims, who began performing their ablutions and rituals on board.

Amma had flown before, but she was overcome with nerves. When the plane shuddered from what Rais called "a little turbulence," she asked him why, with such a big sky, the pilot couldn't find any other, nonshaky path. They were sitting near the wing, which Amma eyed warily to ensure everything was as it ought to be. As the plane swooped down toward Jeddah, a chunk of the wing began, ever so slowly, to detach from the rest of it. Amma became convinced that the wing was falling off. Rais tried to reassure her: it was just a flap coming down, and very much intended.

When they landed, a wave of feeling, which had been rising and gathering force over years, crashed over mother and son alike.

"It was the most beautiful thing in my life," Rais said. "The feeling that finally I'm going with my mother, which was a promise to God—that I wanted to take care of her and to take her with me. So I was crying the day we landed in Mecca. We both, mom and son, were crying, because we never thought that it will come true one day."

✳

Rais spoke of tending to his mother in Mecca in a manner that in his adopted country was reserved for the first days of romantic courtship and the lyrics of songs: anything for you; money is no object; whatever your heart desires. It was part of what still separated him from an America to which he was growing accustomed: a devotion to his mother that would never be diverted toward a woman of different blood—a love that would instead remain a bulwark of resistance against such latecomers, fickle as life had shown them to be. He pleaded with his mother to enjoy herself to the fullest. "Whatever she wanted to do, wherever she wanted to go, I told her, 'You just tell me,' " he said. "Because there are so many holy places around Mecca and also in Medina. I said, 'Well, you just name it. Money's not a problem. Time's not a problem. We're here for a month. We'll do it.' So wherever even the Hajjis cannot go, we went there."

Upon landing on that first day, mother and son boarded a bus from Jeddah airport to their hotel, in the Misfalah quarter of Mecca. After checking in, they went immediately to the Haram Mosque—sprawling over an area the size of several stadiums, its six towers poking finger-like into the sky. It overflowed with worshippers all day. Rais and Amma made their way toward the Kaaba, the giant black cube that is the mosque's centerpiece, decorated with golden calligraphy. Pilgrims worshipped around the Kaaba in rings: the innermost group stood close enough to embrace the cube, their hands pressed into the black stone; behind them, a more populous ring circled it in prayer; and beyond them was the remainder of the visitors, hundreds of thousands strong.

"When we're near the Kaaba, my mom told me to ask something from God when I see His house for the first time," Rais said. "I asked for His mercy, forgiveness, guidance, and paradise in the next life. While I was asking something from God, my mother looked at me with eyes full of tears and rubbed her palm on my face and head." When she drew close enough to touch the Kaaba, she rubbed her hand against it, and then against Rais's face and head. She kissed him on the forehead.

Rais had heard from people that prayers given from Mecca had 2,700 times the efficacy of prayers offered elsewhere. Here, unlike in Dallas, where dealing with server problems often got between him and his ability to pray, Rais set an alarm in their hotel room for 3 a.m. every day. He and his mother would bathe and then walk together to the mosque. Rais relished the sight of hundreds of thousands of people, most of them in white, coming from all directions at that early hour, bound for that one mosque—Muslims from Asia, Africa, South America; descendants of the original Arab Muslims, the conquered peoples, the Western converts; the covered and uncovered, the tunic-clad and shirt-clad, the rich and the subsidized poor—a mesmeric reminder of the power of the faith, of the enduring and transcendent appeal of His message.

Day after day, amid the crowds and the chanting loudspeakers, Rais's churning mind stilled. "Once you're in that mosque," Rais said, "anything, everything except praying to God is restricted. You're not supposed to think anything about this world; you are not supposed to think." He and his mother would stick around until the second prayer at 5:30 a.m. (Sometimes, it was actually Rais's third prayer, because he often woke up for an unprescribed extra-credit prayer in the middle of the night. "If instead of sleeping, because of your love toward God, your respect, you wake up in the middle of the night and then you pray, it is extra special," he said. He offered an analogy to office life: "It's like, I don't have to work at one o' clock in the morning, but if my boss sees that I'm still working, I build trust, right? You build the relationship.")

At an ordinary mosque, Rais and his mother wouldn't have prayed together. In Mecca, however, the sexes could pray side by side, because who on earth would think sexual thoughts in such a place? "That time, you're not in your normal mental stage," Rais said. It was also, presumably, dangerous to part with loved ones in a swarming, seven-digit-strong crowd. What impressed Rais, though, was how orderly the place was. Crime was rare, he heard. The merchants—selling tunics and prayer beads and T-shirts and handbags—left their stalls unattended when they prayed, and no one thought to steal. Plus, everyone knew that around here they cut your hands off for behavior like that.

The pilgrimage was chiefly a spiritual endeavor, but it also gave Rais a chance to show his mother how he had grown since leaving her. Almost every meal of his mother's life had consisted of Bengali food. Now here in Mecca were restaurants from all around the world: Pakistani, Indian, American, European; there was that halal KFC; there was the restaurant at the Hilton, with its tiramisu and chocolate mousse cake. (When they visited the Hilton, his mother suggested that they get one dessert to go with their coffee, but Rais insisted on their tasting several.) He longed to expose his mother to these exotic foods. He suggested they try a different place each day. She was concerned that he was wasting his hard-earned money. He countered that food here was so cheap. If money wasn't for tending to his only mother, then what was it for?

His mother was particularly bothered by Rais's liberal tipping. He had returned from America with a penchant for sheikh-like behavior, spitting out money to anyone who did anything for them, even just pour a glass of water. At one restaurant, the waiter served them coffee, and Rais gave him money in multiple currencies for his trouble. He explained to his mother that the waiter would appreciate this and give them good service, but she was skeptical. Rais couldn't be stopped, though, and had taken to using airline frequent-flyer analogies to explain how God rewarded virtue. "The more you give," he told her, "the better is your mileage." He had also worked in a restaurant himself, and done so in America, where, more than back home, the waiter is recognized as a person with a life and needs and maybe his own children. "I know that I don't have enough money," Rais said to his mother, "but I have the heart to give money. And you know Allah will give me if I give to others."

For Rais, this chance to serve and honor his mother was as important as the journey to the center of the faith. He hoped the month together would make clear to her what separation otherwise obscured: "I wanted to give my Mom the feelings that she raised a good son, and I am at her service. I'm not here to give her company; I am here for her service, as her servant. Because that comes from this teaching that your heaven is under your mom's feet." For Rais, who felt more acutely than most the preciousness of time, the pilgrimage was an opportunity for spiritual multitasking—honoring his mom while ostensibly on a mission to honor his God. "I thought that was the time I should earn some frequent-flyer miles," he said. "My mom is there, I'm showing her Mecca, so I should serve her the best way I can."

The religious instruction of his youth came vividly to life in Mecca. He had known, for instance, of the magical well called Zamzam that had slaked the thirst of millions of pilgrims with the holiest water on earth. It was Abraham's son Ishmael who was said to have discovered it, miraculously, as his mother ran through the desert searching for water for her boy. In the version of the story Rais knew, Ishmael dug his feet into the sand while waiting for her, and there it was: so much water that his mother urged the well to "stop, stop," which is how they say it got its name. All these years later, believers couldn't fathom that it still hadn't stopped, recharged somehow despite the extraordinary demands on it.

One day during the crowded prayers, an old man collapsed and fell on Rais's head, which was inches from the ground. Rais could feel his nose break into pieces. He saw blood pouring out, dyeing his shirt. At the first-aid office, he asked for antibiotics, which they informed him weren't necessary. It was a minor break. Just clean it with the Zamzam water, they said. Within five or six days, Rais said, the nose had healed, without surgery or medication. How great was God. Convinced of the Zamzam water's signal powers, Rais bought two 20-liter containers for five riyals each and filled them at the public sinks for the return trip to Dhaka, where the water would be given to cherished friends and those in medical need. The episode left Rais with a strange feeling. God had healed him, yes. But why did God want to hurt him in the first place—and here, in His own house? It had to have a meaning.

Rais organized some trips out of Mecca to show his mother holy sites nearby. She especially longed to climb Jabal al-Noor, the Mountain of Light, upon which the Prophet Muhammad had received the first of the revelations that would grow into the Koran. Rais pointed out the obvious: her knees, which struggled with walking in horizontal situations and seldom managed a few stories of stairs, could not endure a climb of a few thousand feet. She insisted, and in that insistence Rais saw flecks of himself. "Like mother, like son," he thought. She told him, "If you can, I can." So they did a flash prayer at the foot of the mountain and pushed their way up and reached the summit in less than two hours. His mother felt an unaccountable surge of energy and, she claimed, no pain.

The mountain's Hira cave was what most called to Rais. There, in a dark little pocket among the rocks, too small for more than a few people (and now under a painted red, white, and green inscription), the Prophet had sat and meditated, and early verses of the holy scripture had come to Him. As Rais reflected on the Prophet's time there, and on his wife's service to Him in that hour, it seemed to remind him of the contrasting example of Abida. "How many wives nowadays would make that sacrifice?" he said. "That their husband is sitting in the mountain and she go and drop the food? The hardship, the extra task, that he's not at home, the sacrifice." As Rais interpreted the story, the Prophet had sat high up in that cave and stared down at a tribal world seething with hate. He was "sitting here, thinking of mankind, thinking for mankind, that why do people do these bad things to each other? What is the solution?"

Something in this picture of the Prophet—in His mix of anguish and ambition for a torn-up world—profoundly affected Rais that day. It was something new he felt in himself: a permission he was giving himself, after long years spent pursuing health and stability, to think more broadly about the kind of vengeful world that had hurt him—and what better world could be built.

"When I entered the Hira cave, I felt a heavenly peace in my heart," Rais said. He looked through a small hole in the mountain and managed to see the Kaaba. He prayed and tried to figure out what lay ahead. "I realized that God wanted me to come here one day to seek guidance, and that's why He did not take my life eight years ago," Rais said. "Definitely there is something good going to be done by me and that's why He put me through terrible pain and sufferings first, so that I could feel for others when they go through pain and sufferings—and now brought me here to fill my heart with peace, forgiveness, and love for His creation."

Foreigners visiting Mecca weren't encouraged to roam around the kingdom, but Rais's gallantry toward his mother dismissed such rules. A cousin who worked at the Hilton arranged a car to take Rais and his mom to the city of Ta'if, a few hours' drive away. They drove on the sparkling Saudi highway across the bleak, empty land, past half-done concrete buildings, over low and flaky brown hills, up and around the Möbius-strip turns, and into that mountain city.

Muhammad had once gone there seeking converts. In the version of the story that Rais remembered from childhood, the people of Ta'if were vicious to the Prophet: insulting Him, abusing Him, throwing rocks. He left the town bloody and stumbling. The angel Gabriel came to save Him, offering to bring the mountains crashing down on Ta'if. This the Prophet declined; Rais imagined Muhammad holding His hand up to Gabriel, telling the angel to back down. The Prophet wanted to forgive. "He not only raised His hand," Rais said, "but He prayed the maximum in His lifetime for the people in Ta'if, that God have mercy on them. What they did, they did not understand." The journey to Ta'if, this story of forgiveness, the incident with his nose and the Zamzam water, those moments spent in Muhammad's lonely cave—Rais felt God to be telling him something, but he couldn't decipher what.

⋆

SOMETIMES, IN THE middle of the night, Rais would awaken with a start to find his mother beside him, rubbing his head and crying.

She still couldn't believe that she'd gotten him back: "She used to tell that I miss you so much, and that in all these years I could have been spending time with you, take care of you, cook something good for you, and rub your head while you sleep." They talked and talked the whole time. Discussion of the material world was haram for pilgrims, so they dwelled on loftier subjects. She explained to him the significance of the places they were visiting, the rituals they conducted. They spoke of the afterlife, but also of how Rais might serve God in his remaining years on earth. They spoke of the role of mercy in the faith. Rais told her of a peculiar feeling that had begun to stir in him—a call to do something for others.

These words—"to do something for others"—had played on a loop in his mind throughout the pilgrimage. And he knew where they came from. As he lay dying years ago, he had looked to the sky and proposed a deal: if You save me, I will dedicate my life to doing something for others. This journey to Mecca had reminded Rais that he had strayed from that pledge. Life after the shooting became, more than ever before, about himself. It had to be so. It had been a time for recovery—for surgeries and rehabilitation and the securing of bread and roof. God couldn't begrudge him that. But what he felt now was that he had crossed some invisible line separating the moment of rebuilding from a new phase. What or why or how, he didn't know. The debt was gone. The right eye, mostly blind, was what it was. The more Rais prayed, the more God elucidated the message He had been sending. God was calling in an old favor. He was telling Rais it was time.

Rais's father had told him, before he left, that whatever he asked for in Mecca would be granted. One day Rais and his mother were praying at the Kaaba. His mother was chanting. Rais remembers her asking God: please help my son to fulfill his promises to You. Rais, feeling the summons of a new mission, asked God for the resources he might need to serve others. He asked Him for mental, physical, and financial strength, so that those basics could recede from his attention and free him to concentrate on service. He asked for guidance about where his life should go, knowing that it had to travel in new directions: "I said, 'Help me to lead a respectful, good life, and keep me from all evils. Give me the power and the strength to help others. Once I come back to You, You put me in the highest Heaven that You have created.'"

He had told his mother of his long-ago promise, and she encouraged him to bring it up with his God, which he now did. "Before I close my eyelids forever, I want to do something for others," he whispered.

They were not idle words. Rais couldn't explain it, but as the pilgrimage ended, he felt very different. It was perhaps the prompt for another of his leavings, though he didn't yet know what he was escaping or where he was bound. For now he knew only this: "My heart feels softer than ever before."

Gadfly

"There's not a day that goes by that I don't think of what I'm here for," Stroman wrote in 2008. Six years at Polunsky had given him plenty of time to stew. He felt himself occupying a front-row seat at a spectacle of self-examination. He pondered what he was, what else he might have been. Not that he could have been a lot else, he figured. Not with the "liars" who called themselves his family. Not with the mother who wouldn't come visit him: "Every time I try to write her anything, I always get the same story: 'It's too hard. It's too hard to accept this.'" Not with the boys who were all about him when he was buying rounds but melted away at the first inconvenience. He hadn't seen anybody from the family, besides his sister Doris, whom he couldn't trust after she testified before the grand jury: "I still got love for her because we're blood kin, but that respect's gone." It wasn't that Stroman didn't understand their behavior. They were doing him like he'd done them. That's how they would explain it. He just wished they'd remember that "every flower that ever bloomed had to go through a whole lot of dirt to get there."

If you asked Doris or Mary when they first knew something was amiss with their little brother, they might cite his dreams. He'd had nightmares since he was a little boy. Sometimes it would be an imagined alligator under his bed. Sometimes it would be some crazy thing that convinced him, still half-asleep, to try to rip out the ceiling fan. Mary said, "He would also sleepwalk. I know he would go out the window, and my mom would hear something out the back door, and it would be my brother standing there in his underwear. And he didn't even know how he got there."

Now, all these years later, Stroman's sleeping mind still swam with dreams. He was one of those people who remembered his dreams, though he wished at times he didn't. Sometimes he would be dreaming of life on the outside, sweet and breezy, and then jump up startled: "just woke up from a short sleep . . . what a hellish sleep it was . . . I was dreaming of free life . . . and to awaken in this place and to hear all the insane screams and yelling of the ones around you is almost enough to make one want to exit this sad little existence." He dreamed on other occasions of falling from cliffs and ledges. He dreamed of the gurney—of being strapped down, the sheet placed over his body, amid icy silence.

Sometimes the gurney dream and the falling dream flowed together in his mind—the first creating in him the feeling of the second. Sometimes as he dreamed of the gurney, it went as far as the final moment itself: the needle is about to be injected, and then he hears the strangest screams. He reckoned it to be the "yells of the damned." Was it a glimpse of Satan coming for him? Maybe, he mused, it was a preview of heaven. What did it mean? Was he being warned?

Dreams could also soothe him. Dreams of freedom, of laughter, of loved ones long dead. He dreamed of the 1980s, cowboying around, being the Mark who could set any room alight. Dreamed of his grandpa and running away to him on Old Seagoville Road, which back then felt so far from Plano, and riding a tractor and horses there. It made Stroman wonder if it was God laying out these images, or just the brain's endless churning. "It amazes me that we are able to store these things inside of our minds for all these years and then it's like something HITS the rewind button *WHEW*."

These thoughts found expression when, in the summer of 2008, Stroman became a blogger. Ilan Ziv, the filmmaker, agreed to receive letters from him for this purpose and post them online. If you had someone on the outside willing to do this for you, it was a legal way to publish from prison. (As a result of this process, it is not always clear whether the misspellings that appear are Stroman's or Ziv's.) "This blog is just to open the eyes of the ones who are reading it, to show you what goes on behind these doors of Texas death row," he wrote. He presented himself as "a simple Texan stuck in a freaking hellish nightmare." What he wanted above all from blogging was to establish his humanity in the eyes of his audience: "Most call us animals, not to have any type of feelings or compassion. Well that's wrong and I'll show that in these blogs."

Stroman had served on the Row long enough to understand that death was not a one-time thing. A man didn't just up and die. He died tendon by tendon, vein by vein, synapse by synapse. He died daily in proportion to the number of days he had left, even if the date hadn't been set. He died in and by the act of waiting.

Working through lawyers, Stroman had tried the usual Death Row appeals—with the usual Death Row results: an appeal of the conviction here, a state petition for habeas corpus there; a federal judge's recommendation to deny habeas here, a turned-down certiorari petition to the Supreme Court there. It took years to execute a man because of the opportunity to make these appeals. But you'd be a fool to think you had a chance.

Day after day, Stroman sat and stood and paced his cell, asking difficult questions of what remained of himself. Never in a million years had he imagined his life ending up like this. He wondered how that wild boy had become this caged man. "How did I end up so far away from home I'll never know. Fate? Destiny? Karma?"

Of course, Stroman had arrived on the Row as a double murderer. Sometimes, as he sat inside, casting himself in writing as a victim of fortune, he could seem oblivious to the long trail of victimhood that he had hacked.

His moods could lurch like a truck on a mountain road. Some days he felt happy "to the point I could piss smiley faces." The voices within him and around the Row were quiet; it was a good time to "gather up my thoughts and grab a hold of my sanity." But sometimes, halfway through such a letter, his brain would swerve, and he would declare happy Mark to have exited the building.

He wrestled with apparent depression: "The days blend into nights, the nights turn into days. The ways to battle depression are lost to me it would seem." The isolation was eroding what humanity remained in him. He claimed to be hearing voices in his head, but even they were growing tired: however loud they screamed, there was no one to listen but him. Stroman confessed that he'd contemplated ending things himself: "Sometimes it seems like suicide is the only solution, but I'm not that brave."

He cowered and cried when he received word that his daughter Cassandra had gone missing. He knew to be afraid, because his time inside had taught him to believe "in real time monsters, not the kind that lived under our beds as small children, but real sicko monsters." And then he praised God when He returned Cassandra to her mother.

Anniversaries of September 11 were also hard, because they reminded him of the war into which he had been drafted, only to find himself alone, a soldier without comrades. After these many years, however, he was also able to see the events of 2001 at a philosophical remove—to conceive of himself more as a part of that tragedy than a hero of it. "I myself struggle daily knowing my actions have caused pain just like the attacks on our country have caused pain," he wrote. "This vicious cycle of hate has to stop somewhere."

The hardest thing about the Row was watching men vanish into a destiny that awaited you, too. A kind of empathy grew from selfishness. Stroman lived with a group of men who had, in their own separate ways, arrived at the same fate: who had horsed around in that same cage for an hour a day, lived through the same gassing and shouting and chewy pancakes, learned with him to plug Vaseline into the ceiling to ward off the rain, been stripped by the same guards, herded to the bathroom in the same raids, become as obsessive as he was about the progress of their appeals, despite knowing the wispy odds of success.

The simple parallelism of the Row—people convicted of similar crimes, bound for the same penalty—made it hard to ignore the analogies between your life and others'. Everyone was a future version of someone else. What happened to another today would happen to you tomorrow.

Stroman kept a calendar on the cell wall, and beside it an execution schedule. "That combination of calendar and death list gives the day meaning and purpose," he wrote on a good day, sipping coffee and crossing off another of the calendar's boxes. He wondered about his peers. How did they feel on the day of their death, awaiting the injection that would send them to the "land of Oz," as he called it? Did they feel remorse? Had they managed to hand Jesus their heart in good time? What did a man do as the hours dwindled and the walls closed in? Did he sleep? Did he limp around his cell like a wounded beast? Did he write letters? Did he finally say the unsaid things to his loves? What did he do on his last morning? Did he pray? Did he catch a final sunrise?

Stroman recounted to Ziv how the prison authorities had brought out paper forms from the psych department one day and asked the inmates to fill them out. The forms were seeking to gauge the prisoners' mental health, and one of the questions asked if they had frequent thoughts about death. "It's like a joke," Stroman said. Who could live on Texas Death Row and not think about death?

One of the benefits of the Row for Stroman was his discovery of inmates who'd known lives much worse than his. "I heard someone in our rec cage just yesterday saying that life is a wounding, an accumulation of pains and maiming's and grief," he wrote on his blog. That statement really got Stroman thinking: "There was nothing about love or happiness in his little sermon. I for one have had a lot of negativity in my life, but the happiness and love and good times outweigh anything else."

Over the years, Stroman had been a troublemaker at Polunsky, but of an evolving kind. Six years turned him from flat-out angry to something more like constructively critical. He cast himself in his blog as a monitor of the prison regime. He was that eternally complaining customer who keeps returning to the restaurant anyway. His rage, scalding in the free world, cooled into a kind of nagging. He was Polunsky's little gadfly: a reviewer of its food, a chronicler of what criminals less dignified than he did, an explainer of its overly bureaucratic processes. In his blog posts, he might disclose such things as the organogram of the prison, or the winding path that complaints followed, or the financial arrangement by which the county paid the state for keeping inmates until the death warrant was signed.

When Stroman first came in, he was more likely to write about things like what you should do to a black man if you happen to have a heavy truck and some unused chain at your disposal. As the years wore him down, he sounded more like a high-school-newspaper editor or a professor who thinks himself a contrarian. Stroman complained about the lack of access to televisions or church services. He complained of the guards' behaving like "walking drones" who were "institutionalized in their own way" and "programmed to do as they are told even if it makes no sense at all." He complained about being allowed to shower only on Monday, Wednesday, and Friday. He complained about the security procedures that required them to gas you in your cell before coming in if you'd had a stroke or heart attack or even died. He complained about the cameras on the Row. He cited with approval a ruling by the European Court of Human Rights that cast aspersions on the American penal system. He complained about budget cuts that had the inmates going without dental floss while he heard that the governor, Rick Perry, was living in a mansion. He complained, with particular ferocity, about the raids on the prisoners' cells, in which he claimed they were stripped and cuffed and sent to the showers while the guards rummaged through their possessions, leaving everything in a mess. He complained about the quality of the beans. He complained that the executioners, at least according to what he had heard, were paid by the killing.

There was in Stroman's complaining a kind of citizenship. This was not the raving Mark who had come to Polunsky. He complained now more in the spirit of a cranky, self-important whistleblower: "Today is the 18th of January and so far we have had them horror-story pancakes fed to us 13 days this month. No one hardly gets up to eat these because they feed 'em so much and the end result is a waste of food and money." His criticism was born of a quiet faith that it could, perhaps, be otherwise. The terrorist appeared at times to be reinventing himself as a reformer.

Late in 2008, he wrote on his blog about Polunsky going into lockdown mode: "We 'Death Row' are being punished for the few that have been caught with cell phones and other contraband. And that is not right," he wrote. Then, a few days later, the guards happened to discover in Stroman's own cell a cell phone, a charger, a chunk of metal sharpened into a crude arrowhead, and a substance resembling marijuana.

It was in 2009, by various accounts, that Stroman's letters and blog posts showed signs of a turning. He had been told long ago, as a boy, that he so lacked self-awareness that even therapy couldn't save him. Now, for the first time, flecks of such awareness were becoming evident—and went beyond the flickers of good cheer that he had been able to perform throughout his life.

"I'm no angel by far and I've done some things after September 11, 2001 that still haunts me and by no means am I proud of the pain my own actions have caused," he wrote in April 2009.

He found himself growing more introverted, more eager to dwell in his own mind. A new vocabulary, inflected with the jargon of positive psychology, surfaced: "I've been unraveling, unsure and undetermined but this morning I'm just a man who feels as if he's on top of the world and from where I sit and write this, that's saying a mouthful! How about that folks! Can you honestly say that's how you felt this morning when you woke up? In the land of freedom? I have a lot to be grateful for and that's why I am feeling it this new day."

Stroman's newfound religiosity could be especially striking: "Thank ya Jesus for allowing this ole' Texas Rebel Redneck one more day of life, for no matter where it is I awake or lay my head, I know for a fact that this nightmare is only but a path to a true blessing and I will continue to 'walk it proud' and 'talk it loud' the American way and when I do get to that final destination that cross's me over into the next phase of existence, the learning process of life would have been completed with each day I absorb more knowledge and that shallow minded fool I once was is slowly fading away. Who would have thought that the trail of blood and tears would have opened my eyes so wide?"

This language from Stroman could feel almost put-on, too new. Was it genuine? Perhaps he really was changing with the vanishing of his old influences and their replacement by new influences: a blossoming relationship with Ilan Ziv, the filmmaker; contact with commenters who read his blog; other correspondence with people who wrote to Death Row prisoners out of charity. Or perhaps it was his shrewd understanding of what such people liked to hear to make themselves feel helpful.

Stroman constantly told his correspondents and readers how he appreciated all their letters and greetings and wishes. He felt the strength they were beaming his way. He sent them his blessings in turn and imparted little life lessons: "Never take life for granted and never pass up the chance to smile at someone."

From time to time, he took on projects, like making an album for each of his four children. He told Ziv it would be a kind of "legacy." It would contain pictures, written reflections, and other trifles: his thoughts when he first saw them, stories from their childhoods, answers to questions they might have in his absence, an account of his likes and dislikes and convictions. Sometimes assembling the albums made Stroman cry.

He gave the impression of working on himself and through his past. On darker days, he had learned what to do to calm himself: sit back and probe for a few memories. He had to dig deep. He knew what a mess he had made, but it was what it was. "Into each life some rain must fall," he once wrote.

There were still bad days aplenty, when it felt like he'd breathed in hell itself and those silent demons would awaken as if to remind him that they had been nestled in his organs all along. "I'm unraveling," he wrote in January 2010.

Then the brightening Mark Stroman would resurface. "I was born free, you can knock me down and keep chains on me and try to break and silence me and you can even execute me but I can assure you I'll die with my head held high and I'll still be a true American." He could even play the cosmopolitan: he wished his readers a wonderful Thanksgiving—and then added, "Even if you don't celebrate this in your country or lands, give thanks on November 25th for what you do have, for I can assure you, things could be a lot worse!"

Some weeks later, he wrote, "A person can have all the money in the world, several nice homes, cottages, villas, and a different car to drive every day of the week and still not know what true happiness is. Here it is, I have nothing, but I have everything for at the end of each day, before I go to sleep I know I have lots and lots of people who love and care about me."

✳

"MARK CHANGED," SAID Ilan Ziv, "not because we did anything, but because of who we were. His old world betrayed him, and a new group of people who was more loyal to him than his own family introduced him to our world."

The filmmaker was the pioneer and unofficial steward of this group of supporters and friends of Mark. By 2011, its ranks had swelled to include a network of European and American pen pals, a priest turned journalist, an elderly pastor who ministered to prisoners, a diffuse community of blog readers and commenters, and of course Ziv, who had arrived to conduct one simple interview, only to discover in his subject answers to questions that had haunted him almost since birth. Members of the group corresponded with Stroman, took an interest in his life, cheered him on in his appeals, vowed to be there with him at the execution.

The first time Ziv entered the Polunsky Unit, he walked into Visitation and sat in one of the cubicles. Walls to his left and right sides cut him off from other visitors, and a piece of glass stood between him and this bald, painted hulk of a man. In those earliest moments, Ziv felt something strange coming over him.

"You're sitting at a very uncomfortable proximity," he said. "Suddenly your physical space is invaded. The physical distance where we feel comfortable is invaded by this glass and the need to lean and this artificial focus." He went on, "In that cubicle with the seats, I just see you. There's almost no visual distraction. So you have this very bizarre semiuncomfortable thing that now I am focused only on you, and I'm sitting uncomfortably close to you. We don't have walls between us. And what it does is, I have this very uncanny focus on you, where I feel like I know you and I see a lot of things in you."

Back in 2004, when he first looked at Stroman with that focus, he saw none of the callousness and cruelty he had been expecting: "Everything broke down from the first meeting, because he's a complete mess. He's a completely helpless mess—crying, like, 'Oh my God, I prepared for this interview,' and now he's collapsing." Stroman just talked and talked, telling Ziv as much as he could think to ask: "I mean, the guy is not lying; he's just dangerously honest. Which is very kind of amazing. So he proceeds to tell me how he was going to go to Dallas malls. I mean he tells me stuff that he shouldn't have told me. And he tells me he was very confused. But he's also very charismatic, he's very engaging, and the eyes are very twinkling."

Ziv was not the first person to be charmed blind by Stroman. You could ask Tena or Tom Boston or any of his kids. But Ziv was also a seasoned, worldly documentary filmmaker who knew what he was doing and wasn't easy to dazzle. There was just something in this man that defied his expectations. Throughout the interview, Stroman cried and fretted that he'd messed everything up. Ziv offered him a mulligan: "I said, 'You know what, I promise you I'll come back.'" Did Ziv make that offer because he needed more tape? "No," he said flatly. It was because something strange and ineffable happened between them that day: "I wanted to come back forever."

ILAN ZIV LIKED to think of himself as a man not easily enchanted—certainly not by a murderer. What happened with Mark was different. It perhaps had to do with his discovery that the line separating him from Stroman wasn't as thick as he would have liked to believe.

The history that primed Ziv for their encounter preceded his birth. Ziv's father had grown up outside Warsaw in the 1920s and '30s, an assimilated Jew in a mixed apartment building in a religiously diverse neighborhood. When Hitler invaded Poland, the father realized with shock and bitterness that no one regarded him as the Pole he had always known himself to be. Neighbors were betraying Jewish neighbors, ratting out Jewish friends, watching as

Jews were sent off to the ghettoes. "It's this personal betrayal and an identity betrayal," Ziv said, "because he was a Pole."

His father, then sixteen, disguised himself as a Polish gentile, assumed a false identity, and escaped to Romania. He ended up, by a trail of disguises and deceptions he remains loath to detail, in Israel, and eventually in the Tel Aviv suburb of Afeka, where Ziv grew up. Most of his father's relatives weren't so lucky. "Eliminated," Ziv said simply.

This particular level of proximity to and distance from the Holocaust shaped the young Ziv's worldview. It left him consumed by the question of why his father's neighbors had betrayed him. It also, he figures, left him less ardently nationalistic than he might otherwise have been.

"I never grew up with Auschwitz stories, with the horror of the death camps," he said. "I never grew up with that. I grew up with a surreal escape story." The names to be mourned were names he had never known in the flesh. The losses fed endlessly repeated gossip: "I grew up with who fucks who, who was a closeted homosexual, who stole from who. But nobody exists."

The Holocaust suffused the atmosphere of Ziv's schooldays. He still remembers the school pausing instruction to broadcast reports of the Eichmann trial over the loudspeakers; Ziv was eleven. "Everything was Holocaust," he said. "It was a degree of obsession at that time in my childhood." And he understood that many of his neighbors and classmates had lost much more than he.

As he came of age, he sensed that there were two ideological roads available to an Israeli seeking to make sense of, and transcend, recent history. There were, of course, many trails in between, but to him it was a real fork. One road was hard-core Zionism and nationalism. It was the more particularized interpretation of the history of their people: a systematic attack on Jewishness that had to be answered by a systematic assertion of Jewishness. The other road was built on a more universal reading of what had occurred: the Jews, like so many other peoples in history, were victims of "chauvinism," as Ziv put it, and of the abuse of power; they must now stand with anyone anywhere threatened by chauvinists, caught under power's jackboot. "You can come out to Jewish nationalism and I shall fight and never again," he said. "Or you can come out so sensitive to human-rights violations."

Perhaps it was the abstraction to him of his family's loss, but from the time of high school Ziv found himself among the universalists—a position, as he put it, of "refusing to trust chauvinism and nationalism." An assumption of that worldview was that Nazism wasn't wholly exceptional, that it was the extreme expression of a potentiality that lay within all people. It was something that could hijack you or me, a German or, yes, even a Jew. This belief was the seed of Ziv's career, though he didn't realize it at the time. If we all harbor the germs of evil, why do they infect some of us and spare others? Is evil always a choice, or can it at times be explained by context and circumstance?

As a student at Ironi Yud Daled High School in Tel Aviv, Ziv applied these still-forming ideas to his editorship of the student newspaper. When the 1967 war broke out, he figured he should dedicate the paper to the conflict and publish Palestinian voices, so readers would hear both sides of the story. "Over my dead body" was the headmaster's response. Ziv considered raising money and publishing the newspaper anyway, for the students of other high schools, as a public service.

Then, at seventeen and a half, he graduated and was drafted into the military of a country, his country, whose growing nationalism made him wary. Israel was turning in that direction after the Six Day War, in which it had more than tripled the territory it controlled. Ziv, feeling lonely in his convictions, was mobilized to an elite reconnaissance unit under the Central Command called Sayeret Haruv. In 1968, he finished basic training and deployed with his men with a mission to prevent the Palestine Liberation Organization from infiltrating the West Bank. Ziv suppressed his opinions as best he could in that time. It could really mess you up to keep thinking about how you were against the mission. And he found in the physical challenge of combat an outlet for his competitiveness.

At times, he felt himself flirting with that invisible line, at risk of becoming what he had once assailed. One night a commander offered a deal to Ziv's unit: for a certain number of Palestinian infiltrators killed (Ziv couldn't recall the precise bargain), the responsible team would get a week off. "We were lying on these bunk beds in the barracks—it was a desert down in the valley—thinking, 'Who's going to get the chance to do it?' " Ziv said. " 'Will tonight be the night that we get it?' Because a week off was a big deal, a really big deal—Tel Aviv, your girlfriend, cafés, life."

The next morning at breakfast, another man in the unit whom Ziv recognized as a fellow skeptic said to him, "Do you remember last night when we were all competing?" They couldn't believe themselves. What was scary to Ziv was how little it took to buy into the chauvinism. "I'm not going to put down anyone who crosses moral lines," he said years later. "I understand how you can do it," he added.

One advantage of being a paratrooper was that it insulated you from the intimate realities of occupation. "I didn't put people under curfew; I didn't abuse women at roadblocks; I didn't do any of that," Ziv said. Occupation duty, he imagines, "would have punctured the bubble much earlier." Instead, his unit took missions like dashing over the Jordan River late at night to raid a base. They zipped in and out of the lives they affected: "It's like getting bin Laden—the poor man version."

On later missions, he came closer to those lives. Assigned to a unit enforcing a curfew in Gaza, made to face the human reality of the conflict, he "freaked out" and recoiled. He couldn't get himself to do it. He volunteered instead to wash pots and scrub floors in the unit's kitchen. He got out of the army in 1971, traveled to Europe for several weeks with his girlfriend, returned home, and enrolled in university.

On Yom Kippur in 1973, the holiest day in Judaism, Ziv was hanging out with some of his theater buddies. They had put on a play together earlier that year, an avant-garde work starring Israeli Jews and Israeli Arabs, exploring their differing perspectives on the 1947 UN resolution proposing the partition of the region. The group had stayed in touch and reunited every so often. At this particular reunion, they found themselves desperately hungry. They decided to drive toward Ramallah in the West Bank, Ziv said, because it was Yom Kippur, "which is the most horrible day in Israel because everything's closed."

As they drove, the radio brought the news that Israel had been invaded by its Arab neighbors and was at war. The Jews and Arabs in the same car were now on different sides of the line. Everybody knew they had to return to their corners: the Palestinians in the group back to their families, the Israelis to theirs. The troupe exchanged tearful good-byes. Ziv phoned his parents to ask if they had heard. They told him that a man had come to the house with an order summoning Ziv back into service.

Ziv took a bus to Tel Aviv. "All through the bus, I'm saying, 'I should defect. I really should defect,' " he said. For the rest of the ride, he played the scenarios in his mind. He'll go to the border and escape; he'll fly away quietly. But what would happen to his parents? What would people think of the family? "Everybody will look at me, the worst of the scum," he said. "The country's invaded, and I am defecting. Can you imagine a worse crime sociologically?" Once again, he yielded.

"I mobilized," he said. "And that I always will remember, and that was haunting to me—because there was such a discrepancy between what I should do and what as a person I can do. And how weak I became, or how meek I was forced to become, because of human reality." He counts it the worst day of his life.

When the conflict subsided, Ziv applied for permission to leave Israel. He fibbed, saying he needed only a short break to get over war trauma. "I knew it was a total lie, that I would never come back, even if it was violating the law," he said. The documents signed, he bought a plane ticket to America and flew there in April 1974, to enroll as a student at New York University. There his interests would evolve from theater to documentary filmmaking. In project after project, he would probe the question of why some people, under some conditions, cross moral lines.

In 1982, he returned to Israel for a short visit. War had broken out again that June, when Israeli forces had invaded Lebanon. Ziv received an assignment from CNN to go there with a camera. He went into Lebanon twice. By the second trip, Beirut had been fully besieged, and Israel would soon be held responsible for the massacres in the Sabra and Shatila refugee camps. Ziv returned to his father in Tel Aviv and told him something, long in coming, that closed the circle of his relationship with Israel: "I said to him, 'Father, this is Warsaw.' And I said, 'Don't give me bullshit. This is Warsaw. I mean, ghettoized, exiled people who are terrorized. I don't see how you can make a distinction, an intellectual distinction.' And I don't think he ever argued. My mother erupted, but he didn't argue. But he gave me this look which was very bewildered."

Ilan Ziv never lived in Israel again.

RETURNING TO NEW YORK after his first interview with Stroman, Ziv thought to himself, "I'm a friend of a murderer now; God help me." He wasn't a friend friend, but Ziv had made a commitment. He continued his research and returned a few months later for a second conversation. Arriving at Polunsky, he underwent its particular rituals once again. Your license-plate number and name are radioed to the staff inside to establish your identity. You are searched. You can take inside only your car keys and $20 in quarters. With that, you can buy snacks for your chosen prisoner—a task with its own protocols. You put the money into the vending machine, and the Visitation warden gathers the items, places them in a brown paper bag, and gives them to another warden, who gives it to the prisoner, who by now has been brought from his cell by armed guards and made to sit opposite you on the other side of the glass. Your four-hour slot begins.

This second meeting pushed Ziv further away from objective film-making and into a peculiar friendship. It led to a correspondence by letter, with Stroman writing often and at length in his loopy hand-writing, and Ziv regularly apologizing for being too busy to respond substantively. When Ziv discovered an online service that allowed him to e-mail Stroman and have those messages turned into letters, a brisker back-and-forth ensued.

They talked, in person and in writing, about Stroman's past and Ziv's, about the nature of hatred, about what makes men the way they are. The more they talked, the more Stroman reminded Ziv of something aching and unutterable within himself. "I have the victim and the victimizer in me a little bit," Ziv said. His life story began with his people being betrayed and murdered; then, in a blink of history, enough had changed to turn Ziv into the killer. "I under-stood the victimizer perspective," he said, "and I understood how you could become the victim." This duality attracted him to another, differently divided soul.

In his subject's life Ziv saw a mirror image of the American dream that Stroman's victims had been pursuing. There was some truth in that idea. For those whom the economic dream had deserted, the consolation could be to belong to some walled-off culture or group—bikers, rednecks, Peckerwood Warriors, loud and proud Texans, True Americans—that not everyone could. If you were a native-born white male in postmillennial America, it was possible that you felt the country stagnating more acutely than most. Because however grim it was out there, however scarce the work, however hard it was to get hours, however high one's debts stacked, if you were a woman or black or gay or an immigrant from some punished republic, this time was very likely a better time for you than your parents' time.

Your personal liberty had grown enough to distract you from the nation's broader situation. Your individual graph swung up and to the right, even as America's plateaued.

Somewhere down the line, only because the gods have a sense of humor, a leftist peacenik from Israel developed empathy for a right-wing, swastika-tattooed white chauvinist from Texas.

Ziv was taken with Stroman's boyhood stories of abuse by his step-father, Wallace. "He didn't like kids too much," Stroman said in one of their conversations. "I remember the day that he hit my mother, and I jumped up and I told him that was it, you're not gonna do this no more." Stroman confirmed his sister's memory of being sexually abused, including once overhearing Wallace say to her, "You know you liked it, bitch." Diverting attention from his own racism, he complained of having racists for parents: "I married my wife—she's Spanish—and they disowned me because of a Spanish woman."

Ziv wanted to know when Stroman began to drift in the direction that would eventually lead to the Row. Others had their favored theories—it was Shawna's departure; or there had always been something wrong with him; or it was meth; or it was finding a girl of his in bed with his buddy. But Stroman had his own preferred moment. He attributed it to when he found out about his father.

He was still a boy, on the cusp of adolescence, hanging out at his grandfather's one day, and one of Grandpa's friends, a guy named Eddie Stroman, kept calling him "son." As Stroman told Ziv, "I said, 'I'm not your son!' And my grandfather said, 'You know what? Let me tell you a secret. You can't tell nobody.' He said, 'That's your dad.'"

"So my whole life I'm letting this man, Wallace Baker, abuse me," Stroman said. "Thinking he's my father. Kick me, thump me in the head, do all this stuff. And then I find out that this man's my father." He explained how the revelation shattered him: "The people I've trusted my whole life turned out to be a pack of liars. You know, you grow up trusting your mother, your grandmother, and your grand-father, and you believe everything they say, and then when you find out that your whole existence has been a lie, it's shocking, very shocking."

From that moment, he said, "I automatically rebelled." It was not long thereafter that Stroman had spied that silver pickup truck, with keys lying invitingly in the rear bed, and taken it for a spin. After that incident, Stroman said, "it's my mother and stepfather who put me in a boys' home, thinking it would straighten me up. And from then on shit just went downhill."

Ziv asked about his time in the custody of the Texas Youth Commission.

"Sheesh," Stroman began, for once short of words. "At age twelve and thirteen years old, it's a—you grow up quickly. Especially here in Texas. Texas is notorious for their penal system, and it's just—you know." He cleared his throat. "I witnessed things that I shouldn't have seen at an early age." He declined to go further down that hole.

In one of their conversations, Ziv asked Stroman about his love of guns. Where did the obsession begin?

"I'm an American," he said, grinning wide. "American dream, you know." Asked to elaborate, he added: "You know, right to bear arms—it's in our constitution, you know."

Ziv asked about Stroman's history of nightmares, which others had spoken of in interviews.

"Oh, I've had nightmares since I was a kid," Stroman said.

"You never went to counseling?" Ziv asked.

"No, sir."

Their conversations meandered far and wide, and Stroman told Ziv not just about his demons but also about his taste in music and tattoos and all things Confederate. Somehow this led an immigrant to understand Stroman's intolerance as a worn-down native's desire to claim a sphere of his own. "You might find it abhorrent, but that's culture," Ziv said later. "It's part of somebody's pathology to be different—to be a rebel." Ziv was struck by the absence of community in Stroman's milieu: people unable to lean on those closest to them;

people whose lives had become too chaotic to raise good children; people attached to few of the binding agents—family, company, union, church—of an earlier time. Ziv compared Stroman's world to the wreckage of the car-building communities he had surveyed when shooting a film in Flint, Michigan. There almost all the good jobs had gone, but he sensed some enduring mutuality. "Where Mark comes from," he said, "there was nothing."

It was not that Ziv excused Stroman: "I said, 'Mark, if there was no death penalty, I would vote for you to be life without parole until your last day on earth. Because,' I said, 'I'm sorry, but you've got to pay. I've seen what you've done, and you've got to pay.' "

From time to time, Ziv returned to the subject of that frenzied month. "You accept that what you've done is wrong?" Ziv asked.

"Yes. Yeah, I know it is. I mean, yeah, taking a human life is wrong. But at that time, man, I was doing the right thing in my mind. I really was."

Ziv asked what Stroman would say if addressing not a filmmaker right now but one of the women he had made a widow.

"I'm sorry for causing her grief," Stroman said. "That's just what bothers me, because I know I have caused these people pain and misery. This whole September 11 thing has just devastated every-body's lives, and then here I am—I step in and become an Ameri-can terrorist and start wanting to shoot everybody of the Middle Eastern descent. I had no idea this guy was from India, you know. That was the biggest mistake of my life, you know—for the pain that I've caused their children. That's what bothers me; it bothers me at night. Because I know that what I've caused my family is doubled on theirs."

But then Stroman quickly turned around to argue that he should not be killed, despite all this: "The State of Texas is saying, 'It's not right to kill.' So to punish me, to show me it's not right to kill, they're going to do the same thing I did—a revenge killing. Makes a lot of sense to me. You know, those terrorists who flew that plane in there—that was a revenge-type vendetta. I did the same thing. I started killing people from the Middle East. Oh! The State of Texas says you can't do that; killing's wrong; we're gonna strap you down; we're gonna kill you. The cycle never ends. The men that attacked the Trade Center in the '90s? Enemy combatants to this country." He still thought of himself as their patriotic inverse: "I'm an allied combatant." This thought seemed to lead to an idea: "I'm a combatant to this country, but they want to execute me. You've got young men dying over there every day in war. I'm sitting here perfectly healthy. I want to go over there and give my life, but they want to strap me down, pump some poisons in me, to show me and the public it's wrong to kill."

During one of their conversations, toward the end, Ziv asked Stroman if he'd like to use the video camera to record messages to his children. Ziv promised to edit the tapes and send them to the proper addresses.

Mark choked on his own feelings for a moment. He told Robert, Amber, Erica, and Cassandra that he loved them. That he was sorry for the pain he'd put in their lives, for quitting on them when they most needed him. He was crying. His voice was too broken with sobs to make out the words. Ziv offered him another take.

He collected himself and started over. Speaking now just to Robert, Amber, and Erica, he apologized for leaving the way he had. He begged them to stay out of trouble. He hoped that their dreams would come true. Then he addressed Cassandra and Shawna, and said they were the best things that ever happened to him.

A third take, calmer still, retreaded much of the same territory, but a new sign-off appeared: "Love your country, and you know that's true. God bless America, and don't forget September 11. I love y'all. Good-bye."

Ziv's interactions with Stroman rang in his mind for a while every time he left Texas. Soon Stroman became the leading man of the entire documentary. It ceased to be about hate crimes in general;

it was now about Mark Stroman. The blog Ziv set up for Stroman in 2008 connected the prisoner with a whole array of people from around the world, many of whom shared Ziv's generous understanding of a convicted murderer. Between the commenters on the blog, his other visitors, and his pen pals, Stroman was connected to a wider world than he'd ever known living on the outside.

Small details defined a man's days on the Row. They were also the common ground between Stroman and his far-flung correspondents: all of us, whatever else we lack, have details. So his letters were full of questions about the little particulars of life on the outside. "So tell me about the parking in New York," Ziv remembers Stroman asking. "It's really lousy, right? So you pay $400 to park in a garage? My God, you guys are crazy. Why do you need a car in New York?" There was no factoid too small for him, Ziv said: "Mark was intrigued by elevators and doormen—how does it work? Mark was living in a cell, creating a universe through letters and a universe through all these people who were describing in detail their lives in other countries, what they go through and what they do. And that became sort of his travel, you know?" Stroman's blog went from a few dozen hits a day to several thousand over time. A significant fraction of this traffic came from Europe, where the death penalty was widely considered barbaric.

One day Stroman told Ziv that he wanted him to be responsible for his ashes, when and if they carried the sentence out. Ziv felt greatly moved by the request, and he asked where Stroman wanted them scattered. The Austrian Alps, he said. He mentioned Britain and Ireland as possible backups. How the hell Stroman, who had never left metro Dallas, let alone Texas or the United States, chose the Austrian Alps was beyond Ziv.

"Mark, you're a self-described American patriot who allegedly killed for his patriotism, right?" Ziv remembered saying to him. "You killed for your patriotism. You want your final ashes so far away from America? Fascinating."

Stroman said, "I feel all the people who helped me live outside of the United States. This is where I think I belong. This is where I'll be at peace."

In 2009, Ziv began to sense a pronounced change in his subject. Stroman was becoming calmer, more reflective. A pro forma statement of remorse back in their first interview had evolved into a genuine understanding of the damage he had wrought, and of the means of redemption. "Everything I'm doing here, I'm trying to get my heart right," Stroman told Ziv. "I ask God every day for forgiveness for the people I've killed. That's not something I'm proud of doing, but that's just something I did. There's no turning back. That's one thing that I'm serious about—I've took chances my whole life—but I'm not gonna chance my eternal life. I do fear God."

Ziv knew that their conversations were partly responsible for the change, but he insisted that it had less to do with him and more to do with the A-B switch in Stroman's life. From the moment Stroman entered Polunsky, everyone who had shaped him dropped out of his life. Everyone who came into his life besides his fellow prisoners— the religious advisers in prison, the correspondents from around the world, the blog commenters, Ziv, and a handful of other occasional visitors—was of a very different breed. "On the surface, we have nothing in common," Ziv said. "However, we do. We were all outside of the world that Mark grew up in. We are politically very liberal; we are mixed ethnically; some are gay. Most of us are not Americans. In short, we are the representatives of the world that the younger Mark probably despised and looked down on—or was afraid of. We were the opposite of his redneck biker buddies from the drinking and drug binges. We were very different from his relatives and his immediate family. But the fact is that we were his most loyal supporters." They were the ones who wrote to him, who visited, who bought him commissary items. Some of them had pledged to be in the viewing room at the end.

In one of his conversations with Ziv, Stroman himself made the point about his family: "Not a single Christmas card, not a birthday card. 'Do you need any help down there?' Nothing. I'm not asking for nothing. I'm asking for a little compassion. You know, I'm on my last—if I was on the outside and one of my family members was on Death Row, I'd be going out of my way to make their life easier down here."

For Ziv, perhaps the profoundest moment in their relationship came late in 2009, not long after the attack on the Fort Hood military base in central Texas. A U.S. Army psychiatrist named Nidal Malik Hasan, an American of Palestinian provenance and Muslim faith, had gone on a rampage at the base, killing thirteen people and wounding thirty-two. He had told relatives of his growing discomfort with serving a country at war in the Muslim world, while suffering harassment by comrades on account of his origins.

Ziv had arranged back-to-back sessions with Stroman over two days. On the first day, they spoke of a book that Stroman had been reading and had grown infatuated with: *Man's Search for Meaning*, by the Holocaust survivor Viktor Frankl. It was not clear whether he had read it because of his relationship with Ziv. When Stroman first mentioned the book to his friend, Ziv was surprised by the tastes developing beneath that swastika-tattooed exterior: "I said, 'Mark, you realize I am the son of a Holocaust refugee. That was the popular book of my youth. I was supposed to read it like eight times, and now you're telling me about the fucking book and how you find it so fascinating.' "

They spoke at length about the book that first day. There was much in the work—born of Frankl's years in Nazi concentration camps and his investigation of how people survive in the direst circumstances—to calm a man in Stroman's situation: "Everything can be taken from a man but one thing: the last of the human freedoms—to choose one's attitude in any given set of circumstances, to choose one's own way." Stroman, who used to spout terms like "nigger-loving Jew," now found himself drawn to one

Jewish man's story of inner transformation: "When we are no longer able to change a situation, we are challenged to change ourselves." After Stroman's years of pondering what the world had
done to him, the Frankl book traced a different line of thinking,
centered on responsibility and on the future rather than the past:
"Even though conditions such as lack of sleep, insufficient food and
various mental stresses may suggest that the inmates were bound
to react in certain ways, in the final analysis it becomes clear that
the sort of person the prisoner became was the result of an inner
decision, and not the result of camp influences alone."

Stroman especially liked this passage about living for others: "A
man who becomes conscious of the responsibility he bears toward
a human being who affectionately waits for him, or to an unfinished
work, will never be able to throw away his life. He knows the 'why'
for his existence, and will be able to bear almost any 'how.' "

As he and Ziv spoke that first day, Stroman said the book had,
among other things, filled him with guilt about his swastika tattoo.
"When I read this book—the swastika, my God, I never understood
what that means," Stroman said. "You have to tell me, Ilan!"

On the second day, the subject of the Fort Hood attacks came up.
Mark told Ziv that news of the attack had reawakened the specter
of 9/11 for him and roused his dormant hatred of Muslims, whom
he still thought to be evil. "You know me and Muslims," Stroman
snarled.

"I looked him in the eye," Ziv said, "and I say, 'You know what,
Mark? You're a fucked-up person, and now I see how fucked you
are,' because that's the way we talked. I said, 'I see how fucked-up
because you know what your problem is? You don't see people. You
see groups, right? You see groups, and I see people. And that person who did this killing is a very fucked-up individual. From everyone's perspective, you're a very fucked-up person. Nobody would
say you're white and you're Christian, and all white Christians are
fucked up. *You're* fucked up.' "

Stroman looked at Ziv for the longest time and finally said, "So this is what they did to the Jews, right?" For a moment, it all seemed to flow together: his Holocaust reading, his conversations with an Israeli visitor, the post-9/11 history of terror and profiling, and, of course, his own crimes.

"I had tears in my eyes then; I had tears telling it to my wife," Ziv said. "At that moment," he added, "I really felt he got it."

✳

In late 2010, Stroman could find himself severely backlogged with letters. That plus the blog posting and the legal papers he had to review—it took more time than he had. He knew it was a good problem: "I am an extremely lucky man. I can count on both hands the ones I love and still need many more fingers." His correspondents seemed genuinely to care for him. More than that, they gave him a chance to test out different iterations of the new man he was striving to become.

One of his new correspondents was Michael, a Briton who was a police officer of some importance over there. Like many others, Michael had come to write to Stroman through an organization that matched Death Row prisoners with pen pals. The one he used was called Human Writes, based in the English town of Wetherby. For pairing you with a prisoner, its website listed a membership fee of £18 a year. ("The organisation needs some money behind it for unavoidable expenses," the site says, including an annual conference and occasional "socials.") The fee also bought you access to the local Human Writes representative in the state where your pen pal would be executed: "Typically, your co-ordinator would be in touch with you several times before the date and would try to be available to you on the evening of an execution. They will then inform you if it has gone ahead. In the following days and weeks they are there for you too." Should grief overwhelm a pen pal, the group had a network of trained counselors—a perk that it noted gave it a competitive advantage in a crowded market: "It is worth mentioning that the support we offer is obviously not available on the more impersonal internet sites for pen friends."

Michael, like other pen pals, found in the letter-writing an intimate form of charity. "My particular motivation was to provide some contact with the outside world to any person who has to tolerate being stuck on Death Row," he wrote. "I'm against the death penalty, but was more motivated by simply wanting to hold out a hand of friendship than by crusading against another countries' penal code and policy. I had expected to be allocated some petty criminal who used a gun badly or domestic violence perpetrator so was surprised when I learned of Mark's profile, but we did hit it off, and we exchanged over 15 letters each way in the brief time we corresponded. I genuinely came to like the guy, he was respectful, gracious and well mannered, but I was not blind either to the fact what he had done, whether by madness or character fault or just shear stupidity was horrific."

As in his long-ago letters to the Templetons, Stroman liked to adorn his letters to Michael with stickers. His handwriting was greatly improved by the years inside. His language had far fewer mistakes of spelling or grammar. His reading and corresponding appeared to have borne fruit. And his tone, as on his blog, was now unrelentingly positive:

Oct 11, 2010—3:50 AM

Dear Michael,

As always, this letter is being 'sent' and 'wrote' with respects and my kindest regards and my hopes and prayers are that you and all the loved ones are in the best of health and the highest of spirits and safe from all the evils of this world. As for myself, I'm just trying to make the best out of a bad situation. But I'm alive and where there's life there's a small glimmer of hope.

There were complaints here and there, of course, but he was a man who sounded almost unaccountably at peace with himself—and bordering on saccharine: "Thank you for your awesome and kind letter and I was pleased to see that my last one reached you safely and that you had enjoyed the photos."

He told Michael all about himself. How his life began in Dallas but had ended, as far as he was concerned, with the faraway events of September 11, 2001. He wrote of having spent all his life "in the 50-60 mile range of the Dallas area—and to me, it's the best town in Texas ☺." He wrote of turning forty-one in a matter of days and commiserated with Michael about getting older, about how fast the years crept up on a man.

He was grateful for Michael's description of a typical morning and now had follow-up questions: "I see you drink tea—I would assume hot tea—right? In Texas we drink our tea 'iced tea.' Yes, you'd raise some eyebrows if you asked for hot tea."

He appreciated Michael's bits of praise, including about his positivity. He didn't want to mislead his friend, though: he assured him that he still had dark moments aplenty. He was just trying to get by, to stay focused: "I'm just trying to keep my mind from wandering—too much drama & chaos and petty issues to deal with . . . At times I actually believe this place does it deliberately to keep us un-balanced." But enough of his dislikes, he said again and again in his letters to Michael. He wanted to be positive: it was another damned day of his caged existence, but he would find a way to hold his head up high!

He wasn't proud of everything he'd done. He knew he was far from perfect and had made grave mistakes. And yet when Stroman spoke about his crime, which wasn't often, at least not with Michael, he still tended to make up justifications. And he could flat-out lie to some of his new pen pals in a way that he could no longer to, say, Ilan Ziv. He told Michael that he did what he did to avenge the death in the Twin Towers of a sister. "Out of love, anger and stupidity," he wrote, "I lashed out at the Muslim world—and became what I hated the most—a terrorist." He could still, for all his evolution, betray a macabre sense of self-importance about his actions: "My case is very high-profile since I'm the 1st man in AMERICAN HISTORY to retaliate after SEPTEMBER 11th 2001."

He struggled with the feeling that at this stage of life he should be serving his progeny, and here he was locked away. Instead of guiding and protecting his children—and now even his lone grandchild—he was wasting his days, useless to all.

But he was determined not to stew in his own worry. Life was full of other people and more important things. A budding man of the world, Stroman claimed to be hooked on international news. He shared with Michael his concerns about the weather over there: he had heard it was Britain's coldest winter in more than four hundred years. He mentioned learning of the tragic explosions at the Pike River Mine in New Zealand, which trapped and killed twenty-nine workers, and seemed to hear in their condition echoes of his own: "the feeling of being trapped . . . the feelings the loved ones must have . . . helplessness." The geopolitical scene filled him with worry: "I fear what's boiling up as we speak—China, Iran, North Korea, Russia—troubled times indeed."

One story that especially troubled him was the news from Japan of an earthquake, a tsunami, and now a nuclear disaster. He had an idea to offer, though he figured that Michael was probably in no position to do anything about it. What if they let some Death Row prisoners like him go over there and into the contaminated zones, where they could work to contain the leakage? "Why be foolish and not send us to do the task at hand . . . willingly and with pride."

✳

THE NEWCOMERS IN Stroman's life could be a little too credulous. Having come into his life when they did, they could minimize his darkness. Stroman's sister Doris didn't personally know most of these do-gooder types who had fallen in love with her brother, but she knew of them and got a good laugh thinking about them. She loved her brother, but she loved him with eyes wide open, knowing everything she knew, knowing what he was and what he'd never be. These people—Ilan Ziv, the pen pals, the blog readers—they seemed to her to be begging Mark to con them.

Ever since the trial, but before it, too, Doris and Mary had believed that Stroman would say anything to save himself. He wasn't your regular criminal. He was a cunning one.

The sisters rattled off the misinformation they had heard in the news or from Mark's lawyers or at the trial. Their mother couldn't have had Mark at age fifteen, Doris said: "That means she would have had me at age nine." Further: "There was one thing that I read, that his mother was found in a ditch pregnant. That's not true." They said it was the same thing with the sister in the World Trade Center: "There wasn't one." Doris denied that Wallace had hit them, although her exoneration contained a different accusation: "He never beat any of us. But I was sexually abused by him." Mary denied that Wallace was a heavy drinker, though Doris remembered otherwise: "I remember he used to drink those tall ones." Mark wasn't the victim in school, Mary said: "My brother was not bullied. He bullied." Nor, she said, had Mark run away to their grandparents eleven times—maybe once or twice. The sisters questioned whether Mark and Tena were ever legally married: "I've never seen a marriage license," Mary said. She denied that Mark had inherited any of his racism from the family: "My stepfather was not a racist. Neither was my mother. Or me or my sister." They dismissed claims she'd heard attributed to Mark that they had a pet monkey named Tarzan as children. Nor did they buy the 9/11 warrior thing: they just saw their brother as a screwed-up, possibly brain-damaged or bipolar guy with an untreated drug problem.

Though she accused him of many fibs, Mary was particularly

exercised about Mark's self-depiction as a motorcycle man: "He claimed to ride, but he didn't. He loved Harleys, but he never had a bike. I had a bike. He never had a bike." She added, "I tell you, I think there was something wrong with my brother's mind. I think he lied so much, he believed what he lied."

She continued, "It was always hard with my brother, because he was such a good con man. He could tell you something and make you believe it. So it's hard for me to believe anything that came out of his mouth, just because he always conned his way out of everything."

Doris thought Mark had figured out what these kindly liberals helping him wanted to hear. She did believe, from what she gathered by letter and on occasional visits, that he was becoming a better man at Polunsky: "He was going back to the old Mark—the kindhearted Mark," Doris said. What made her wary was how her brother had become a vessel for all his helpers' ideas about the world. Perhaps they needed to believe Mark had changed in order to recoup a respectable return on their investment of time and feeling.

Doris was right that the people who had grown fond of Stroman saw him through their own lenses, tinted or smudged as they might be. They tended to fixate on the idea of his abusive childhood and awful parents. They seemed to see a man whose choices they judged to be less real than their own had been—a victimizer who, if you looked more closely, was a victim of his circumstances. They flirted, as his sisters resisted doing, with the idea that Stroman was not wholly his own problem—that his failure was also somehow ours.

To Doris and Mary, their brother was a remarkable shape-shifter who knew how to promote himself. He had become almost like a brand, with a small but fanatic cult of consumers. Doris realized this when she went online, on Facebook and elsewhere, and left comments trying to correct the record. She claims to have received a death threat over the phone not long thereafter—"All of you are gonna die," the person said—as well as a great deal of backlash from other Internet surfers, who were defensive of Mark's reputation.

Doris and Mary, of course, had their own biases. Some time ago, they had told Ilan Ziv a very different story than this one, portraying their childhood in considerably bleaker terms. They seemed cannier now, and determined to prevent any of Mark's reputation from spilling on them. "I truly believe he's a sick man," Mary said, "and I'll always believe that. And the system failed him."

⁕

On JANUARY 20, 2011, Mark Stroman's lawyer paid him a visit at Polunsky, bearing some long-awaited news. The system had decided that Stroman would die on July 13 of that year.

Less than a month later, Stroman received a letter from the state. He opened it during the recreation hour, and as he began to read the death warrant, which graciously added an extra week to his life, he couldn't stop "laughing like a crazy man," perhaps out of fear, perhaps at the absurdity of receiving a letter from your own government informing you that it plans to kill you:

> It is hereby ordered that the defendant, Mark Anthony Stroman, who has been adjudged to be guilty of capital murder as charged in the indictment and whose punishment has been assessed by the verdict of the jury and judgment of the court at death, shall be kept in custody by the director of the Texas Department of Criminal Justice, Institutional Division, until the 20th day of July, 2011, upon which day, at the Texas Department of Criminal Justice, Institutional Division, at some time after the hour of six o'clock p.m., in a room arranged for the purpose of execution, the said director, acting by and through the executioner designated by the director, as provided by law, is hereby commanded, ordered and directed to carry out this sentence of death by intravenous injection of a substance or substances in a lethal quantity sufficient to cause the death of the said Mark Anthony Stroman until the said Mark Anthony Stroman is Dead.

Ten days later, he was minding his business in his cell, typing a letter to his attorney, when two guards showed up at the door. They said Stroman was wanted at the major's office. As he walked down the hallway, it felt different from before: he could see people talking but couldn't hear them; the only sounds were the blood pulsing in his head and his own footsteps. Awaiting him in the office was a stack of papers: all the forms he had to fill out to get to the next round, so to speak. Everything around him seemed to echo; the world was swirling in slow motion. He returned to the cell with the packet of death. The men around him were unusually silent. No screaming, no barking, just some quiet acknowledgment: "I receive a few silent nods of the head, which we are all aware of in this place of death meaning 'take care' and good luck," Stroman wrote. He packed up his things, had a last turn at recreation with his buddy Olsen, and then migrated to his new death watch cell, where they kept prisoners awaiting imminent execution under closer scrutiny. He felt like some kind of reality-TV star, with that camera staring at him from the wall. The unit had four death watch cells. When you were placed in one of them, you could safely assume two things: that someone else had just died, vacating a spot; and that you were going to die before long.

Stroman knew that everything that happened now might be for the last time. Earlier that month, for example, he had savored what he knew might be his last encounter with rain, and then written about it. Out he went with his friend Olsen to the rec cage. He had heard of an arctic blast aiming its wrath at Texas, but it was supposed to be in the sixties still, so the men wore shorts and T-shirts. A faint drizzle blessed them, and Stroman savored its smell. Then the drizzle exploded into a torrent. The temperature plunged, and it felt a lot like that arctic blast that was supposed to be far away still. The lights above them began to gyrate. The wind, which almost never came down into their high-walled cage, ducked and thrashed the men. It was the first time Stroman remembered feeling wind in

nine years. The rain blew in every direction. "We laugh like two little kids enjoying our morning time," Stroman recalled. After twenty
minutes or so, he and Olsen were numb, and the guard accompanied
them back inside.

Stroman headed for the showers at once: "I undress and am
instantly hit with the hot water and my whole body tingles. Almost a
painful feeling; the coldness had numbed me just that quick. I show-
ered and thawed at the same time." It was enough excitement, Stroman concluded. He swore he wasn't going to leave that cell for the
rest of the day if he could help it: "No more movement for me unless
I'm called out to get my death warrant or a visit arrives."

The New American

"I hereby declare, on oath, that I absolutely and entirely renounce and abjure all allegiance and fidelity to any foreign prince, potentate, state, or sovereignty, of whom or which I have heretofore been a subject or citizen; that I will support and defend the Constitution and laws of the United States of America against all enemies, foreign and domestic; that I will bear true faith and allegiance to the same; that I will bear arms on behalf of the United States when required by the law; that I will perform noncombatant service in the armed forces of the United States when required by the law; that I will perform work of national importance under civilian direction when required by the law; and that I take this obligation freely without any mental reservation or purpose of evasion; so help me God."

In November 2010, not long before Stroman received his date, Rais—wearing a purple shirt and black trousers—spoke those words in a ceremony that made him an American. From filling out his N-400 through uttering that oath, he felt the process remolding him. Now thirty-seven, he was offering himself up to his adopted country. "It's not only a status change," he said. "It's also made me more responsible, and I took it in this way. It's not just a certificate they gave me today. It's something that I have to treat myself in a different way. From now onward, I'm more responsible, and I have more duties." Had he been a native-born American with a special occasion to celebrate, he might "just go and party around and throw some Champagne bottle," as he put it. (He had clearly been watching American sports.) But for Rais it was less a celebration than a coming into his own. From the moment of his arrival, he had known that it was a country of boundless anythings, but he had also come to know its ailments. Citizenship brought the opportunity to talk of such things without fear, to try to improve the home he had chosen: the people he wanted to address were now, legally speaking, his people, and they couldn't just kick him out if they didn't appreciate his message. "Now I think that I have a voice," he said.

RAIS'S FOCUS THAT day was, as it should have been, on himself. He was part of something larger, of course: part of the vast infusion of new blood that kept the country young and churning, and that defined its essential being. This was America's strange, stirring commitment: to keep itself vital by allowing itself, again and again, to become somebody else's. Immigration had made, and continued to make, America; immigration ever seemed poised to tear America apart. The people were asked to celebrate this recurring passage into new hands. But in hard times those who had only the glory of their pasts could choose to cling to them—even if it meant sending the country to hell. Yet if you survived their wrath and remained, you would become as much a part of the scenery as they. You would become old blood, too. And, as sure as dawn, you would calcify into what needed further refreshment. Thus the country, having become yours, would become somebody else's.

It was becoming Rais's country now. Dallas had been good to him, mostly. To the outside eye, especially the northern eye, it could be dismissed as a gussied-up, diverse, but ultimately narrow backwater. If you had failed somehow to be white, you could feel the eyes on you when you walked into a nicer restaurant. You knew that you were welcome, legally and otherwise, but you also had the feeling of being done a favor, the sense that you moved about the city at other people's pleasure.

To see Dallas in this way, however, was to bring to it a view that many of its own immigrants, including Rais, didn't share. Enormous numbers of them genuinely loved it, and they continued to arrive by the planeload. They loved, for starters, the sky and the roads and the low taxes that had brought Rais to the city long ago. But it was more than that. A newcomer like Rais could find in Dallas a kind of acceptance that New York or Washington or Los Angeles didn't give.

There was an ad running these days in Rais's former home that captured the difference: "NYC: Tolerant of your beliefs, judgmental of your shoes." Dallas was, you could say, judgmental of your beliefs, tolerant of your shoes. This contrary equation wasn't without its advantages. For the immigrant who was not coming for a cultural transplant or new belief system, who just wanted a chance to rise without meddling or to arbitrage the price of her labor, it was perfect. A city tolerant of your shoes was a city easy to understand, master, and ascend. It was a city without elusive codes. You didn't have to wonder how to dress in public, for almost any semirespectable way of dressing would put you above average; or what knife to use with which course, because that wasn't really how they ate down here; or what subway carried you where, since most people had their own bubble of a car. What many immigrants found in Dallas was a dimension of America's tolerance that was the tolerance of casualness and convenience more than of open-mindedness: an ease of living that became its own kind of welcome.

Dallas, like its immigrants, was don't-look-back new. Its landscape seemed to have no legacy that needed reconciling with modernity. It looked like the sum of millions of private pursuits of happiness: as though everyone had conjured a dream, grabbed as much of it as possible, and not conferred with anyone else. In its absence of nostalgia, in its solipsism, the city could resonate with a certain kind of immigrant. The folk memory that Texans often called up to explain their culture was of pre-political solitude—being alone out on the land all those years ago, days from anyone who could save you, far from the law, under brutal heat, on angry soil that required taming or would fold you into its layers as it had assimilated many others before. It was a strange memory to apply to modern life, as the rest of the country was regularly reminded during national arguments. But it was a narrative that overlapped with how some newcomers, from settings far afield, saw their lives.

For the immigrant, even listening to the radio in Dallas was to hear, on station after country station, cowboy-accented reminders of the values that you had sworn not to desert when you left the old country: to stay simple no matter how fortune blessed you; never to forget your God; to distrust the temptations of the corrupting metropolis; to live for family; to grow better than you used to be.

✲

MANY YEARS BEFORE Stroman received his death warrant, a university professor and anti-death-penalty activist named Rick Halperin received a letter from Polunsky. Halperin was a gregarious teddy bear of a Texan who taught peace studies at Southern Methodist University. He was well known for his work against capital punishment and had a reputation among Death Row inmates as a guy on the outside who would help them. When he saw the envelope, he recognized the sender's name at once: Mark Stroman. He had followed Stroman's trial. Now Stroman was writing to ask for Halperin's help in researching end-of-life arrangements, should it come to that—basically, calling around to some undertakers in Dallas to compare prices. Stroman also made sure in the letter to voice sincere remorse for his crimes. Halperin gladly followed up, sending back a letter with options. As was not uncommon, he didn't hear from the inmate again.

Late in 2010, when Stroman's expected execution date popped up on his calendar, which was the kind of thing that popped up on Rick Halperin's calendar, the professor had an idea. The execution was to be in July of the following year. Coming as it would so close to the tenth anniversary of 9/11, the execution was a suitable moment to raise larger questions about America's decade-long struggle with terror. Like many activist academics, Halperin was the kind of guy who spared no opportunity to organize a modestly attended panel discussion. Plans for one, on the execution day itself, began to take shape.

Despite his personal geniality and good cheer, Halperin's office overflowed with just about the most depressing books in the world, about prisons and justice and death, death, death. Books served as the furniture, the artwork, and, when stacked knee-high on the floor, the slalom poles one had to navigate to get around to the professor's desk. Post-it notes obstructed the view of other Post-it notes. No decent liberal cause lacked for space on the walls, which featured exhortations against torture, a Code Pink sticker, a "Caution: Children at War" poster, signs in support of gay rights and the war on poverty and maternal health care, and signs in opposition to the "racist" mascot of the Cleveland Indians baseball team, the killing in Darfur, and hatred in general.

Halperin was among those Americans who felt his country had gone off the rails after 9/11: "We had to hurt somebody after 9/11, and by God we're still doing it." In fairness to his country, he had always found it a little off the rails, but he genuinely believed that America had strayed from its nature and forgotten things essential to its being in fighting this vague new enemy called "terror." He thought that Mark Stroman somehow captured the country's turning.

"He encapsulated everything about 9/11," Halperin said. "He acted because of 9/11. He lashed out with violence to kill others in the name of his dead half-sister. Watching the Twin Towers collapse brought out a visceral reaction in Mark Stroman—who had no history of killing anybody, of shooting anybody before that—to kill Arabs at the point of a gun. It was the visceral, typical Texas/American response. And what was America's response? To go invade. To go against the evidence. We ignored the evidence that there were no weapons of mass destruction in Iraq. We ignored the truth and went hell-bent into Iraq to cause upheaval and violence. Well, Stroman had no evidence that the people he attacked were Middle Eastern. He looked at them and thought they were the guilty ones. But he was wrong, and America was wrong."

Not long after Halperin began thinking up his Stroman panel, an activist friend of his asked if he would meet a nice young man who wanted to see him. The young man soon e-mailed and then paid Halperin a visit in his office suite. The visitor was short and slender, with a prominent nose and thinning hair. Half of his face was covered with bumps, and his right eye was gently adrift. It was a strange coincidence. His name was Rais Bhuiyan, and he was the man Mark Stroman had shot. He, too, wanted the professor's help.

※

AFTER THE HAJJ, Rais had dropped his mother back in Bangladesh and returned to Dallas. The new stirrings within him, to do something for others, grew stronger still, but he couldn't figure out what the something was: "My heart is telling me that, Rais, now you are in a better shape, because all this time you've been struggling to survive, to come to better shape. So now you're in a better shape—physically, mentally, financially. And now you came from Hajj, and you had a promise to God that you want to do something. So why I'm waiting more? Why don't I start right now? Who knows when I'm going to die? Because we don't know that when our time will be over."

He felt his vision growing wider than ever before. He was filling up with questions: How can I make the most difference? How can I use my talents? Whom will I need to know? Whom can I serve? Where do I begin? He considered himself "just a normal human being, a very, very poor and normal human being, a simple ordinary person." If he was going to achieve anything for others, he would have to do his homework and choose carefully.

Thus Rais spent a good part of his free time in 2010 online. Many ideas came to him. He thought about starting a charity focused on the developing world's poor. He thought about doing something to aid other victims of hate crimes, to speak and lobby on their behalf. He researched the case in which he had become entangled, studied victims-rights policies in Texas, examined case law, perused the sites of peace groups and other civic organizations doing all manner of social work around Dallas, poked around the pages of Muslim groups.

Rais worried that his knowledge of how to get things done in America was very limited. "It's not like I was born here, I know the culture, I know the people," he said. "So I had to go through a learning process to understand how things work here. Am I doing the right thing? Or am I going to make people pissed off or upset by doing this kind of thing? Because I had no idea."

He needed guidance and direction of a kind the Internet couldn't furnish. Rais needed, he realized, to network. So all that year he did. Community meetings. Peace conferences. Political fund-raisers. Human-rights dos. If Dallas hosted it in a ballroom with stackable chairs, Rais attended it. Here, too, he sensed his skills lacking, but he tried to learn: going up to people he figured were important, telling them his story, asking advice if they seemed open to him. He carefully followed what he perceived to be the American rules— for example, giving people only a hint of what you do the first time you meet, then hopefully running into them again at another event and making a fuller-court press. "You don't really give them a lot of information the first time," Rais said. "You don't want to make them panic. It's also creepy—that, 'Why this guy is talking everything at the first point?' That was a learning curve for me. Because in this culture, this is how it is practiced. Even if you like someone, a girl, you don't just tell everything about you the first moment, right?"

Rais followed this precise approach when meeting Hadi Jawad. Jawad was a respected elder in the Dallas peace community, a seasoned activist quick to call a march or lead a delegation. Rais knew of Jawad from his research and ran into him one day at a fund-raiser for Farouk Shami, a Palestinian American personal-care tycoon who had parlayed his claim to have invented the world's first ammonia-free hair dye into a run for governor of Texas. When Rais first met Jawad, he told his story, to which Jawad intently listened. As it happened, the two met again on the Dallas circuit, a short time later, at a Muslim Legal Fund of America event. Rais now moved in. He told Jawad he'd been wanting to do something for others out of gratitude to his God, and he had an intuition that this something he was after should have to do with the man who attacked him. He wanted his service, whatever it was, to involve Mark Stroman.

It was, to say the least, an unlikely conclusion. Nevertheless, over these months Rais's exploration and reflection had converged in one particular theory: of all the things he could do, intervening in the cycle of mistrust and enmity between his religious community and his adopted country—between Islam and America—would be the most valuable. "Hate is going on in this country since 9/11," he said. "And where this hate is taking us? Nowhere. Our life is becoming more and more miserable every single day since 9/11. It has to end somewhere." After his long research, Rais had decided to devote himself to helping to bring about that end.

He realized, the more he read, that he was seeking the impossible —to change deep habits that stretched back far beyond the present conflict. "If you look at the history, starting from the native Indians, what they went through; then the blacks, what they went through; the Irish—all those potato-famine people, they came to this country —what they went through; then during the Second World War, what the Japanese went through," Rais said. "And after them you see what the Jews went through. What the Arabs, they went through in this country, what the Latinos are going through, and now the Muslims are going through. It's like, you see, a pattern—that a group of people is always under the bus. And another group of people is waiting in the pipeline."

Rais continued, "I'm saying it not out of my anger, but I see the pattern. We have a long history of hate and violence. I think the time has come to stand up and say enough, because at the end of the day we're all Americans living in this country. Why can't we stop that cycle? That's why I think this message is very powerful, because we have to end this cycle. The cycle is going on starting from the day the country was built."

When Rais shared some of his thinking with Jawad at the fund-raiser, the activist was taken by this young man and his strange idea. You have to meet Rick Halperin, Jawad said.

So now here Rais was. Since the encounter with Jawad, Rais's idea had developed further. He had started to focus on the possibility of forgiving Stroman as the centerpiece of his approach. Was this not what the Prophet had done when the citizens of Ta'if attacked Him? Was this not the logical implication of what Rais's mother had always taught him about mercy? Was this not what God had been trying to whisper in Mecca, by smashing Rais's nose, then healing it? Rais felt an urge, from the deepest place within, to forgive. He felt that it would cleanse him somehow, and of course multiply the God-given frequent-flyer miles of an imperfect man. He also had the feeling that forgiving Stroman, so close to the ten-year anniversary of 9/11, might nudge Americans to look anew at the notion of mercy—and reflect on their own thirst for vengeance.

From there, the idea continued to blossom. For a man as furiously ambitious as Rais, forgiveness—simply to excuse—began to feel necessary but insufficient. To forgive was almost an absence—to declare the passing of bad feelings. That was fine, but God hadn't saved Rais Bhuiyan just so that, all these years later, he could tell some deadbeat man, "Now it's OK." When the saving had happened, he remembered what he'd told himself—that he should "do something better and bigger not only for myself, for others as well," that he should educate the Americans: "There are so many things they can do, but they're not seeing because of their lack of self-esteem or lack of stamina, lack of energy—lack of something. But if you can fulfill that side of whatever they're lacking of, it will be a life of worth."

Ever since his arrival in America, a part of Rais—at first a small part, swollen by time—had wanted to grab these people, shake them by the shoulders, and wake them from their misery and depression and self-loathing and family-breaking and money-grabbing and loneliness and violence. He wanted to tell them: "Look, why you guys are still suffering? If I can overcome, if I can turn around my life, with the mercy of God, in this country, from that negative point to this point—you guys are born here, you guys speak better than me, you understand the culture better than me, you have more networks, more resource. Why can't you stay in the same place—even going down day by day? Why you have to struggle on a regular basis, just to survive?"

He wanted, he said, to save them from childhoods with "no peace at home"; from an idea of life centered on "sex, alcohol, and drugs, starting from your teenage until when you grow up"; from people staying poor "generation-wise because of lack of education"; from members of an overclass that "never even know what is happening in the poor people's life"; from "lack of in-touch with family"; from stressed and fragmented parents, "busy with their own lives," who tell their young to "just feel comfortable, just make your life happy" and thus nudge them toward things like drugs; from people who are "free, but the way they're living their life, they're losing their freedom."

"If I can do, you can do," he wanted to tell them. These words were not a criticism of the country at large, because the country had served him so well. They were a criticism of how other people made use of the country. Now that he was ready to do something big, now that he had this kernel of an idea of forgiveness, now that he saw a chance to intervene in the stalemate between Islam and the West, he wanted also to stay true to this vision of waking his countrymen up.

With these ideas swirling within him, Rais inched toward his epiphany: he would first forgive Stroman before all the world, and then he would wage a struggle to save Stroman's life.

The idea verged on the bizarre, but it fulfilled many of Rais's desires: to apply Islam in the fullest way; to show the faith at its best to the Americans; to practice the mercy his mother had counseled all his life; to get great PR for the cause of ending the cycle of hatred; to spare another man that horrid feeling of impending death that Rais had known himself. There was another motivation, too, which Rais wouldn't have come to but for a class he once took at the University of Texas at Dallas with Kevin Mitnick.

Mitnick was a reformed computer hacker who now taught computer security. He had flipped and, in flipping, done a lot of good for the technology world. He had, to Rais's mind, done more good than he would have done had he been good from the start. "Who can teach better hacking than Kevin Mitnick?" Rais said. He dreamed of making Mark Stroman the Kevin Mitnick of American chaos, of degeneracy, isolation, and hate. He imagined a radical act of forgiveness and a battle for Stroman's life that would turn that ex-warrior into a symbol of better ways of being.

"I did not see him as a killer or a murderer," he said. "I looked at him as a human being like me. Yes, definitely he made a terrible, terrible mistake and crimes. But we all make mistakes. We are not angels. We're human beings that make mistakes, and there are some human beings that learn from others' mistake and some learn from their own mistakes. Mark's definitely the head of a horrible crime. But I thought if he was given the chance, he might become a spokesperson. He might warn people: 'What I did, don't do that.' And who could do better than Mark Stroman?"

Sometimes Rais imagined himself as a speaker on a dais somewhere, at the kind of event he had spent that year attending, talking about hate crimes and relations between Islam and the West. Midway through his speech, he would unveil a surprise: Mark Stroman, ladies and gentlemen, is now joining us live via Skype from prison! "You could ask him any question you want—how powerful that would be," Rais said. He even found himself imagining what Stroman would say: "Guys, I'm still behind bars. I'm not in the free world. What I did, that was wrong, and I'm grateful that I was not executed. But now I've dedicated my life for educating people."

Rais said, "If I go and talk to rednecks, if I go and talk to white supremacists, do you think they're going to listen to me?" He could imagine Stroman lecturing on so much—hatred, parenting, sex, drugs: "If he used his own terms, the way he talked, his local Texan terms, people will listen to him more than if I go and talk to them with my foreign accent."

It was a curious, stunning vision—and, whether or not Rais would admit it, a vision befitting all the things he complicatedly was: his ambition and selflessness, his piety and sense of specialness. Here was a way to be everything at once: to cast himself as the Dallas metroplex's prophet of mercy, and yet to be, as his mother had taught him, one step behind others, a servant rather than master.

PERHAPS IT WAS his long habit of reinvention that primed Rais to forgive. Perhaps he could leave behind the grudge of those pellets in his face because he had left so much else—left so many things that in the moment seemed total and unleavable. His family, his mother, his Abida; the Air Force, New York, the food mart, Salim; the Olive Garden and Zale and the various employers who got him on his feet. His life was measured in leavings. He could pick up and go with a light-ness not available to men like Stroman. He could be this, then that, then something else, without suffering loss. It has been true of many of the millions who over the years have made themselves Americans.

History felt heavier to Stroman. It had been that much harder for him to escape it: the circumstances of his birth, his parents, the nightmares, the early bad choices that narrowed the spectrum of future choices, jobs that felt designed to keep you right where you were. When this was your destiny, prestige and self-belief came from holding on—to the past, to a sense of tradition, to where you belonged before Johnny-come-latelies like Rais showed up. Think of how Stroman had reassured Michael in his letter that Dallas, the only city he knew in Texas, was Texas's best city. To another, less tethered being, it might seem like a contradiction, because bestness implies comparison. But for the anchored who had only their anchors, the best city was the one that was yours: the one whose back streets you memorized as a boy, whose traffic reports you yearned for in prison.

There was, for a man like Stroman, no tension between the spe-cialness of a place and one's lack of exposure to other places. To love a place was an act not of judgment but of commitment. It was like loving your mother, not choosing a wife.

Stroman called himself a biker even though he perhaps never owned a bike. Here, again, pause and suspend judgment, because there is another way to see it: as a commitment, a statement of belonging and tribe and fellowship. What Stroman was really say-ing when he called himself a biker was that he was a certain kind of person and that others of his kind had his back. He wanted you to know that without having to spell it all out.

The past and his oases of belonging were just about all Stroman had—especially now, living in prison. In this he was not so differ-ent from the more reverent and rooted countrymen whom Rais had left back home in Dhaka, who would have lacked the stomach for his adventures and gambles.

On the Row but also for many years before, Stroman had been stuck in the ditch of his own past. He had a forward visibility of inches. Rais's visibility stretched out for miles. He nodded to his past, his heritage, his faith. But nowhere did he dwell more comfortably than in his own, incandescent future. He was one of those men who value themselves not by what they've held on to but by what still looms. The ambition swelling within him now was to save a life that had been so profoundly unlike his own.

PROFESSOR HALPERIN COULDN'T believe his good fortune. Sitting before him was a devout Muslim who was saying, if he understood him, that he wanted to take on the Texas death establishment and promote to Americans the idea of mercy. "He said he wanted to lead an effort to try and save Mark Stroman's life, and could I help or how could I help him or would I help him," Halperin recalled. He told Rais about the panel in the works—and the coincidence of receiving that inquiry from Stroman some time ago, then planning to trigger a discussion using his case, and now meeting his victim.

Rais arrived with no specific ideas about how to save Stroman; that was why he'd come to the professor. Halperin, for his part, had learned to temper his hopes of interrupting the state's machinery of execution, because it almost never stopped grinding. But the professor had been around long enough to perceive in Rais a rare opportunity. The case didn't implicate one or two of Rick Halperin's pet causes; it seemed to implicate nearly all of them. It provided a new weapon to deploy against the death penalty. It argued for religious toleration, by portraying Islam in a way that would surprise many Americans, as a religion of mercy. It was a natural gateway to a larger conversation about America's response to 9/11, and the other ways it might have answered the attacks. And the case forced one to think again about the meaning of patriotism after a decade of chest-thumping and fear-mongering.

"I thought that his story was profound and compelling," Professor

Halperin said. "Here's somebody who happened to be a Muslim, who was the survivor of a hate-crime rampage based on the worst crime in America since Pearl Harbor, talking about forgiveness, compassion, and healing."

Halperin added, "I don't know any other story that would raise the issues to make America look at itself the way this case does."

✳

On the second Thursday of every month, Chapter 205 of Amnesty International, representing Dallas, met on the SMU campus. Halperin had long been involved with Amnesty, and he invited Rais to come to the February meeting, to share his story and his big idea.

Perhaps ten people attended; few knew of Rais, though some vaguely remembered the shootings some years earlier. Rais spoke for forty-five minutes or so, explaining why he wanted to save Stroman's life. Halperin remembered stunned silence, followed by a volley of questions for Rais. Then nearly every attendee signed up, giving their names and contact details, to contribute however they could. Some days later, Halperin invited Rais to give another presentation, this time to the Dallas chapter of the Texas Coalition to Abolish the Death Penalty, which met on the third Wednesday of every month. Once again, most of the fifteen or so audience members signed up to help.

Now a campaign had to be designed. This was Halperin's specialty. His proposed approach was to tap into the power of Rais's story. It was a long shot, but perhaps Stroman could win clemency from the state if the authorities heard this message of the victim who wanted to save him.

The professor sat Rais down for a long talk about what would happen if he pursued this course: "I told him that this was going to be a grueling, demanding process for him, both physically and mentally. And that people would come at him, and he would feel like a piece of

Turkish taffy being pulled in all directions by people with knowledge and without knowledge, with criticism and with support, who did or didn't understand." Halperin wanted Rais to know "that he was going to be questioned for his motives."

There was the further complication of the other two families. Rais was the lucky one who had survived Stroman's wrath. Waqar Hasan and Vasudev Patel hadn't been so fortunate. What basis did Rais have to call for mercy for a killing spree that spared him, in a murder case that technically didn't involve him?

Even before coming to Professor Halperin, Rais had thought about this. He decided to approach each of the families and seek their blessing for his campaign. He claimed that Alka Patel, the widow of Vasudev, had given a tacit endorsement of his effort, although she never publicly affirmed or contradicted his statement and has consistently refused to speak about the matter to outsiders. Still, long after the campaign, Rais and Alka remained friends: he often stopped by on a weekend to greet and check in on her. The Hasan family, publicly represented by Nadeem, Waqar's brother-in-law, was more explicit in its support. Nadeem said his sister had been persuaded by Rais's argument that Stroman "might convince other people in jail who would get out eventually not to be racist and to kill or hurt people based on religion or the color of their skin." He also thought that the campaign would depict Islam well: "People always quote the 'eye for an eye' line in the Koran, but the next line, the line right after, is that 'He is closer to Me who forgives.' " Nadeem liked the idea of exposing Americans to that further idea.

Halperin and Jawad, who had become Rais's wingmen and principal advisers, now focused on a media campaign. Halperin had contacts at the *Dallas Morning News,* and he fixed a meeting with its editorial board for May 16. Jawad knew a reporter there named Dianne Solis, who agreed to attend. Rais, Halperin, and Jawad walked up the stairs and under the building's massive stone inscription: "Build the news upon the rock of truth and righteousness.

Conduct it always upon the lines of fairness and integrity. Acknowledge the right of the people to get from the newspaper both sides of every important question." Several of the editorial board members came to the meeting, along with a photographer. Halperin introduced Rais, who once again shared his story, which was getting more polished through repetition. Then the board rained questions on Rais: What did he hope to accomplish? How did he feel as the execution date approached? Where did he envision this campaign heading? Why was it worth saving Stroman's life?

"We hung on every word that Rais had to say," said Keven Ann Willey, the editorial page editor. People often dashed back to their desks after the meeting, but this time Willey remembered her colleagues lingering. "We were so struck by the emotion of it and the magnitude of the capacity for forgiveness, we wanted clearly to write on it," she said. "We talked about, we have to write about this in a way that will communicate with our readers. We talked about how not to sound like glassy-eyed idealists and how to translate the capacity for forgiveness into an essay that will resonate with our readership."

The editorial page's opposition to the death penalty was well known in a city where many readers vehemently supported it. The board's challenge on the issue had always been to find new ways into a debate in which the sides were pretty well fixed. Rais struck Willey as just the thing: "I do remember hoping that, because here was a victim who gets it, this editorial might touch some people who hadn't been previously touched by this argument."

Rodger Jones, another board member, found Rais "doe-eyed," earnest, and sincere. "This is a nation built through the hard work and the contributions of immigrants," he said, "and a person like Rais is the kind of person you want to continue to build the nation on."

The next morning, the *Morning News* ran its first article on Rais's quest, under the headline "Victim Seeks Stay for Gunman." Ms. Solis wrote: "Bhuiyan wants to forgive. He'll be asking for a stay of

the July 20 evening scheduled execution of Stroman, and a stop to
the 'cycle of violence,' as he calls it." It was an apt time to call for
such a stop: that month an era seemed to be passing with the death
of Osama bin Laden.

Days later, the newspaper published an opinion piece by Rais
titled "Why My Attacker Should Be Spared the Death Penalty."
"There are three reasons I feel this way," Rais wrote. "The first is
because of what I learned from my parents. They raised me with the
religious principle that he is best who can forgive easily. The second
is because of what I believe as a Muslim, that human lives are precious and that no one has the right to take another's life. In my faith,
forgiveness is the best policy, and Islam doesn't allow for hate and
killing. And, finally, I seek solace for the wives and children of Hasan
and Patel, who are also victims in this tragedy. Executing Stroman
is not what they want, either. They have already suffered so much; it
will cause only more suffering if he is executed."

A few days later the board published its impassioned editorial:
"With his attacker set to die in Huntsville this summer, Bhuiyan has
begun a quiet campaign to spare the man's life. We wish to give that
campaign voice. It delivers a potent message to a nation still torn by
the loss of 9/11. It resists the cycle of revenge that doesn't stop until
someone has the courage to say enough." It continued, "Despite the
ugliness that festers in this country, Bhuiyan's belief in America has
not withered." The editorial praised Rais's "thoroughly American
optimism" and argued that the "nation should embrace it regardless
of the country and religious faith it comes from."

It was a brazen attack on received opinion in a state where faith
in the Death is almost a civil religion: a half-blind immigrant citing
the values of Islam in his plea that Texas not execute the white racist
who sought to kill him.

Halperin made sure the *Morning News* coverage crossed the desk
of an Amnesty colleague in New York who had good contacts in
newsrooms across the country. That led to Rais's going on National

Public Radio to plead his case, which ignited the story. Rais asked the professor if he would handle the incoming interview requests, which started arriving from all sides. "My phone didn't stop ringing for several weeks," Halperin said. As May became June and the execution date—July 20—drew closer, news of Rais's gambit was spreading.

Rais was working full-time as a database administrator for an online travel company. Until the campaign's launch, he had been exercising most days, at the gym or with games of tennis or soccer. Now the exercise abruptly stopped. On many nights, Rais struggled to find sleep. But he also found this new struggle quite exhilarating. The mission seemed to make his hardships feel more worthwhile than before: "I didn't come to this country just to live hand to mouth, or just to live in this country, or for money. I had a glorious past back home, but I came here to do something better." There was some vindication of his struggles and leavings in this swirl of activity.

When one of Rais's interviewers contacted Stroman's attorney seeking his reaction to the campaign, Stroman reportedly said, "This is the first act of kindness that I've ever known." He was stunned by Rais's act, which he said left him more content than he had ever felt before.

"There is a man out there that has every right to hate me for what I did after the 9/11/01 events that rocked our world," Stroman wrote on his blog. "This man, Rais, has come to the forefront in an effort to show the world how forgiveness and compassion overrule the human nature of hate. I'm envious of his actions and his kindness speaks volumes. He is an example that the human race should follow. Rais, I'm deeply touched by all you have said and that's from my heart and soul."

On another occasion, Stroman wrote of Rais, "Fate has joined us together in a very strange way." He told Ziv that he wanted Rais to continue battling hatred and prejudice even if he couldn't be there to help. "We need to make sure," Mark Stroman said, "there is not another Mark Stroman."

*

"Saving one life is like saving the entire mankind," Rais wrote, borrowing from the fifth surah of the Koran, in a June 2 letter to Craig Watkins. Watkins was Dallas's dynamic young district attorney. A few weeks after their *Morning News* triumph, Team Rais had managed to land a meeting with him. He was the first African American to hold the job and a breaker of molds. Though a supporter of the Death, he'd become known for his pursuit of exonerations for the wrongfully convicted. In many cases, he had prevailed. The team felt good about their chances with him. They would ask him to withdraw Stroman's death warrant. By now they were armed with new reasoning: in addition to the forgiveness argument, they had found a provision in Texas law that gave violent-crime victims a right to mediation with their attackers. The idea was to sit face-to-face, victim and attacker, and discuss the crime from both points of view, in the hope of helping the victim process the event and move on psychologically. Rais wanted to engage in mediation, which required months to prepare and carry out. The death sentence, if not commuted to life on compassionate grounds, should at least be delayed to accommodate Rais's emotional healing, the team planned to argue.

Rais, Professor Halperin, and Nadeem went to the meeting together. They were waiting in the anteroom when one of Watkins's aides emerged and invited them in. Rais and Nadeem entered the room, and the aide then blocked Halperin from following them. "Not you," he said. Watkins knew all about Rick Halperin, and they had sparred a few times.

Having invited Rais and Hadeem in, Watkins heard them out. Nadeem found him sympathetic and attentive, but the DA confessed that there was little he could do. Let me get back to you, he said. Rais pleaded for a decision by week's end, so that, if it came back negative, he could try the parole board next.

It took two whole weeks, with time dwindling, to get their answer—and the answer, as it so often was down here, was no.

IT WAS TIME to take this campaign on the road: this was Team Rais's conclusion. And, oddly enough, those roads were in Europe.

Stroman had carried on with his pen pals all this while, slowly weaving his own little global network. One correspondent was a British woman in her mideighties named Margaret Meakins. Some years earlier, widowed and depressed, recently placed in an old-age home, Meakins seemed to her daughter to be losing her desire to live. The daughter tried several things and eventually alighted on the idea of her mother's writing to a Death Row inmate over in America. She became, as Michael had, one of the fair number of Europeans, aghast at American capital punishment, who correspond with Death Row prisoners—rather like all those nice people in Kansas City and St. Paul who occupy themselves with the finer details of girls' schooling in Afghanistan and abstinence campaigns in Botswana. The Meakinses reported that letters had been arriving from Mark for the last seven years, often twice a week—newsy, funny, sweetly teasing. The daughter claimed that the letters had helped her mum to vanquish depression and, eventually, to return to the family home.

As the daughter, Linda, followed Stroman's march toward execution, she wondered how she might repay her debt. She contacted a British charity called Reprieve, led by Clive Stafford Smith, a lawyer who had made his name through twenty-five years of work defending the indigent and mentally unbalanced in American death-penalty cases. He had also represented several inmates at the U.S. facility in Guantánamo Bay, where, incidentally, he was once accused by the authorities—incorrectly, he insists—of smuggling Speedo swimsuits and Under Armour briefs to his clients.

Ordinarily, Stafford Smith would have turned the Meakinses down. Reprieve was tiny and barely able to manage the cases it already had. It took hundreds of hours of reading, interviewing, brief-writing, and litigating to help a prisoner who probably didn't have much of a shot. Two years earlier, however, Reprieve had taken on a project, funded by the European Union, to locate and assist foreign nationals facing the death penalty in the United States. And there was, believe it or not, a case to be made that Stroman was more than just a true American.

It was a precarious case, but Reprieve came across adequate suggestion—"evidence" may be too strong a term—that Mark's father, Eddie Stroman, had in actual fact been Eddie Ströman. The umlaut, that pair of dots that non-Germans struggle to fathom, now carried the potential to save Mark. Eddie Ströman, if that is his real name, was said to have come from Lower Saxony—how distantly, it wasn't known. Reprieve reached out to the German consulate in Houston, seeking to have Mark deemed a German national. But Stafford Smith didn't wait for that decision. He had somehow managed to convince himself that Mark Ströman, as Mark's legal filings would now spell it, qualified as a European stranded on America's cruel Death Row. Armed with government financing from the EU, Reprieve jumped aboard the spreading effort to save his life. A case that started with a militant American seeking to exterminate foreigners had somehow flipped: it was now framed as a case about a European prisoner hurtling toward death despite his model American victim's campaign to spare him.

Reprieve volunteered to bolster the legal work of Stroman's attorney, Lydia Brandt, which she found welcome. She had been pursuing appeals on the more conventional grounds, but Reprieve shared Professor Halperin's assessment that Rais's story was perhaps the sharpest, most attention-getting spear for their cause. So its people contacted Halperin and offered him and Rais an all-expenses-paid, four-country tour of Europe, where they would raise awareness of Stroman's Strömanness and lobby ideologically sympathetic governments (the death penalty is banned across the European Union) to call on Texas to spare this European prisoner.

Because Rais needed a week's vacation, the trip compelled him to do what he had thus far avoided: let his boss at the travel company know about his new moonlight life as an activist. "He was shocked to hear that I was a survivor of a hate crime of 9/11 and was shot in the face," Rais said. "He was more shocked and surprised when I told him about the campaign." Vacation granted.

So, on July 4, the pre-umlaut Stroman's favorite holiday, Rais found himself in Copenhagen, in a meeting room at the headquarters of the Danish pharmaceutical company Lundbeck. Three days earlier, the company had made a headline-grabbing announcement: it would stop shipping its drug Nembutal to American prisons that conducted execution by lethal injection. Nembutal was intended to control seizures in patients, but some American executioners had turned to it earlier that year, when a company called Hospira announced that it would stop selling its sodium thiopental anesthetic, the usual drug of choice. In the meeting Rais applauded Lundbeck's efforts and asked for support for his specific case. In a sign of the hubris that was beginning to attach to Rais's work, he and his team suggested afterward that Rais had been responsible for the company's announcement. "In large part, they did it because of his visit—that's pretty phenomenal," Halperin said. "They'd said that they wanted to make changes, and when he came I think it solidified what they wanted to do." That Lundbeck's statement had preceded Rais's visit by three days became somewhat irrelevant.

Onward to France and the European Parliament. The next day, in Room 3.5 of the Louise Weiss Building in Strasbourg, Rais, standing alongside like-minded lawmakers on the Subcommittee on Human Rights, gave a press conference. He was hosted by Baroness Sarah Ludford, a Liberal Democrat member representing London. He urged European officials to pressure the authorities in Texas to grant Stroman clemency and again raised the drug-exports issue. Then it was onward to Germany for meetings with members of the Bundestag. Another victory: Tom Koenigs, chairman of the body's

Committee on Human Rights and Humanitarian Aid, was quoted in a local report as vowing to challenge the execution. "We've written letters to the governor and not gotten a response," Koenigs said. "We're trying to make contact with them. This is about human rights and we have a mission to promote these values."

With each meeting, Professor Halperin could see Rais maturing. Rais came to this work already conflicted between his very real humility and his very real sense of grandness. Selling himself like this, becoming a brand, packaging his story into juicy morsels for hungry reporters—these things widened the gap between how he conceived of himself and what he now had to be. A man who professed to be primarily interested in the next world—and continued to pray several times a day while abroad—was ever more determined to leave his mark down here, and seemed willing to sacrifice his health and tranquility to do so.

"Not only did he not lust for Mark to be killed," Halperin said of Rais. "He took the lead in a very emotional way, because he had to talk. Every time he speaks, he has to talk about what happened to him. He has to relive being shot in public. Every time a microphone's before him, he has to relive that anger, that hurt, that blood. And he's still got thirty-five pellets in his face, in his head! He had to relive his own victimization every day because he wants to get us to a better place."

As a high schooler at the Sylhet Cadet College, Rais had a public-speaking class every Thursday. All he had to do was stand and say something for three minutes, maybe five max. He was so shy then that he could barely manage. Now Rais found himself able, against all odds, to speak extemporaneously without any trouble. "It came automatically," he said. "I didn't push myself to go and have to prepare myself. It was a flow; it came out of me."

Rais learned to be unfazed by the cameras and microphones jammed in his face. Halperin noticed that his protégé stopped needing notes. He began to trust in the power of his story. He mastered the politician's art of foreswearing irony and irreverence, revealing nothing of himself but his devotion to the cause. He learned to open sentences with "Well," to buy himself that extra second. He started pushing his hands out in front of him when he spoke, to underscore a point. In his pursuit of holy mercy, he had acquired something of the American hustler about him.

While most of his audiences were totally sympathetic, Rais was tested when, on the final stop of the tour, he met a skeptical, even faintly hostile, crowd in London.

The event was in the evening at the West London Islamic Center in Ealing. The large rectangular room was packed with fellow Muslims—perhaps a hundred or more—seated in two clusters of chairs. A few women sat in front, but the room was dominated by young men. With hardly any seats remaining, some of them were standing by the windows. It was the first time since the campaign was launched that Rais was addressing kin of the faith. He stood at a table with a lectern and began to speak. When he got to the part about forgiveness, justifying it in the name of his God, their God, Halperin remembers a man in the back raising his hand. The man, without being called on, began to talk, challenging Rais, who at first didn't acknowledge him. Halperin recalled the moment like this: "He said, 'Who are you as a Muslim to forgive a Christian? What right do you have to do that?' Then this man went off on American policy in the Middle East and 'Where is the forgiveness for all the Muslims that Americans were killing or had killed in Iraq and Palestine and Afghanistan?' "

Halperin added, "When he finally stopped, I remember, he was just angry and emotional and loud. And Rais said, 'I'm not an Islamic scholar. I know that the Koran teaches forgiveness.' And he recited a passage or two, and that obviously was not the answer the man wanted to hear, and he started interrupting Rais again as he stood up and walked out."

Rais remembered it this way: "I thought it would be easy to share my story of forgiveness with them and didn't have to explain the message of forgiveness in the light of Islamic teachings. But at the beginning, some in the audience thought I was speaking on behalf of the U.S. government." He could understand their feelings but tried to steer them otherwise: "I told them my trip is completely personal to share my own story; it's not a politically motivated trip."

When the time came for questions, hands soared. Not every questioner was supportive. "It was the only audience where that large a percentage of the questions were critical of him for his act of forgiveness," Halperin said. He figured it was 50-50 positive-to-negative; Rais estimated 70-30. Some people rose and told Rais that they totally disagreed with him about forgiveness, for many of the same reasons as the angry man who walked out, but that they respected what he was trying to do for the faith. When the event finished, Halperin was astonished to see virtually the entire audience line up single file to shake Rais's hand. Some just thanked him; others stopped and talked awhile. Whatever they thought of his campaign, several of them told Rais, he had placed true Islam on display for the world—a religion of love and mercy, not bloodlust.

"Thank you for doing this," they said over and over, shaking Rais's hand and that of his Jewish-Texan-American sidekick. A few of them, Rais said, asked for his autograph.

✶

UNTIL THAT MOMENT, Rais and his team had followed two interlocking strategies: to move public opinion to their side, and meanwhile to petition the Texas authorities to either commute or delay Stroman's execution. The first strategy was working, but the second was having little effect. They had gone to the DA, had contacted prison officials to seek mediation with Stroman, had asked the Texas Board of Pardons and Paroles to recommend clemency to Governor Rick Perry. Each path dead-ended.

"Not only in our state in Texas but around the country and around the world, people were overwhelmingly in support and awe of his actions or his desire to save Mark Stroman's life," Halperin said of Rais. "They supported him wholeheartedly. So in the court of public opinion, we seemed to be winning. But we weren't gaining much ground with the death-penalty apparatus here in the state of Texas."

At Reprieve, Clive Stafford Smith was convinced that Rais had a compelling legal case in America if he wanted one. The asking-nicely strategy was failing, and as Rais returned from Europe, Stroman had less than two weeks left on the planet, barring some miracle. Reprieve suggested that Rais file a lawsuit claiming that he had been denied his right under Texas law to victim-offender mediation. Stafford Smith saw in him, as Halperin did, an unusual commando in the long-running war against capital punishment. Rais agreed with the plan.

He researched his options for a lawyer and came upon one named Khurrum Wahid. Wahid was a high-profile defense attorney based in Miami and had made a name for himself representing Muslims caught in the antiterror dragnet. Like Stafford Smith, he had gotten himself involved with Guantánamo cases, which wasn't necessarily the association Rais needed for his campaign. Wahid offered to take the case for free, though, and they had a deal.

On Wednesday, July 13, a week before the execution date, with Stroman's team working in parallel on more conventional appeals, Rais went to court with the help of his new attorney. He did so with characteristic ambition, filing a lawsuit that would come to be known as *Bhuiyan vs. Perry.* That very week, the state's square-jawed charmer of a governor, Rick Perry, was much in the news. A flailing Republican Party, worried by the ongoing presidential contest, was looking to transfuse fresh blood into the race. Perry had said he was thinking about it. He had recently announced that he would be going ahead, despite protest, with his massive prayer event for evangelical Christians at the Reliant Stadium in Houston. He had also let it be known, lest anyone think he had fewer foreign-policy bona fides than Herman Cain, that he and his wife had just lunched, in Austin, with former President and Mrs. Musharraf of Pakistan. In a month's time, he would be a full-fledged presidential candidate, and even a front-runner. And in that moment when his star was beginning to rise over the country, he became a defendant in an obscure case in state court. The plaintiff was Rais, whose lawsuit made some of the more unusual arguments ever to land before a Texas judge.

"THE MEANING OF this Shariah law is not bad," Rais said. "It's really, actually, good. But we people in this country, we give the word a bad name." Across the country, fear of Shariah was ascendant. Just in the previous year or so, half of American states were said to have considered formally prohibiting judges from relying on Shariah, the ancient Islamic legal code, or other foreign law—even though actual evidence of judges doing so was hard to come by. Oklahoma had amended its state constitution to bar Shariah from its courts. Texas was especially hostile terrain for arguments citing Shariah. But Rais was a serial survivor who wrote his own rules, and he wanted his lawsuit not only to save a life but also to bend perceptions of Islam and, specifically, of Shariah. He called it "taking back the word." If you used the word in the good way before a court, maybe people would begin to hear it as Rais did.

So Rais's legal team filed a few dozen pages of briefs that suggested, among other things, that Governor Perry should consider what Islamic law had to say about the situation.

As if to set the tone for its arguments, the first item in the lawsuit's "Statement of Material Facts" was this: "Plaintiff is a United States citizen who is Muslim."

In the usual manner with such cases, the strategy was to throw all kinds of arguments at the judge and pray that one would stick. Broadly, though, the lawsuit advanced three claims in support of its plea that Stroman not be executed the following week.

The first was the most conventional, and where a less gumptious plaintiff might have ended. The suit noted that Article 56.02 of the Texas Code of Criminal Procedure lays out certain victims' rights, of which one is "the right to request victim-offender mediation coordinated by the victim services division of the Texas Department of Criminal Justice." Rais argued that no one had informed him of this right around the time of the attacks, and that, once he learned about it, he was thwarted from making use of it. "Plaintiff is a victim," the lawsuit said. "As such, he did not want to rush into a public spotlight. Had he only known his rights, he would have been quietly pressing for his rights for a long time." The suit said Rais needed to meet Stroman—and, more than that, to succeed in changing him—in order to heal: "Plaintiff's own ability to reach a cathartic point in his own recovery depends very much on his being able to make full efforts to help Mark Ströman to reach his full potential, and to overcome the very negative lessons that he was taught as a child."

The second line of argument was that Rais was being denied his constitutional rights as an American because of the state's refusal to honor his right as a Muslim to offer mercy. "As a Muslim, Plaintiff is of the belief that when he forgives or promotes mercy for his attacker, the government should no longer have a duty or a right to exact the ultimate punishment upon Mr. Stroman," the lawsuit said.

Rais's brief offered a tutorial in Shariah law to make his point: "The first lesson that might come as a surprise to many people is that Islamic law does not call for mandatory killing of everyone who commits murder, or the chopping off of hands at the first opportunity. Rather, while murder is obviously strongly condemned, mercy is vigorously upheld." The brief then gave this quotation from the Koran, chapter 5, verse 32: "If anyone kills a . . . it would be as if he killed all people. And if anyone saves a life, it would be as if he saved the life of all people." The quotation's stray "a" followed by that ellipsis was easily overlooked, but if the judge had Googled it, he might have been surprised. The "a" was the beginning of a clause that Rais's legal team redacted, and that clause read: "any person who

had not committed murder or horrendous crimes." The full version
(in a slightly different translation from that in the legal brief) read:
"Anyone who murders any person who had not committed murder
or horrendous crimes, it shall be as if he murdered all the people."
Rais was right about the Koran calling for mercy, but this citation
didn't apply to murderers like Stroman.

More solid support came from the famous "eye for an eye" passage, in chapter 5, verse 45: "The life for the life, and the eye for the
eye, and the nose for the nose, and the ear for the ear, and the tooth
for the tooth, and for wounds retaliation. But whoso forgoeth it in
the way of charity it shall be expiation for him."

The lawsuit argued that, in light of these passages, it was Rais's
religious duty to seek mercy. It acknowledged that this was an uphill
battle: "Perhaps it has been true in Christian society at various
times, but the process of showing mercy is more integrated into the
Islamic legal tradition today than it is in many Western legal systems." The suit went further in suggesting that Rais would suffer
religious discrimination if Texas denied him the chance to exoner-
ate his attacker: the state often listens to victims whose beliefs lead
them to seek vengeance, it argued, but ignores those whose faith
calls for mercy. The suit also claimed that Rais was being denied
equal treatment under the law because Texas granted mediation to
victims of lesser crimes but not as readily to those ensnared in capital punishment cases.

The third, and perhaps most surprising, argument was the suggestion that Texas revert to the good old days when victims and per-
petrators, without too much meddling from the state, resolved their
differences bilaterally. This argument, too, emanated from a reading
of Shariah law. It was an idea that endured in many Islamic societ-
ies, where victims have some influence over a perpetrator's punishment, with an option in some cases to reach a financial settlement
or grant mercy instead of sending the accused to prison or death.
Bilateral justice was also, of course, how an earlier era's disputes

were resolved right here in Texas, as shown in all those movies that had made Abida fear the place years before. The lawsuit argued that in the shift away from a direct victim-perpetrator connection, the virtue of mercy had fallen away. And it had an interesting source of support: a growing movement in the United States itself in favor of so-called restorative justice, of which one component is a greater emphasis on the victim-perpetrator relationship.

"The move towards recognizing victims' rights has come about primarily in the last quarter century, representing a shift back towards the way that the judicial system used to operate when the United States was founded, and for some time afterwards," the lawsuit said. It was quick to distance itself from a return to simple vigilantism: "Obviously society must excise corruption from the system of justice; it may well be that society should discourage the cycle of revenge; but there was never any room for the criticism of victims who were interested in restorative justice, or who advocated compassion." This the suit wanted to change, and Shariah law, it submitted, offered a way forward. It offered an elaborate explanation of the rules of diyat, or blood money: a practice under Shariah law of compensating a family for its dead relatives, often as a substitute for prison time or execution. (Incidentally, and unbeknownst to Rais's team, four months earlier, in a court in Lahore, Pakistan, a jailed CIA officer named Raymond Davis had been freed by diyat: 200 million Pakistani rupees in exchange for forgiveness from the relatives of the men he shot.)

So Rais, a victim of an American version of tribal law ("We was wanting justice," Stroman had said), was now reaching back to the ideas of his own, Islamic tradition of tribal law to seek support for showing Stroman forgiveness. A violent notion of bilateral justice—justice unmediated by the state—was being met by a nonviolent one. Rais's arguments could come across as a call for kangaroo justice, and yet they had many strange echoes. They resonated with Stroman's idea of taking matters into his own hands, but also with theories gaining ground in the restorative justice field and even with the movement across the nation, and in Texas especially, toward more robust victims' rights. But it was in Shariah law that the idea had its amplest expression, the lawsuit said.

"In Islam," the lawsuit said, "the victim is hugely respected. This has not been Plaintiff's experience of the judicial process in Texas to date."

✳

THAT OLD "TRUE AMERICAN" manifesto, which Stroman had loved and circulated from prison, declared: "My uncles and forefathers shouldn't have had to die in vain so you can leave the country you were born in to come here and disrespect ours and make us bend to your will." But a man whose hours are dwindling can become flexible, or at least allow his lawyer to be flexible on his behalf. Which is how Mark Stroman went on record calling for the application of Shariah law in a Texas court of law.

As Rais pursued his case, Stroman's lawyer, Lydia Brandt, was mounting her own appeals. The two sides were collaborating, and it showed: certain arguments appeared in similar form in both sides' filings, so that the two became almost indistinguishable at times. The two litigants, who had faced each other in hostility all those years ago at the Buckner Food Mart, now copied ideas from each other's documents, plagiarizing shamelessly, as if to underscore that they now played for the same team.

One of Stroman's briefs spoke, as did Rais's, of reviving what was lost in the evolution of modern justice systems: "In enforcing the criminal law, the judicial process has evolved over hundreds of years primarily to replace vigilantism and the terrible cycle of revenge. Society gradually sought to place limitations on the degree of punishment so that a blood feud between two families would not continue wreaking havoc for generations." However, the brief said, this process had perhaps gone too far, shutting out a victim's voice when that voice wants to show kindness instead of anger: "There is nothing illogical about a system where society does not always fulfil the victim's desire for revenge, but always respects the victim's desire for mercy."

Perhaps the most unusual strategy Stroman's lawyer employed was attempting reverse psychology on the Texas judiciary. Failing to spare Stroman's life, she argued, would amount to Texas accepting the moral superiority of Shariah law—and we can't let that happen, can we now?

"It is perhaps ironic, given the 9/11 spark that precipitated these tragedies, that Islamic (or Shari'a) law would not permit executions under these circumstances," Stroman's brief said. "The essence of a judicial process is that the victims cannot unilaterally demand vengeance—the state procedure is placed between the perpetrator and the victim to avoid the cycle of revenge. However, at the other end of the pendulum, there is no moral basis for suggesting that the victims cannot exercise mercy. If they called for mercy in an Islamic court, their wishes would be respected."

The brief opined, "It would be sadly ironic if the law of Texas were unable to show respect equal or greater to Shari'a law for a compassionate victim of crime." Stroman's lawyer now went a step further, arguing that it was unconstitutional to execute Stroman because doing so would admit American inferiority: "The U.S. and Texas Constitutions do not permit the execution of a person when the victims oppose it because the law of the United States and of the state of Texas is not somehow inferior to Islamic or Shari'a law."

Mark Stroman had to be saved, in other words, because not saving him would admit that his beloved country was second-best.

Bro

This was, Stroman was certain, either the end or the start. "If I'm allowed to live past the 20th of July, I will take that as a sign from God that my work has just begun," he wrote on his blog. As the days dwindled, he was full of motion—corresponding, thanking, bloviating, advising, giving interviews, taping statements for his loved ones, welcoming visitors.

"Mr. Rais, thank you for your inspiring message. You have forgiven me; you have forgiven the unforgivable," Stroman said in a video message. He added, "What do I want you to carry on? What I want you to do today, I want you to get out there, take center stage, and give the world their rights. It's a remarkable thing you're doing. And just continue with the human rights, because you are touching so many people."

Despite what loomed, Stroman's mood was upbeat. Sometimes he fixed himself one of his signature "Death Row lattes," using a pint of Blue Bell vanilla ice cream, three heaping spoons of coffee, and some sweetener. Sometimes he just listened to the radio as he tried to gather his thoughts, which could feel like wild eagles streaking the sky.

Stroman was overwhelmed by how much was being done for him. "I've seen so many people worldwide trying to save my life in the last few days and weeks and it's a surreal feeling," he wrote. The pen pals, the lawyers from Reprieve, Rais Bhuiyan, and, even more unbelievably, organizations representing the Muslim community in Dallas—Stroman felt blessed to have all these people wanting him to live. It was more than his own family was doing for him.

Sometimes the guys on the Row made snide comments about Mark's public declarations of regret. "They're calling me a pussy, but I look at them like primitive apes," he told Ziv.

"The closer I get to my death," Mark wrote, "Peace I seem to find." Even as he encouraged those seeking to save him, he was preparing himself for the end: "In the final hours when they do come, I'll blow out the candle of life with no bitterness for I have tasted life, lived, loved."

✳

WITH THE DEATH, the legal drama is often saved for the end.

On July 13, Rais had filed his suit against Perry in state court in Austin. He later stood on the courthouse steps, under sweltering heat, giving a press briefing and taking questions. He returned to Dallas. The case was set for a hearing on Monday, July 18, just two days before Stroman's possible last.

An hour or so before that hearing, Rais's side received word that the matter had been transferred to federal court, at the suggestion of the Texas attorney general. The reasoning was that Rais had claimed a violation of his civil rights, which was more properly examined by a federal judge.

Rais's team rushed back to the law firm to write fresh documents, and his lawyer, Khurrum Wahid, sprinted several blocks to the federal courthouse, getting there just before closing time at 5 p.m. He filed the documents required to request an injunction against the execution, and they were told to check in on Tuesday. And then on Tuesday Wahid was informed that the case would at last be heard by a judge—but now only on Wednesday, the day Stroman was supposed to die.

That morning, Rais woke up thirteen hours before the scheduled end of Stroman's life at 6 p.m. He dressed for the day and gave some interviews, including to a Japanese media outlet: another hopeful sign of how far the story was traveling. At 9:30, Team Rais gathered in the hotel lobby, from which they headed to the federal courthouse.

At 10 a.m., in an ornate courtroom decorated with paintings of jurists past, Judge Lee Yeakel heard arguments from both sides for a quarter hour. He promised a result by afternoon. Rais and Wahid returned to the law offices to wait. Then, in the early afternoon, word came from the court that the judge had turned Rais down. They had one remaining avenue in state court—but this time civil, not criminal. The lawyers now had to produce yet another crop of motions: an appeal of Judge Yeakel's order to a federal appellate court, a draft appeal to the U.S. Supreme Court should the appeals court decline, and their renewed bid to the state court to delay the execution.

The lawyers' scrambling that afternoon reminded Rais of "a perfect *Law and Order* episode." There was some hope for their new bid at the state level, but anxiety dripped from every face in the office. The dozen or so of them sat in a large conference room, around a long oval table: Rais, his lawyers, some interns, a handful of reporters who'd asked to trail them. Rais observed the interns "typing 100 miles per hour"; people getting up and leaving the room and returning every few seconds to print or fax or receive some document or other; cell phones ringing nonstop with calls from colleagues and news reporters; one of the journalists snapping pictures.

Rais, normally unflappable, was tense. "It was too much pressure on my shoulder," he said. "My heart became very heavy. And I said, 'Well, God,'—the way that I was praying on 21st September—I was praying that, 'Right now, there's another guy, another human being like me, he's in the same situation. He is thinking is he going to die or is he going to survive today, and I can understand what he's going through in his mind. And at least have mercy on this guy, and at least let him live for a better world. Let him live to make a change.' "

As the team frantically worked, a message bearing luck arrived from the court. A judge in the state civil court—one Joseph Hart—had, at long last, become the first one willing to hear the case on its merits. He would see them at 5 p.m.

✳

"Don't cry. don't cry, baby," Erica remembered him saying. Stroman was soothing his daughter Erica and even managing a few laughs on the other end of the phone. He was in good spirits for a last day. "He said, 'I'm going to be in a better place,' " Erica recalled. "And he was like, 'I know what my sins are,' and he was telling me, 'I'm fine. I'm OK.' " He was even a little excited, having been treated to his first Coke and first cigarettes in an eternity. He apologized for coughing like a virgin from the smoke, which may have had something to do with cramming three cigarettes into fifteen minutes.

Erica, Amber, and Tena were sorry they couldn't make it to Huntsville, life being what it was and all. But at least they each got a few minutes with him on the phone. When Amber got a turn, she got right down to it: "Dad, I'm not CNN news; I'm not your publicity crew. I want to know where you're at in your spiritual life. Because I worry about that, and I stress on that. I mean, after you're gone, where are you going?" Not that she was exactly where she wanted to be in her spiritual life, but she at least had time. She remembered her father, who had said little about God to her when he lived on the outside, sounding now like a true believer:

"He said, 'I know where I'm going. I made peace with God. I asked for forgiveness.' I was worried about him going to hell—you know, because 'Thou shalt not kill.' He felt in his heart that he was going to heaven, no matter whatever he done. He knew what he done was wrong, but he had built a relationship with God."

He also kept repeating that he was "at peace" with everything, which started to irritate Amber: "I just wanted to say, 'Are you serious? *You're* at peace with this?' But I didn't. I told him, 'That's good, Dad.'"

When Erica spoke to him, she could barely contain herself. When he was gone, who would call her freckles kisses from the sun? "Don't cry, baby girl," she remembered him saying. "Let tears of joy flow down." She remembered his parting advice: "I'll always be the same fucking knucklehead that I've always been. But if you don't know God, let Him into your life."

He said something else to both daughters that stayed with them: "This saved my life." It was the same thought that he'd shared with Ilan Ziv, but his family more easily understood it. Out there, their father had lived impulse to impulse, sense to sense. He hadn't possessed the idea of God, of being fallen, of a higher and lower way of being. He had existed sucking from life the marrow of beers and girls and powders, then calling it a night, waking up, and sucking some more. On the Row something had clicked and had given him the chance, as he saw it, to reserve a table in heaven. "It took him this to realize how to really live," Erica said. "I do agree it saved his life."

Amber, who, though a Christian, also spoke often of karma, agreed: "I think everything happens for a reason. Because if my dad would've stayed out on the streets, if he wouldn't have done this— and I'm not saying that what he done was right; it's far from right— but I believe in my heart that if my dad would've stayed out in the street, he would have either been killed or . . . And at that time in his life, he wasn't saved. He didn't pick up the Bible. I know he woulda went to hell."

Tena, who spoke to Stroman as well that day, concurred: "It sucks that those families had to be the price to pay for his eternity, but I believe it took this happening for God to get him where He needed him. Otherwise, I don't think Mark would have stayed still long enough for God to give—because God's a gentleman. He ain't gonna force Himself on nobody. He's a gentleman. He's there for us if we need Him, but He ain't gonna force Himself on us."

Tena had talked to Mark about Rais's campaign. Mark, she said, was flabbergasted: "This man's going everywhere, all over the world, trying for my life, and I tried to take his from him," she remembered Mark telling her. He said he didn't know there was that kind of forgiveness and love in the world.

Stroman had the chance that afternoon to speak to his only grandchild for the first time. Amber put her daughter on the phone, and she cooed, "I love you, Grandpa Mark." Everyone on their end was bawling. "You know what I said?" Tena recalled. "I said, 'The State of Texas thought they was trying to take Mark Stroman off this earth and out of this world,' but I said, 'They forgot he had three kids and a grandbaby that look just like him.' "

There was still a chance of deliverance that afternoon. In case it all failed, Stroman promised to his kin that he'd run up to their dead relatives in heaven and give them a kiss. Tena, who so long ago struggled to hold him down, remembered him telling her that their joint legacy was in her care now: "He said his destiny was to meet me, me have his kids—that was his destiny. That now it's up to me to keep. Each one of our kids is like a link on a chain. Every time we'd have one of the kids, we'd add a link to that chain, and he said that that was his destiny, to meet me and have kids. And he said, 'Tena, when the chain breaks and a link falls off, people don't pick up the link and put it in their pocket to get the chain fixed. More likely, it's gone.

That chain's wrecked.' He said, 'Tena, keep our chain together. You be the missing link and keep our chain together.' "

✳

ILAN ZIV, WHO in the course of seven years had gone from chronicler to friend to designated spreader of Stroman's remains, was in Huntsville to witness the death that he still hoped would be averted. He was joined by a small handful of Stroman's chosen visitors, including a former priest from Britain and a Texan named Laura, who had become interested in the case more recently. In the midafternoon, Ziv and the others made their way to the Execution Suite, a large house run by a local church where friends and family of the waiting-dead could wait themselves in the final hours (and even stay overnight, if necessary). In this particular case, it was only friends and no family.

This was how Stroman claimed to want it at the end, though perhaps it was an adjustment to the inevitable. "I don't want no family," he told Ziv in one of their Visitation talks. "I'm allowed visits the last week for eight hours a day, for five days a week. You know, some of my kids here in Texas were saying that they wanted to be present. I'm not gonna traumatize them. When they strap me down, we're going to be as close as me and you are. You're gonna be looking. I don't want them to see that and remember that. And for the other family members who say they want to be here for me during my execution—I don't want them here for that. If you can't be here with me while I'm alive and breathing, don't dare when they're fixing to kill me. I need you now. I don't need you when I'm fixing to leave."

So it was just friends in the end. Ziv and the other visitors received a hearty, home-cooked lunch from the church volunteers, including "homemade Jell-O with real fruits," as he later reported. Then the group sat in the living room and waited. Despite their common cause, people were mostly quiet; Ziv figured they were all focused on Mark in their minds rather than one another. Stroman called them

three or four times; he had between 3 and 5 p.m. for final conversations. From time to time, the hovering people whom Ziv called
"functionaries of the execution machine"—pastors and prison officials assigned to the suite—offered to pray with their visitors and
explain the steps between now and execution.

Ziv knew that he and the group were being treated as well as could
be, but something about the Execution Suite sickened him. Something about its saccharine, Jell-O-abetted gentility: "I loathed this
place and was furious at all the wonderful people who surrounded
us from nice church volunteers to at least 2 chaplains and Mark's
spiritual advisor," he later wrote. "I know it is irrational and also
unfair to be angry with people who tried to make our stay, given the
circumstances, as pleasant as possible. But it was in the 'Hospitality
suite' that I understood for the first time how this wonderful 'cover
up' allows the State of Texas to execute so many people while still
claiming to be moral and Christian. Execution, in the 'Hospitality Suite,' was treated as some terminal disease from which Mark
was going to die in few hours. We were the assembled relatives and
friends to be with him in his last moment. None of us had any power
to change anything. Execution like death itself was an act of nature.
We just had to accept it and all these wonderful people around us
worked very hard to ease our 'acceptance.' "

Ziv was full of nerves and anger over his friend's fate, and in his
state he found himself despising the church volunteers for their
kindness. He knew it wasn't their fault. He compared the present
way of killing to the executions of another era, and somehow reasoned that the old ones were more honorable in their forthrightness:
"I wished the Guillotine was back in service with hooded executioners hoisting the head of the condemned, showing it to the cheering
crowds. It was so 'uncivilized' in the French Revolution or Elizabe-
than England hundreds of years before, but it was a much more honest event showing execution for what it is."

Shortly before 5 p.m., when the group would be moved from the suite to the prison, Ziv got on the phone with Rais, who needed some help. Rais could sometimes rub Ziv the wrong way; he wasn't sure why. It was perhaps that Rais seemed to get all the media credit for reforming Mark when it had been Ziv and his crew who invested years in him, not mere months. And it was Ziv's suspicion that Rais was in this for something more than Stroman's life: "I always felt that Rais could have had a shot at sainthood on this side of heaven if he had not become such a self-promoter," Ziv said. Now here Rais was on the phone. He was calling because he'd quietly been hoping to speak to Stroman during his phone window today. It would be their first encounter since the one at the Buckner Food Mart. Rais would, inshallah, have a fuller opportunity to speak with Stroman if the case succeeded and he got his mediation sessions. But, just in case, he wanted to try now. He was calling Ziv because he had tried reaching Stroman directly at the prison but had been unable to get through. Rais suspected that the authorities were thwarting him because of his legal campaign.

Rais was in luck. Ziv had been talking to Stroman on the Execution Suite landline, and he put his cell phone on speaker and placed it near the other phone, so the two men could have their first conversation since the one beginning with "Where are you from?" a decade earlier:

Mark: "Rais. How you are doing, Rais?"

Rais: "Hey, Mark. How are you, buddy?"

Mark: "How are you doing, man? Hey, man, thank you for everything you have been trying to do for me. You are inspiring. Thank you from my heart, dude."

Rais: "Mark, you should know that I am praying for God, the most compassionate and gracious. I forgive you, and I do not hate you. I never hated you . . ."

Mark: "You are inspired, Rais."

Rais: ". . . and this is from the bottom of my heart."

Mark: "You are a remarkable person. Thank you from my heart. I love
   you, bro. I love you with all my heart. Thank you for being such an
   awesome person. I mean it."
Rais: "You will always be there."
Mark: "You touched my heart. I would have never expected this."
Rais: "You touched mine, too."
Mark: "Hey, Rais, they are telling me to hang up now. I will try to call
   in a minute."

And that was it. Stroman's phone time had ended. Now he would
have to prepare for the last meal and other formalities. He had
reportedly ordered chicken-fried steak with gravy; an omelet with
ham, cheese, onions, and tomatoes; bacon; fried potatoes, squash,
and okra; pork chops with eggs sunny-side up; Dr Pepper; and a pint
of Blue Bell vanilla ice cream.

Over in Austin, Rais's team was again due in court. The legal
papers had multiplied into the thousands of pages, which they
stuffed into cardboard boxes and carried from the law firm to the
courthouse. As the group made its way there, everyone roasting in
a sweaty glaze, Rais kept replaying one moment of the phone call
with Stroman in his mind: "Once he said that word, 'I love you, bro,'
I could feel already my tears were coming out of my eyes. The same
person, ten years back, he wanted to kill me for no reason, for my
skin color, because of my Islamic faith. And now, after ten years, the
same person is telling me he loves me and calling me his brother."

What Stroman didn't tell Rais, but did tell Ziv, was that a certain
part of him wanted Rais to fail. He was in love with all this love, this
forgiveness—even from the Muslims! But victory would bring a life
sentence, which he figured meant getting off the relatively placid
Row and going back to the general population, where Stroman, after
his earlier periods inside, had sworn he would never return. He had
been thinking. "I'm ready to go," he told Ziv. "It's not a life to live. I
have enough faith in my religion to accept what's coming." He even
called his sentence "a blessing." Ziv pushed back, but Stroman was

clear: "Compared to a life sentence, I'm blessed. I'm not going to live like this for the rest of my life."

Stroman knew, however, that he couldn't openly admit to this fear. "Because he was so overwhelmed by the love and the fact that all these people cared for him, he was not going to be the party pooper and say, 'Guys, just leave me alone,' " Ziv said.

It reminded Ziv of something he had learned in making a different documentary. He was filming an indigenous community in South America when a man gestured to a sloth nearby and said, "This animal doesn't know when to die." Ziv didn't see his meaning. The villager explained that with certain animals, you wallop them once and they die: simple for them, simple for you. That sloth, though, dies only if you hack its throat. "That's the reason why we don't eat its heart, because then we will not know how to die, too," the villager told him. That seized Ziv. "It took me three days of contemplation—how profound this thing was. I think Mark felt it was time to die."

BACK IN AUSTIN, at the Travis County Courthouse downtown, the hearing came to order shortly after 5 p.m. It was past business hours, so the building was mostly deserted. A dozen or so people sat behind the lawyers' tables in the viewing space on humble blue seats.

Rais had arrived in the city that Monday, two days prior, without even a toothbrush or shaving cream. He had figured he would make his case and go home. Now, at last, after a whole lot of kicking around, his argument had a hearing. As the proceedings began, however, Judge Joseph Hart said he would hear the matter only if the state agreed to delay the execution until after his decision. The execution window was to open in less than an hour. The government lawyers refused. The two sides bickered about why the governor wouldn't delay the killing even for a few hours. At 5:50 p.m., ten minutes before the deadline, a reporter in the courtroom heard Rais wonder aloud if Stroman was already fastened to the gurney.

Eight minutes later, with the lawyers now in closed chambers with the judge, the reporter noted Rais swaying back and forth in his seat, his hand slowly crushing a white plastic cup. Two minutes later, at the precise execution hour, Rais muttered, "This is how easily lives are torn apart. Just like this cup."

Around 6:40 p.m., Judge Hart emerged from his chambers. "All rise. Court is now in session, the Honorable Judge Hart presiding," the bailiff declared.

"This is D-1-GN-112192," Judge Hart began. He looked over to Rais: "You'll have to help me with the pronunciation." Rais softly obliged.

"*Bhuiyan vs. Rick Perry*," the judge said.

The judge said there would now be a brief hearing on whether he in fact had jurisdiction in the case. The arguments from earlier that morning were rehearsed, and again the judge disappeared into his office. He returned a little after 7 p.m., offering good news for Rais's side and a solution to the impasse. The state had paused the execution and agreed to keep it on hold during the hearing, with one condition: the state's Court of Criminal Appeals could immediately and in parallel consider if Hart's court had jurisdiction to hear this case. It was a shrewd compromise for the state: its attorneys showed respect for legitimacy by participating in the hearing; and, in now requiring two judges rather than one to stop the execution, they were no worse off than before the deal.

Around this time, Wahid got the news that the federal appeals court had turned Rais down on another of their tracks. Wahid messaged his colleagues to submit an appeal, already drafted, to the Supreme Court in Washington. Justice Antonin Scalia would receive their plea and decide on its merits. All this while, Stroman's own direct, and more customary, appeals had been bouncing around some of the same courts, but none was getting anywhere.

The hearing was operating under an unusual protocol. "The normal local rule is not to have cell phones on," the judge explained, looking over to the state attorney. "You may have your cell phone on because you may get a call that I need to know about."

That call, if it came, would be from the Court of Criminal Appeals, which was now simultaneously reviewing this court's jurisdiction.

This hearing was Rais's first and only chance to make his case for Stroman before a judge. First Khurrum Wahid, representing him, framed the issue in terms of timing rather than outcome. Although Rais had battled to save Mark Stroman from the death sentence, the request was more narrowly described now. "The bottom line," Wahid said, "is that, under Texas law, Mr. Bhuiyan, as a victim, has rights. And if those rights are not enforceable, then there really are no rights. And we simply need the time to allow him to enforce those rights and execute what he wants, which is victim-offender mediation dialogue." He said Rais had spoken to other targets of violent crime who had undergone mediation and "found closure to the hole that was created when they became victims."

As Wahid spoke, he couldn't help but look past Judge Hart to the wall clock behind him. He felt each minute's passage acutely. To litigate an execution an hour and a half after it was meant to occur was to walk on strange, unfamiliar terrain. In the middle of his argument, the state attorney's phone rang. He picked up, but the other court had no news as yet. "I apologize, Judge. No updates at the moment," the state attorney said.

Wahid quickly sketched the facts of Rais's life—his coming to America, his being shot, his surgeries, his professional reinvention. He explained that it had not occurred to Rais until very recently to seek mediation, and could not have occurred to him given all he confronted. If Judge Hart didn't block the execution tonight and allow for mediation with Stroman, Rais would "never have that opportunity to be fulfilled"—an experience, Wahid added, that some participants had compared to "starting life over again." On the other hand, if the judge blocked the execution, all it would mean for the state was postponement of the inevitable: "The harm to the defendant is they would have to re-set up for this particular execution. And all things being equal, that happens pretty often for other reasons in the State of Texas."

Wahid addressed head-on the inherent strangeness of his plea: "I think what confuses everyone in this whole event is that he is the victim of that defendant, and that's why it's so unusual. No one has seen this before. Why would the victim want to save this person's life? Well, look at it another way. The victim wants to save his own life. That's what he's trying to do. He's trying to go through a process where he can come out and hit the reset button."

Now the state attorney rose to argue that Rais had in fact received multiple communications from the government, right after the shooting and then after the trial, giving him a chance to request mediation with his attacker. Rais had never answered, the state attorney said.

It was time for testimony. "You may call your first witness," Judge Hart told Wahid.

Rais walked up to the stand, swore the oath, and spelled his name for the court reporter. Under questioning by Wahid, he began by denying that he had received any invitation to mediation with Stroman. Even if he had, he would have been unable to process it: "I don't remember at this moment any of these documents, because after I was shot I was going through a tremendous amount of depression and a tremendous amount of trauma, and I don't know what was going through that time in my mind."

Rais's voice was low and melancholy, without any of his usual energy. But it wasn't until Wahid asked him to retell some of the story of his recovery that he gave in and cried as he spoke: "Well, this crime put me into a situation—I never would have imagined that I would be going through this thing in my life in U.S.A. I was going through one after one disaster mentally, psychologically, physically, where I got my life back, but I was in a situation that I didn't know where the money was coming from for the surgery. I had no money in my pocket. Many a times I called the doctor's office to get some sample medicine."

His voice was shaking and cracking into sobs. He spoke now of Abida, trading in his usual term "fiancée" for "wife," as she had been technically and on paper but in no other sense: "My wife was under tremendous amount of parental pressure back home, because her parents didn't want her to be with me, and they were pushing her to marry somebody else, and she was keep calling me and putting on me lots and lots of pressure that I had to go back, but I couldn't go back because of my eye surgery. The doctors didn't want me to go, because they thought that I would have lost my eye forever. It was tremendous amount of pressure that my dad had a stroke and he survived, because of my shooting incident, and I could not go and see my parents. I mean, I have no clue how I survived that couple of years after I was shot. And the pain I was in"—now his crying grew fierce—"was unbearable. The way Mark Stroman completely destroyed my life. And I could not think straight and think clearly, that I had to go through all this kind of situation in my life in one of the best countries in the world."

He again denied that the state had apprised him of his rights as a victim, or even about the execution date, which he said he had learned from Rick Halperin. Rais had become calmer, but he broke down again when Wahid asked what he imagined getting out of meeting Stroman a second time.

He paused for long seconds. "I came to this country"—that phrase made him cry harder—"to fulfill my lifelong dream to have education"—he was almost wailing now—"and to experience the American dream. Before in my country, I had vision 20/10 back home. He took that thing from my life. He put me in a situation that I would never, ever be able to fly. I lost the vision in my right eye. And the trauma he caused, not only in my life—my parents' life, my entire career life."

His voice became inaudible through the crying for a moment.

"I want to see him," Rais suddenly declared. "I want to talk to him personally. I want to connect to him in a human way. I want to see that he's a human being like me. I want him to explain many things, many questions which I don't know at this moment—to find out in course of time if I get a chance to talk to him. I would love him to explain why, what, how. When he shot me, he was standing, looking at me. What was going through his mind, before he pulled the trigger? Did he ever thought about his kids? That I am someone's kid as well? When I was crying 'Mom' again and again, what was going through his mind?" Rais's voice quivered here again.

"I want to know all these things, to close this chapter and move on with my own life, for my own sake, for my mental peace," he went on. "If Mark Stroman is gone, who is going to give me this answer? And as a victim I have the right to talk to him, to get from him all these answers—for my own sake, for my mental peace, so I can move on by closing this chapter and open a different chapter—and leave this one in peace."

Wahid had gambled their case on this moment, and his bet paid off. For the first time in a long time, things seemed to be turning their way. Maybe Rais's luck had returned. The judge was clearly sympathetic, interested in Wahid's argument, hanging on Rais's every word. Rais could see it in the judge's eyes. He even noticed the court reporter weeping.

"Thank you," Wahid said. "Nothing else."

IN HUNTSVILLE, ZIV and the others had taken a short car ride to the prison around 5 p.m. They were led to a cafeteria in its administrative building, where a guard and a Texas Ranger watched over them. They would remain there until all the appeals ended and it was time for the execution. Most of their possessions, including their phones, had been taken away, and so there was little to distract them. The cafeteria had vending machines, but the visitors had no money. Ziv and the others remained mostly silent. They knew only that cases were being heard, arguments being made, about Stroman's fate in various forums—in state and federal courts, from Austin to New Orleans and all the way to Washington, D.C. But they had no idea which way things were blowing. "You just sit there like an idiot," Ziv said.

What they did know was that the execution was supposed to occur at 6 p.m., which meant their having to move again, to the death chamber, before that. When 6 p.m. came along and nothing happened, the silence broke. People started wondering what was going on. Ziv went to chat up a guard about how they would know, when they would know. The man was what Ziv called "guardy-looking": genial, with a crew cut and the all-American appearance of a marine. He told Ziv that he was awaiting a call from something called "the office of the unit," which would give instructions.

As 6 p.m. ripened into 7, for once there was hope. Ziv's guard friend now told him that it was unusual to have such a delay. If it went on much longer, given the extensive protocols involved, they would likely have to withdraw the death warrant: the whole business had to be complete before midnight on July 20, in order not to violate the law. Ziv and the others were thrilled. It could, Ziv figured, mean Mark's going to the back of the line, having to get a fresh date. It would be a miracle. "The last time this happened, a couple years ago, the guy was not executed," the guard told Ziv.

It wasn't everything, but it was something. Rais would at last get his occasion to meet Stroman. Ziv, whatever his reservations about Rais, now marveled that the man's desperate move might have worked. The consensus in the cafeteria shifted its weight toward optimism. Maybe, even probably, it wouldn't happen tonight.

BACK IN AUSTIN, the judge offered the state attorney a chance to cross-examine Rais.

"Mr. Bhuiyan," the state attorney began, "I know you've been through a lot, and I really hate to put you through anything more, but I was just wondering if you ever received any compensation from the state victims' compensation fund for your injuries?"

Rais explained that he had, thanks to his doctor's office applying on his behalf.

"Thank you. That's all the questions I have," the state attorney said.

Wahid now requested a chance to ask something further from Rais. It had occurred to him that the support Rais had corralled from the families of the other two victims might be important to the judge. Rais claimed that both families were "absolutely" supportive of his campaign.

Wahid asked Rais, "To your knowledge, and I can put them on as well, but if you know, just to expedite things, did they ever get any notice of any victim-offender dialogue?"

"OK, hold on just a second," the judge interrupted. A phone had rung in the court. It belonged to the state attorney.

"This is it," the state attorney said to the court. Then he was talking into the phone: "OK. All right, can you send me that document? OK. Great. Just e-mail it to me. All right. Thanks."

Rais stared at the state attorney as he spoke. "I could hear his voice was louder than ever before," he said. "He sounded very happy and he kept telling, 'OK, OK, great, great.' So then I realized that he is getting some message which is going to help him to kill this guy today."

After hanging up, the state attorney addressed the judge: "The Court of Criminal Appeals has granted a writ of prohibition preventing this court from moving forward."

Silence fell on the courtroom. Rais looked around, confused. Hadi Jawad remembers the incredible stillness in the room in that moment, and the feeling of breath being punched out of you.

The judge looked to Wahid. "Counsel, you understand that. Is there any question about that in your mind?"

"No," Wahid said.

"OK. Based on that, then, I cannot proceed," the judge said. "I am prohibited from proceeding by the Court of Criminal Appeals. And this hearing will be terminated at this time." He looked over to Rais. "You may step down. Thank you." Rais was sobbing in his hands.

"Y'all be at ease," the judge said. A moment later, he added, "You all are excused—except I'd like to . . ." And here he came down from the bench, walked over to Rais and shook his hand. The court reporter, the tears welling in her eyes, approached Rais and said how sorry she was.

Rais's mind raced. He pressed Wahid: There must be something we can do. What can we do? Anything? What if . . . Rais now thought of that Clint Eastwood movie *True Crime*, where the execution is interrupted after the lethal injection has begun. So there had to be a way to reach the governor, the parole board—someone, something. As Rais shuffled through these strategies, he was awash in tears. Whom we do know? What connections can we use?

Wahid recalled Rais's optimism even in that moment: "He kind of said, 'OK, what's next?' because we kept having a 'what's next.' And everybody was like, 'What's next?' Even my own legal team were like 'What's next?'

"There's no next," Wahid told them.

A FEW MINUTES later, around 8 p.m., in that cafeteria in Huntsville, a shrill ring blared out of a wall-mounted phone. It was that "office of the unit" phone. The guard walked down the corridor to pick it up, and Ziv followed him, now that they were friends. The guard listened, then turned to Ziv and summed it all up: "We need to go."

The room broke out in tears and the spontaneous holding of hands. The group set out toward the execution chamber—across the street, past television crews with their bright lights and a crowd of people who had come to witness the evening's events and/or protest against them.

In that crowd was Rick Halperin, who had brought a few carloads of activists down from Dallas—including many who had signed up after Rais's earliest presentations at the Amnesty and Texas Coalition chapter meetings. A prison spokesman had emerged a little before 6 p.m. and said there was some kind of delay. A delay was rare—any deviation from plan was rare—and optimism had rippled through the crowd, as it had through the cafeteria. What everyone was now waiting for, and dreading, was the sight of the prisoner's guests emerging from their waiting area and walking into the killing chamber. When Halperin and the other activists saw Ziv and the other witnesses leaving the cafeteria for another building, they knew it was over, and many broke out in tears.

Ziv walked into the main prison building, past the visitation area, through the courtyard, past the buildings full of cells. It was a walk not of seconds but minutes, enough to feel the gravity of the occasion. Then on the left Ziv saw it: a low-slung building "completely architecturally different," devoted solely to ending lives. The sight of the building stirred in Ziv a distant memory; he couldn't quite pinpoint it. It hit him: it was the gas chamber, as plain and nondescript as this building, that he had visited with his father at the Majdanek concentration camp in Poland.

They were guided into the viewing room. Ziv remembered it as improbably small, with a low ceiling. The darkness of the room focused one's eyes on the glass window of import, beyond which was the green-painted chamber of which Stroman had sent the Templetons a photograph years earlier. By the time Ziv arrived in the viewing room, Stroman was already strapped to the gurney, ready to go. He could only nod at his friends from the world after he saw them filing in. A dark-suited warden stood behind Stroman, wearing sunglasses indoors. Somehow the scene made Ziv think of the Madame Tussauds wax museum: everyone frozen in place, playing their little role.

The chaplain blessed Stroman with whispered prayers and caressed his ankle to soothe him. After a time, the green wall in the death room mysteriously opened: it had a scarcely visible door that Ziv hadn't noticed. A suited man ducked in, said "Warden proceeds," and retreated without turning around.

The theater of the Death is just about perfectly rehearsed and directed, and Stroman knew this was his cue. "The Lord Jesus Christ be with me," he said into the microphone. "I am at peace. Hate is going on in this world, and it has to stop. One second of hate will cause a lifetime of pain. Even though I lay on this gurney, seconds away from my death, I am at total peace. I'm still a proud American—Texas loud, Texas proud. God bless America. God bless everyone. Let's do this damn thing."

With that, his last-words time officially ended, but Stroman had a few more to share, these perhaps unscripted: "I love you, all of you. It's all good. It's been a great honor." Because this was unauthorized riffing, the drugs were already pushing through the tube as he spoke, down the needle, through the white-bandaged hole in his skin, and into the busy traffic of his veins.

"I feel it," he said. "I am going to sleep now. Goodnight. One, two, there it goes . . ." His eyes shut.

A doctor emerged from what seemed to Ziv like another hidden door. He placed his fingers on Stroman's neck and looked for a pulse that wasn't there. He bent toward the microphone into which Stroman had spoken and confirmed that the Death had claimed Stroman at 8:53 p.m.

Ziv and the others were, before they knew it, back at the Execution Suite, in its parking lot, meeting with the chaplain who had caressed Stroman's ankle. He needed to hand over the worldly possessions that Stroman had bequeathed to them. Out of several bags of meshed net they emerged: a Swintec 2410CC typewriter, an electric coffee machine, legal documents, dozens of letters that Stroman had been too backlogged to answer, the pictures he had begged the free world to send, and some food items from the commissary that he had perhaps miscalculated being able to finish.

RAIS AND HIS team, who had wanted to be in Huntsville on this day but couldn't because of the appeals, had returned to the La Quinta Inn around 8:30 p.m. They slumped into chairs in the lobby. The news soon arrived. Rais sobbed and sobbed. That pitiful, tattooed man to whom God had strangely bound him had left for "the other side of the light," as Stroman once put it: "pumped full of toxic bug juice, in the name of justice."

Uncle

T he phone rang in the thick of night. He picked up: it was Western Union on the line. After all those hours he put in earlier, they still weren't done with him. They were calling to say that, yes, they may have charged the $17 transaction fee twice but, no, with this there would be no refunds.

For once, Rais snapped: Did they really need to wake him up for that? As long as the Stroman girl received the money, he was at peace.

It had been one of those "crazy busy" days, as Americans called it. A month had passed since Mark Stroman left the world, and Rais was balancing the resumption of normalcy with his new duties as a campaigner against hate crimes. He was building a website for his new organization, World Without Hate, and was hoping to raise money for it. But he was also determined not to slack off at work, lest he lose the bread and butter that made this other pursuit possible. So on this day he had put in long hours at the office, then gone for an interview with Swiss television about his campaign to save Stroman. He had finished working, as was now customary, around 10:30 p.m.

One last task awaited. He drove to a nearby Western Union outlet to make an urgent money transfer. The timing wasn't ideal, because his team of engineers was still working and ordinarily he would have rejoined them after the interview, but this transfer was important. Now the system wasn't working at the shop. He decided to go home and try online. He had to finish quickly to make the day's last prayer. He had missed too many already that week. Now even the website was betraying him. What was happening? It wouldn't give him the MTCN code, and without it the transfer wouldn't go through. A task of minutes stretched to fill two-plus hours. Prayer time came and went. Western Union put him on hold, but no one would pick up. All of this turmoil, he thought, just for wanting to do good.

Finally the transfer went through, but the system somehow charged Rais the $17 fee twice. Who cared. He sent the information to the recipient and went to bed—and then that phone call.

He was just happy he could help. The transfer was for $50 and was desperately needed. The recipient was Amber Stroman.

✶

As the campaign to save Stroman had unfolded, Rais sent word to the daughters of his attacker that they should let him know if ever he could help. It was a genuine offer, but it was also his manner of speaking. The Stroman girls had remembered.

Not long after the execution, Rais drove to meet Amber at a Starbucks in Arlington. She brought some friends along for support. Amber wanted to be honest with Rais: "I said, 'I've been mad at you; I've been mad at the people my dad shot.' Because in my head I'm thinking I don't have the right to be mad at Dad." She felt fear crawling all over her, but the man before her calmed her down: "I was scared and I said,

'How can you sit across this table, buy us coffee—from Starbucks on top of that, and y'all know Starbucks isn't cheap—buy us coffee, everybody, sit across the table and look me in my eye and tell me that you forgive me?' He said, 'Because I do.'"

Amber continued, "He was telling me about his religion—is it Muslim? And I asked him, 'I know you had to be somewhat mad in the beginning.' He said, 'You know what, I was for a short amount of time,' and he said, 'Does being mad really solve anything? Not only am I a victim. I believe that you and your brother and sister are victims just as well.'" Amber had never thought of it like that, and it gave her relief. Ever since her father's war, Amber's rage had fired unpredictably in every which way. She was mad at her father for getting into this mess, but she also seethed at the dark-skinned Them he was after: "I found myself mad if they were from Pakistan, if they were from India. I don't know if it was because I didn't want my dad to think I was a traitor. I don't know."

They went afterward to a nearby Chipotle, and Amber again appreciated Rais's generosity in paying.

A month or so later, Amber called Rais. "I asked her, 'How are you doing? How's everything going? Everything fine? Do you need anything? Any help?'" Rais said. He could sense her reticence: "She was not feeling easy to come out. I said, 'Do you need anything? Is there anything I can do for you?' But then she said that, yes, she needs some help, but she feels shy to ask for it. I said, 'No, don't feel shy.'"

Amber poured out her troubles, which involved (a) the grandmother of her daughter's father taking the toddler away from her; and (b) the grandma's insistence that Amber go to rehab in Fort Worth, which she had; and (c) Amber's now lacking the money to go visit her daughter back in Stephenville. Rais shuddered to imagine what a solitary, uneducated woman must have to do in America to come by money: "I said, 'No, women should not live a life like this, especially in this country. If it would be one of the poorest third-world countries, I understand; there is no other means. But a human being in this country living a life like that—no. I was crying in my heart. I said, 'What do you need? How much do you need?' "

Amber thought for a moment. How about $50?

Rais's extensive effort to wire the money that night was more than simple kindness. It reflected the postexecution strategy that was slowly gelling in his mind. The immediate cause had been to save Stroman's life; the larger cause, to use Stroman to deter others like him from shooting other Raises and Waqars and Vasudevs. Now an even broader mission was coming to Rais. He had observed in his years here that the American dream had stopped working for people like the Stromans in the way it had worked for him. He saw a dream threatened by a rot at its core, and he realized that for his project truly to succeed, he would need to help others live the dream as he had. "Once I came to this country, I did not take things for granted, though most of the people here, they take things for granted," he said. "So I was thinking that in one part of the world, there are people with so much less, and this part of the world, people with so much. Still, why they don't make the best use of their lives, of the resource they have? It's not like back home, that there is nothing. There are a lot of opportunities here. But you just don't see it."

He wanted to challenge this habit of not-seeing, and the generation-to-generation transmission of selfish, isolated, anarchic lives. "The people I saw in this country need help," Rais said.

This was, of course, far too much for one part-time activist to take on. So Rais figured he would begin with a test case—the Stromans. Could he prevent Amber, Erica, and Robert (whom Rais hadn't met, because he was in a maximum security prison for aggravated robbery) from going down their father's path? "I was thinking that let's break the cycle here," Rais said.

"Now if Amber doesn't get any help, if the boy, once he comes out of jail, doesn't get help, they're continuing in the path that Mark Stroman and his predecessors laid for them—nothing but the SAD life, and not doing anything in their life," Rais said, reprising his acronymed critique of sex, alcohol, and drugs. "If Amber doesn't get help, her daughter will follow the same lifestyle as her."

Rais had come to a country that nearly took his life and then generously gave him the means of retrieval—a country that seemed to him ever to contain the cures to its own ailments. But it was a country whose own people seemed to Rais to have lost their life force, ceased to see their potential, ceased to value the connection to other lives, ceased to look into the future and see the truth that made people like Rais come here—the knowledge that here, more than anywhere, they could die differently from how they'd been born. Rais wanted to wake them up. It was part of his idea of service. He wanted to tell them that if he, then they: if a foreign-born, half-blind ex–gas station clerk could make it here, they could, too. He wanted them to know life's preciousness without having to go through what he had to discover it.

"We immigrants, when we come to this country, we feel pressure to be successful, to do something good, because of our family teaching that we have to make our parents happy," Rais said. "But here Amber never felt that she had to make her mother or father proud, right? So there is no urgency—there is no need—to do good. There is no pressure."

To Rais, this was one of the differences between the poverty of Texas and the poverty back home. It was an argument that immigrants sometimes made toward their less fortunate new compatriots, without fully understanding their realities, and it was a doubly complicated stance for Rais: a devout Muslim telling the Americans to become more like some supposed previous version of themselves, which also happened to mean their becoming more like him. For now, though, Rais's ambitions were modest. All he wanted was to help the Stroman children escape their trap.

For Amber, the arrival of that $50 was a shock. She couldn't believe it, just couldn't. Fifty dollars from the man her father tried to kill. She felt now that she'd been stupid, allowing her father's prejudice to become her own. Why did Rais deserve her wrath? She got the feeling that he would be there on the other end of a phone line if ever she needed him. And she knew that she just might someday.

Amber kept thinking of something Rais said to her on the day of their first meeting. It rang in her ears still. She couldn't really understand it—couldn't fathom the depth of the heart it came from. "You may have lost a father," he said, "but you've gained an uncle."

⋇

Mark stroman's dying wish was that his children would not become him. But it wasn't so easy.

Amber's temporary address these days was in a forlorn section of Fort Worth, on a street lined with well-used trucks and overgrown lawns seemingly mowed once per foreclosure. She emerged from the house, a dead ringer for her father, albeit a rounder version, with chipping black nail polish on her hands and flip-flopping feet. Her face was quick to smile but could easily switch to nervous.

Amber was like her father in more than appearance: she, too, was a convicted criminal, having done time for burglary and forgery—committed, she said, in pursuit of meth. She had known her father only in glimpses. He had always been someone to conjure more than savor. His death some weeks earlier made that truer. Amber was haunted by his being gone, though gone was what he'd always been, one way or another. She was rearranging her memories the way one redecorates a room, trying to make him more understandable in death than he had been in life.

Amber was headed to Stephenville, seventy or so miles away, where her sister, Erica, was waiting for her. Joining Amber was Maria, a stout, heavily constructed, silent young woman who vaguely gave off an assassin's air. The glare coming out of her eyes was omnidirectional, singling no one out. She was Amber's girlfriend, reflecting a switch from men to women that had come to pass after the baby's birth. She stepped into the car and began staring silently out of the window, which she would continue to do for the next hour and a half.

"My dad was a very hateful man in the beginning," Amber said, "I guess to where he was so hateful and miserable, he probably hated himself." As she processed him now, she realized that losing a father was especially complicated when he hadn't really been a father. She remembered his taking them to the biker bar he loved, the Texas Trap: "Back then, that was all we could get with him—we took it." They would sit at the bar, drinking Cokes and eating peanuts, and he'd have his Budweiser, and for a time all seemed well. He took them to the state fair sometimes, and to Celebration Station once in a while, or brought them Christmas presents or fireworks in garbage bags. Then he would disappear again, either to a girlfriend or to his new wife and daughter, or to some other unknowable pastures. Amber gradually grew bitter about playing second or fourth or fourteenth fiddle in her father's life, or whatever fiddle it was.

"I was more, I guess, a titty-baby," she said. "Or I felt like I deserved his full attention. I guess because he never gave us his full attention."

Stroman's elusive presence had given even the smallest act of generosity the glow of heroism. Amber remembered the night, years ago, when her father had been kind enough to let her sleep in his bed, instead of his girlfriend of the moment. The girlfriend was there all the time; Amber was in Dallas only briefly; it was only fair. "He had his arm like this," Amber said, sprawling hers out for the narration, "and I remember putting my head in his armpit. And, oh man, it was the awfullest, awfullest smell. To this day—that's kind of gross, whatever, call it what you want—but I'll remember that forever. I'll remember that forever."

Sometimes she asked herself if he ever loved them; sometimes she went a step further to wonder if he even knew what loving was. He certainly didn't show it. But maybe it was she who had blocked him out. Maybe it was her blinders.

She knew, despite everything, that she was "his pick," his favorite. "I'm the only one that looks identical to him," she said; that had to count for something. It also made her proud that her daughter, Madyson Michelle, had Mark's combustive red hair.

Amber was still grappling with her father's transition from barebones presence to surefire absence. Now he would be a thing to define yourself by, and also define yourself against. She was still sorting out what would be the "by" part and what would be the "against."

She didn't know how she felt about him: "Let me tell you this: I love my dad." Her tears broke through. "But for instance, when I talked to him the last time, I lied to him. I told him, 'Dad, I don't blame you for nothing. I'm not mad at you.' And I was. But I didn't want that to be the last thing I said to him. I didn't want him to know how disappointed I was or mad. I mean, it just hurts."

Amber added, "It's shitty the way he done us, really."

Should she have seen "that stunt," as she called her father's war, coming? It was hard to say. Most of the times that she saw him, he was just a wild, fun-loving dad. She remembered chomping those weed brownies with him and not waking up until 6 p.m. the next day and her father having pizza waiting for them. She was thirteen, maybe fourteen. She remembered when he got her a bracelet made of pot seeds, and her mother and stepdad seized it and threw it in the trash. She remembered how when she was giving birth to her baby girl, her father kept calling and calling on his smuggled cell phone, waiting to see if it had happened, and then finally heard her wail in the birthing room. In his last hours on earth, he said to Amber, "I'll never forget hearing my grandbaby cry for the first time. That was the best feeling in the world—until I got to talk to her today."

Still, yes, there were many things she'd known, many things she'd seen. She didn't know, for example, that he loathed Middle Easterners, but she had known since childhood his feelings about the blacks. He hung around with bikers, for God's sake. It was only after he went away that she realized what a figure he'd been among Dallas-area racists: "I've met people in the free world that they found out who my dad was, and they had me on a pedestal." People he had been in prison with, people in the Aryan Brotherhood. She might run into them at a bar, and tell them her name, and they'd tell her how much respect they had for her old man, how he was a "true American."

She confessed that she was struggling to reach Rais's level of forgiveness for her father. She told Rais, "I'm not a good person like you, I guess. Because I still do have hate and animosity towards him." Part of her still thought he had manipulated his little international tribe of holy rollers, made them think he was what he wasn't: "That's what pissed me off about him, too, because in so many ways he was so fake—I mean, so fake."

She still carried the memory of that story her father once told her about the black lady: "There was this one time he picked up a black. She was walking down the road, and he picked her up. She gave him a blowjob. They were driving the road, and after she was done, he opened the door and kicked the lady out of a moving vehicle." He had told Amber this story, back when she was just a girl, because he figured it would impress her. At other times her father could be totally the opposite. Like when Amber's best friend in ninth grade was black, and Amber warned Stroman before introducing them, "If you disrespect her in any way, I will never talk to you again." He treated her fine. Treated her, Amber said, "like she was white."

Stephenville was drawing close. It had been a while since Amber had seen Erica, who was now helping the grandma out with Madyson Michelle. Of course, Erica had her own troubles—she didn't touch meth, as far as Amber knew, but she loved her drink.

"Would you call her an alcoholic, babe?" Amber asked Maria in the backseat. Maria said nothing. "I would," Amber said after a moment. "If she don't have beer, she don't have alcohol, she gets the shakes. She smokes weed. I mean, that was a trait we got passed down from him himself."

Amber knew that all too well. She said she was clean now, but only barely: "I haven't used in a long time, but I consider myself an addict because I think about using all the time."

She wanted to stop in the local Exxon station. She needed a smoke. Entering Stephenville was making her anxious; she could feel the energy of her daughter somewhere not far from her. She bought some Marlboro 100s and sat on the bench outside smoking one, as Maria looked on. Amber knew this gas station well, because it was a favorite hangout of Stephenville's late-bird meth heads.

It was painful to come home. A reminder of her failures as a mother, of the fact that her own flesh was living with the grandmother of a no-good man. Still, Amber had seen the wisdom in the grandma's ultimatum: go away, get clean, and only then get Madyson back. Having herself been kidnapped as a child and raised by a grandma, Amber knew that this was normal. She looked around Stephenville and saw a town that to the outsider might seem quaintly Western but that she knew had been eaten inside and out by meth. You knew it was bad when the teachers at junior high would deal you dope. "If I stay here," Amber figured, "I see myself going downhill faster than what I could climb the damn hill."

In that sense, Madyson's great-grandma was a kind of savior, because her grandson was as reckless as Amber. He'd been in prison for almost the entirety of Madyson's three years alive. He was in there now for deeds that Amber recalled involving the theft of a car and evasion of arrest. It was something else before that, and would be something else after. He wasn't really part of Madyson's life. Of course, Grandma mentioned him to Madyson, but the little girl knew that Amber and Maria were her parents. It got to the point, with Madyson only being around them or Grandma or Erica, that Amber saw an "eerie" look on the little girl's face whenever a man entered the room. It was as though, by the age of three, Madyson had understood the bane of her life: that the men accessible to girls like her would almost uniformly disappoint them.

Where, and how, would the Stroman cycle break?

✴

Stephenville held more promise back when the dairy business was still around and thriving. Now it was mostly fast-food joints on the roads. It was hard to fathom how a town full of people could survive on so many citizens serving each other fast food and being served fast food in turn. It was what was available, though; moreover, it wasn't illegal. There were other opportunities—a local research and extension center of Texas A&M and a well-regarded rodeo, among other things—but they were many social light-years above the Stromans. People of the Stromans' station couldn't really aspire to those.

The Stromans were somewhere above the bottom but below the middle of American life. They claimed not to touch welfare, mostly out of pride, except for a brief time after Tena had the children. They were sophisticated enough to realize that they needed improvement. They were, in their own estimation, above white trash, with its food stamps and trailered living, but below monthly cell phone bills and the fixedness that they implied. They were above having no phone at all but below keeping it on at all times. They were above homelessness but below addresses that persisted longer than a year. They were above hunger but below access to food that actually nourished.

The first restaurant Amber had chosen didn't work, because it didn't serve alcohol. Erica needed a place where she could drink. The Bull Nettle sports bar, dingy inside even at noon, was a natural second choice. Everyone sat on high stools at a wobbly table, beneath vinyl posters that underscored the beer offerings on the menu. There was a lot for everyone to catch up on—though Maria mostly just nodded or mumbled as the others spoke. When the food came, she kept ashing her cigarette into the ketchup on her plate. Erica, meanwhile, was nervous and fiddling with her phone, but also eager for a drink and some talk.

She, too, was processing her father's legacy, trying to organize the facts about him into some kind of edifying narrative. But she was less fluent than Amber, and more guarded and injured still.

What kind of a man was he? "He was a dad, I guess," Erica said. What would he want for them now? "To not end up where he did, and put God in our life."

Amber seemed to be growing distracted by something but chimed in here: "I feel that he wanted us to be a better parent than he was to us."

For Erica, as big as her father's death was, it felt at times like just another thing that wasn't going right. She spoke of many rival goals at present, all jousting for priority, each insisting that another be achieved as a prerequisite. She wanted (a) to take her niece back from that woman, (b) to get her GED so that she could get a half-way decent job, and (c) to start the job at McDonald's that she'd been offered, which her boyfriend had told her might pay fifty cents an hour extra for the night shift. "It's just McDonald's," she said, "but it's something, and it's overnight—it's going to be graveyard shift—so it's probably going to be more. I just need something to start, or at least something to get that $75 to pay for GED." That could bring a high school diploma.

Poverty, in Erica's experience of it, was an unwinnable game. It was more than a deficit of funds: it was a set of distinct, interlocking impossibilities. It felt as if some of the impossibles had to flip to possible in order for the other impossibles to follow, but no impossible was willing to flip first. "It's like one thing after another," Erica said, "and you can't worry about taking care of this because you gotta worry about taking care of this first—and where you going to be next week? You can't jump ahead."

What was especially hard was that everyone in the family was simultaneously down. Robert was in a maximum security prison down in Kenedy, Texas. Mom was addicted and shifting from place to place, often out of reach. They couldn't take turns being each other's rock, Erica said—"like, OK, you may be down, but I'm up, so let me drag you this way for a little bit and then you can bounce back up." No chance of that, since at any given moment so many of them were either high or in withdrawal or short of cash or wondering whose mattress they could sleep on—and therefore in no position to offer charity and guidance. It wasn't success that Erica was seeking from God, just the diversification of failure: "It's like, where she can't do it, I can do it. Where she can't do it, Mom can do it. You know what I mean? Back where we're the backbone for each other, instead of trying to help one another at the same time."

Erica added, "Something's gotta give. Something's gotta happen, somehow."

She was nibbling on batter-fried jalapenos. She had brought her own little yellow box of lime salt with her and was now sprinkling the salt onto a slice of lime and sucking it off, resuming the cycle over and over with the same worn-down slice. Amber, meanwhile, wasn't touching her food. Something had gotten into her.

What emerged was that it had been a big mistake for her to visit Stephenville. She thought she could handle it, but now she saw her error. "I hate being this close and not being able to see her," she said. She felt an almost gravitational pull to Madyson, but Amber had decided that she didn't want to raise her baby's hopes by seeing her, only to dash them by leaving. Madyson had known enough disappointment already. Now Amber was having second thoughts after all.

It was too late, because if she stayed a few days, she wouldn't have a ride back. Then a new possibility emerged: if she could secure the money for bus tickets, she could spend the night in town, see Madyson, and then return. Yes, this would be her plan.

The question arose of where to sleep. Though she had lived in Stephenville all her life, until a short while ago, Amber could not think of anyone to ask to shelter her and Maria for the night. Her sister was living with a current boyfriend, who was in turn crashing at a friend's. Hopefully, within two weeks, everything would be different with their situation, he assured her, as men around here often did, but for now it wasn't an option. It was like that with many of the living arrangements of people they knew—many layers of transactions and understandings between the person inhabiting the space and the person who could give permission.

The table now became a situation room tasked with finding an open bed in Stephenville. They called relatives: no. Called friends: no. The explanations of why not seemed to lurk in that no-man's-land between an excuse and a reason. As Amber continued to dial around, as Maria broke her silence to try her own contacts, as Erica called hers, a solemn loneliness crept into Amber. She began to see the situation for its larger implications and started to cry. Was this how low things had sunk? She seemed to see that it wasn't illogical that people didn't want her around. Was it maybe, just maybe, that she was a bad mother who had lost her baby girl? Or that she was an addict? Was it that she'd been in prison? Or that she'd abandoned the abandoning sex for a woman, seceded into her own little matriarchy? Or maybe it was all the recent television news of her father's ignoble end.

Between phone calls, Amber said, sort of to the table but mostly to herself, "I've turned out to be just like Dad—to the T."

Erica snapped back at her, "Well, you're not on Death Row."

Amber was no longer listening. "I chose dope over her," she muttered, thinking of Madyson.

She tuned out again, looking away from the table. Erica wasn't giving up so easy. She clearly had more numbers she could call, and plainly had done this kind of thing before. It was no biggie. They would find something. Her mind lurched from one man she could ask to another. (She seemed to call no women.) Erica knew how to play up the charm before asking the favor. Amber, far plainer than Erica, swelled up over the years, and now a lesbian, couldn't push through the doors on which her sister was knocking. It might have made a difference, one suspected, if Erica alone had needed a bed.

"I've lived here my whole fucking life," Amber said, "and I can't even find somebody to stay with."

They ran through names—Eddie or Craig, J.R. or Chip, maybe Michael—or what about David? Yes, why not try David.

"Hello," Erica's side of the conversation began.

"Nothing. What you doing?"

Pause. "Nothing. We're at Bull Nettle, drinking—eating and talking with my sister."

Pause. "Yeah, for a little bit."

Pause. "Hey, I have a favor." Here, a nicely placed giggle. "I have a favor. OK, it's kind of a way long story and I really can't explain it all, but my sister's down right now, and she's gonna have a bus ticket to go back on Monday, Tuesday, whenever. She's gonna have the money for that. But I was gonna talk to you or J.R. and see if it would be OK for y'all to help me with the place for a day or two, so they can stay. And they'll have the money for a bus ticket or whatever to go back."

Pause. "Well, it's her and Maria. And I'll probably be with them."

Pause. "I mean, just for like today and tonight really—and tomorrow. And they'll probably leave Monday. They'll have a bus ticket and everything." She tried to reassure David that this bus ticket would definitely materialize. The man had clearly been duped before. "They wanted to see if they could stay longer to visit Madyson for a little bit," Erica explained.

It sounded promising, but David wanted to talk to Amber directly. Who knows what he already knew about her, and what more he needed to understand. Erica passed the phone, and Amber left the table for a quieter spot.

When she returned, call over, she reported the verdict: "He said no."

"HE WASN'T SOME evil, cruel, no-caring guy," Erica said of her father. "He wasn't like that. He was a father." She had heard all the talk about what was wrong with him. She'd heard people say he was bipolar. From the barstool where she sat, though, pretty much everyone was bipolar. By the definition going around, her mom was bipolar and her uncle was bipolar and there's a fair chance her father was, too. What difference did it make? "I think he was a normal person got hurt," Erica said.

Erica's great regret was a simple one. Because she'd been the youngest of the three, her father had always protected her. He might have fed Amber or Robert a weed brownie, but not Erica. She remembered how they'd walk into the Texas Trap on those rare evenings together. The parking lot had no cars, only motorcycles. She would sit towering above the ground on a stool, and her father would proudly introduce her around. All the guys would come up and fuss over Mark Stroman's freckled little daughter. From the moment Stroman walked in, he was in five conversations at once, midsentence with this guy when that guy called out to him, an impresario more than a customer. And for Erica he would always and only order a root beer or a Cherry Coke, maybe nachos. No alcohol. Erica regretted, more than she could express, not breaking the alcohol barrier with her father. It was a substance that had become so important to her—and always been important to her father. It invisibly bound their lives, and yet they never shared it.

"I never drank with him," Erica said. "I never smoked a cigarette with him. And that's what makes me mad, too. I wouldn't mind sharing a Budweiser with my dad or smoking a cigarette with my dad. Just doing anything with my dad to say, 'Oh, I did it—one time I got really wasted with my dad and he's carrying me home and I'm puking on the sofa'—you know, something, just to say I did it."

✳

"You're a big girl, huh? Nuh-uh, you're Mama's baby. Are you a big girl or Mama's baby? Mama's baby? Yeah." Amber sat in a chair in the corner of Madyson's grandma's place, blessedly lost in her daughter.

Amber's luck had struck at last. They had found a bed at a friend's place, which made it OK to visit Madyson. So they headed to Grandma's home in a small development outside of town, packed with identical cramped dwellings.

Grandma, who was wearing a Lady Liberty shirt and playing Farmville on her desktop, seemed happy to see Amber. She had just returned from visiting her grandson at the penitentiary. Her matchbox of a condo was decorated by a "God Bless" poster and fake flowers. The curtains were drawn in the early afternoon—protection from the vengeful heat that was especially unkind this summer.

Madyson was running around in a green dress with pink frills. She offered her new audience a basket of hairbands to choose from. After a time, she got bored and turned to her Etch A Sketch. Her intelligence and spark were evident. Amber's mother often said of Madyson, "Two idiots make a genius."

There were already small hints of how this innocence could be lost, how the trajectory of Madyson's life could fall back to where she came from. She appeared to have learned, for example, that she was being passed around so much, day after day, to people who weren't aware of her full history, that she could angrily throw a new toy while at one house, get scolded for it, even spanked like last evening, and then move to the next house, with the next people—sometimes Erica, sometimes others—and try the same antic again. She had learned to exploit the absence of a unified witness to her life.

When Grandma told the story of yesterday's spanking, Amber wasn't really listening, still lost in her little girl's gaze. So Amber didn't hear, or maybe didn't want to hear, the subtle ways in which Grandma was undermining Amber's position. Grandma told of how, after the spanking, Madyson had been crying on the floor, gasping, "Oh, Mama. Oh, Mama," to her—to a woman certainly not her mama. Grandma added that she had been unmoved, having seen these tricks before. She left Madyson alone for half an hour, and when eventually the child toddled over to Grandma, she said, "I love you, Mummy."

Yet Grandma wasn't unkind to Amber. She reassured her, once again, in front of everyone, that she promised to give the child back. She just wanted Amber to get on her feet again. What went unsaid was that, in a matter of days, Amber was going to have to start paying more than $200 a month in child support to Grandma for Madyson's maintenance, in keeping with the custody agreement. This made it essential for Amber to get a job while going through outpatient rehab. If she didn't pay, she could be arrested and end up back inside.

When Amber and Erica arrived, Grandma had been playing on the computer. She was a big Facebook person, in addition to her love of Farmville. She presently offered some advice on the game to Erica—to stop building so many buildings: "Just spend your time on animals and trees. You get more money off of animals and trees." Erica moaned that she'd been doing it all wrong. "Get you some stuff planted," Grandma said. "That's how you're making money every day."

Madyson was staying with her grandma that night, as usual, and Amber, Maria, and Erica at their friend's. It was probably their last time around a computer that day, and they decided to research bus tickets online.

Madyson, seeing the room's attention turn away from her, took it as a cue to bring toys from all over the house and dump them on the living room floor. She was bright, full of joy, with so much evident promise. Even so, it was hard to ignore the miserable cyclicality of things. Sandra and Wallace had struggled to care for Mark, leaving grandparents to pick up the pieces. Then Mark and Tena had struggled to care for Amber, leaving grandparents to pick up the pieces. Now Amber and Maria struggled to care for Madyson, leaving grandparents to pick up the pieces. On and on it went, and it was difficult for anyone with any sense to look at the girl and assume that this time would be different.

Amber, Erica, and Maria said their good-byes, then drove over sparse, hilly country, and at last arrived at a trailer park. They said there was a good party going on there tonight. It was also where they had found a bed.

✳

ALL THE WAY down 181 from San Antonio, the road swells and shrinks between four lanes and two, across the flat plains of southern Texas, past one-off barbecue joints, past the parched yellow ranch land for sale or lease, past the signs soliciting prayers for rain. A left on Farm to Market 632, and the John B. Connally Unit rises from the dust, shimmering through the curls of ground heat, a vast and squat hive of dues-paying.

Connally was maximum security, and still haunted by the bizarre and elaborate escape of the so-called Texas Seven in 2000—or, as they were alternatively known, the Connally Seven. To get to Robert Stroman, who had been inside six years, you had to cross a gate with a sign warning "No hostages beyond this point." What it meant was that the good guys—visitors, ministers, even the guards—went among the bad guys at their own peril. Once you entered that gate, if a prisoner took you hostage, no deal would be made for your freedom, no prisoner release negotiated to win you back. It was said to apply even to the warden.

A prison official with a big smile and chirpy enthusiasm explained that Connally housed "the worst of the worst." The corridors were weirdly silent, and the centralized air-conditioning sounded shrill amid the absence of other sounds. Occasionally, one heard a concerned groan: the opening and closing of the electric gates that locked the prisoners in. The place was eerie and sad—and also, for those in the industry, ripe with promise. On the wall, a poster reminded the guards of the possibilities: "The overtime earnings are increasing, last month one employee received $1919.88. Sign up now!!!!!"

Mark Stroman's son, Robert, was waiting in the visitation room, a tattooed hulk, though much lighter than the four hundred pounds he claimed to have been when he got in. He was dressed in white, with a freshly shaven head. He had less of a facial resemblance to his father than Amber did, but the overall resemblance—the way he talked, those massive arms, the extensive ink work on his body— was just as striking. His most recent tattoo was of a Viking, with his father's initials on it. He got it done on the inside by a fellow prisoner, which you're not supposed to do because of the hepatitis risk, but which everyone does anyway. He chose it after he found out his father's execution date. He hoped it might make him like the Viking, he said: "wise and hardened by going through it."

Robert was twenty-four and hadn't seen Amber in six years. He had seen Erica a few times, maybe. The family was too scattered, he explained. He didn't blame anybody. Maybe everything would be different when he got out in a couple years.

Like his sisters, Robert was undergoing a change he didn't fully understand in his relationship with his father. Stroman was once for Robert an elusive man to be longed for when he was away and relished when he came around and mimicked as much as could be. Now he was becoming something else: a ghostly reminder of a way of life that Robert knew would tempt him again and again but had to be avoided. It was perhaps useful to have this kind of foil in a dead father.

His father was, like the men at Connally, like Robert himself, a stew of good and bad. What Robert admired in him, and hoped to find in himself one day, was his way of loving by protection. "I want to be loving," Robert said, "because if you grew up with him and you was his friend, he loves you and he'd go to bat for you any way he could—any way." Like the time they all went to the state fair together and Robert vanished among the rides and then saw, perhaps more plainly than ever, the depth of his father's feeling.

"I knew he loved me because I could see the fear and the panic in his face when he realized I wasn't around," Robert said. "And he started hollering my name—'Robert! Robert!' And I said, 'Here I am.' And I remember him grabbing my arm and shaking me and saying, 'Don't you ever, ever . . .' And I knew then."

Robert was aware that his father was a racist, and this he wished to reject, but prison had also made him understand where his father was coming from: "When I grew up, I was never around blacks or stuff like that, so it was like a culture shock, you know what I mean—like, man, took a while to learn how to talk to them and stuff, and understanding why they act the way they do." Robert claimed that it was the little things that alienated the races from one another: "I say 'Yes, sir,' 'No, sir' to everybody—my age, older, younger, because that's the way I was raised up." In prison the blacks, especially, behaved differently, at least as Robert saw it, often leaping into conversation too directly for his taste.

Robert came to Connally for aggravated robbery at eighteen. "It was a drug deal gone bad," he said. "That was all. I didn't know the people. My homeboy ripped them off and—Amber, it was her first car—they chased us, and they ended up running into my sister's car, and the guy jumped in my window, and he started hitting me. So I stabbed him with a knife." It was not all that unusual for a methland case. There were defense lawyers in Texas who reported that such cases now accounted for the majority of their work—if you included the various things people did to sell meth, buy it, smoke it, and protect their persons and honor.

"If I could change anything, man, it'd be doing drugs," Robert said. "It's definitely the tool of the devil, for real—it twists your mind." With meth he remembers floating in the clouds, high above the earth but not flying, just floating, all the words coming at once, awake for days, invincible and alive.

Now Robert wanted to remake himself. This year he could feel the end drawing near. He had two years left if his behavior remained solid. He had so many ideas of how he could be. It was going to be different now, he swore. He wanted to figure things out: "Since I'm getting a late start on life, I'm gonna have to work. Maybe go to school, get a trade." Maybe he would avail himself of the classes inside to learn a skill before he got out, but it was complicated: "There's certain stipulations." Those stipulations involved how much time you had done, when you were due out, and the quality of your behavior. This last had gotten Robert removed from a class once before.

Above all, Robert wanted a family—and a family that was "normal," as his had not been. "To an extent, we won't ever be perfect because we've already made mistakes and stuff in life," he said. Still, he felt a need, even before he had the rudiments of a good life, to have children of his own: "I want kids, man, and I want my kids to know their aunts, my sisters; their grandma, my mom—all that. And I want them to see me doing good. And I want them to love their aunts, and I want my sisters to love my kids, and I want it to go on for generations and generations." He stepped back and considered where he was: "I want none of this, man. And I regret these tattoos and stuff I got."

A moment later, he tempered his enthusiasm for his future children's contact with his relatives: "I know the errors of my way, and I know I messed up. And when I have kids, I'm not going to—I'm going to be there. And I'm not going to allow them to be around anything, and that includes—if my sisters and my mom's messing up, I don't want my kids or nothing to be around it, because I don't want them to see that. And that's why I worry so much about my sisters and hope they get everything together before I get out, man, because I'm going to try help them as much as I can. But I can only do so much because it's time for me to start my own family."

All this talk of a new life as a protective family man seemed to make Robert zoom out and think of politics. "America's losing it, man," he said out of nowhere. He was referring to "morals and stuff like that."

"Same-sex marriage and all that?" he said. "That ain't right, you know what I mean? That's like that Sodom and Gomorrah: men was laying with men and all that. And what happened after that? Got blasted—you know what I mean? And now everything's being accepted."

✶

THAT EVENING RAIS was at the mosque in Richardson, the one where Mark Stroman had dreamed of slaughtering dozens of Muslims all those years ago. The congregants were celebrating the end of Ramadan. Rais wore a blue embroidered shirt in the back-home style and donned a golden cap as he entered the building. The worshippers ranged widely in age, ethnicity, and even dress, wearing everything from T-shirts and shorts to dress shirts and khakis to mesh Cowboys jerseys. Children were everywhere, frolicking in knowing and unknowing defiance of the solemnity.

Rais joined the other men in the waves of bowed prayer, in a building whose decor blended the acoustic ceiling tiles of institutional America with an Islamic dome painted pastel blue. After the prayer, the crowd spilled out into the heat, which was relenting at last, into a courtyard where sweets were on offer to mark the fast's end. Volunteers gave out plates filled with Japanese party snacks and quarter doughnuts and such, to be washed down with a syrupy pink juice.

Sitting in the courtyard, Rais was talking about work—his job at the travel company. He was thriving there and had climbed to the point where he supervised a small army of engineers in Britain, the Philippines, and India. His phone endlessly rang with calls from foreign numbers: people needing his troubleshooting skills. Something that worried Rais, though, was that only his kind of position—supervisory work—seemed likely to stay in America. He saw it in his own company.

The managers were here, but all the new engineers they hired were overseas. The low rungs on the career ladder that had allowed him to build his American life were disappearing, and what good was a ladder with rungs only at the top?

Sometimes it had been Rais's job to figure out how to shift work from his adopted country to countries not unlike the one he had left. He did what he had to do. But he said, as the sunlight slipped from the courtyard, that his campaign to save Stroman and his deepening understanding of, and commitment to, America had prompted him to push back against offshoring whenever he could. He had pressed his boss to consider more local hiring. If his engagement with the Stromans had shown him anything, it was that people starved of life chances are faster to hate. Rais had realized, much to his alarm, that he might be toiling at night to heal wounds that he was responsible for cutting by day.

Then, rather suddenly, he stopped speaking. He closed his eyes and began to pray. After some minutes, returning to this world, Rais observed that the end of Ramadan was "sweet and sour" for him: sweet because he could eat with gusto again; sour because the time of blessings had passed.

PowerPoint

The following May, ten months after the execution, Rais found himself on tour in the woodlands of central Connecticut. These had been punishing, exhilarating months for a new fixture on the lecture circuit. Any gathering discussing peace or interfaith harmony or the like seemed to want Rais Bhuiyan on the platform. It wasn't quite his dream of co-lecturing with Mark Stroman, but it was something. There were high school events in Dallas itself; talks at Stanford and DePaul; an Amnesty International anniversary in Los Angeles followed by an Amnesty International anniversary in North Carolina; a foundation gig here, a United We Change event there, a talk at Georgia State University, and of course repeated panels at Professor Halperin's own Southern Methodist University. Fueling the invitations was press coverage: Rais had granted interviews to everyone from the BBC to NPR to CBS to a Farsi channel in Iran. He had taped his first thirty-second television advertisement, advocating peace and forgiveness on behalf of an Islamic charity. He had received various honors, including from the Council on American-Islamic Relations, the Dallas Peace Center, and *Esquire* magazine, which named him one of its Americans of the Year for 2011. He had taken his roadshow to Italy, where he spoke about the themes of hate and mercy in high schools and town-hall meetings. He had more trips planned for the summer—Indiana and Alaska. He dreamed of Israel and Africa, although the requisite speaking invitations had yet to come.

"Since I can't afford to go anywhere on my own," he said, "people ask me, and I go."

The event in May, in Middle Haddam, Connecticut, was especially thrilling to Rais. An English teacher at a local high school had learned of Rais's story and written a play about it. The play was to be read aloud by a group of students this week at Christ Episcopal Church. The day before, in preparation, the church was hosting a Q&A with Rais, followed by a wine-and-snacks reception. This was the kind of impact Rais had once only fantasized about: a devout Muslim from Bangladesh talking in the middle of Connecticut to a church full of Christians about peace, Islam, and mercy.

Rais was staying at the home of the teacher, Linda Napoletano, and her husband, Dick, in the nearby town of Portland. It was a charming exurb with homes in the Federal and Colonial styles, set on rolling acres of green, which had been enhanced by recent rain. The area was actually rather dense—this was hardly rural living—but its planners had cultivated the illusion of frontierlike solitude and rugged independence, with plots just big and shaded enough to make you feel wholly your own. People came together, of course, as they planned to do that very evening in church, to cook things and pray for things and raise money. Still, the landscape spoke of an American longing that bound Connecticut to Texas despite all their differences: a dream, which had outlived the frontier itself, of being alone.

Rais was sitting at the kitchen table pecking away at his laptop. His phone, tethered to a hands-free cord, was right beside him in case India or Austria or the Philippines called, which they often did.

Rais's focus these days was on building his organization, World Without Hate. He had invested $1,000 of his own money in hiring a Web designer for its site. He had poured a few thousand dollars he had earned through speaking engagements into the organization's coffers. The goals of his effort were becoming clearer by the day. World Without Hate would undertake a number of endeavors: to host speeches by Rais and other anti-hate-crime campaigners; to develop an anti-hate curriculum for school-age children, in a workshop format; to stage an annual essay and art competition for high school and college students; to create a conference on hate crimes; to develop a robust online and social media presence for the group; to provide scholarships "to students who wish to pursue studies in human rights at the college and graduate level who are committed to bringing peace to their place of origin upon completion of their studies"; to offer financial aid to hate-crime victims who struggle to get help; and, underpinning it all, to raise funds to support this work on a sustainable, ongoing basis.

Rais had recently tacked on to these extensive ambitions a further one: becoming a teacher of human rights. He was hoping to enroll part-time at Halperin's SMU in its brand-new program granting bachelor's degrees in human rights. Unfortunately, they were saying it would cost $55,000, which he did not have. He was hoping Halperin might be able to help him devise a solution. One idea was to get the media relations people at the university excited about Rais's attending as a kind of human-rights brand mascot, to "carry the logo of the program on my back," as Rais put it.

He had continued to hear from Amber, although his optimism about being able to help her had waned. A few months earlier, she had texted him. She was planning to move back to Stephenville and said something about needing gas money to move her trailer down there. Rais had heard all about Stephenville and its meth heads, and he advised her to stick with her treatment. She asked for $15. He sent her $50. A few weeks later, she called again. This time, she was hoping she could get Rais's help to buy a uniform she needed for a new job. Rais had begun to worry that his money was funding unworthy causes, and one of Amber's aunts had actually called and asked him to stop giving Amber cash. Thus Rais suggested that Amber ask her new boss to lend her the uniform money, and then he would drive to Stephenville himself to see her and pay the boss back. This offer Amber declined.

Rais, meanwhile, had emerged as a sought-after public speaker. From the earliest days of his campaign for Stroman, Rais had struggled to balance the inherent humility of his quest with the need to get attention for it, to play by the rules of this below-world that he knew to be a mere trailer for the real show. In time the balance had tipped toward attention, and Rais was ever more comfortable in his role.

Rais remembered that when Halperin was advising him the year before, the professor warned him not to get used to this attention, predicting that it would all vanish if Stroman were executed. Rais had responded, "Rick, you know that I'm not doing all what I'm doing right now for any media connection. Purely what I'm doing, it comes from my heart. I won't be surprised if no one even calls me after Mark is executed. I'll be fully fine. I'll be OK with that." Now Rais was happy to note that Rick was wrong: "It seems like people are getting more and more interested around this story because it's something unique, and last week Rick was telling me that, 'This country has a history of four hundred years of killing and revenge and hatred. And your message is coming something new, that we had enough. Starting from the founders of this country, we needed more forgiveness and peace than killing and revenge.' So it's a unique message and people are getting that."

Rais was learning the tradecraft of the public speaker: how to customize his speeches to be funny for high schoolers, logical and evidence-based for college students, inspiring and hopeful for old people. He had learned to handle Q&A sessions and the pressure of riffing on hot-button topics he knew little about. But his multitasking and feverish scheduling seemed to be levying a toll on his health.

The previous November, he had been speaking at SMU, in the student forum, when he went, as he put it, "from standing to boom." He collapsed flat on the floor midspeech. An ambulance fetched him, and an electrocardiogram found ominous news: his heart seemed to have an extra, irregular beat amid the lub-dub-lub-dub. The doctors said it wasn't anything to be excessively concerned about, so long as he ate healthily and slept eight hours every night, which was between double and quadruple what he was currently doing.

This time at Linda's presented an opportunity: some days away from Dallas, a chance to get more than the usual amount of sleep. Linda, a cheerful bear of a woman, kindhearted and sharp, had taken to calling herself Rais's American mother, to which he readily assented. Their distinct stories of reinvention perhaps created a natural affinity. You could trace Linda's back at least to New York, where she was once a schoolteacher. Dissatisfied with the benefits and retirement plan, and needing to be closer to relatives, she returned to Connecticut, where she had grown up. She taught English and desktop publishing and journalism, among other things. As she approached retirement, she figured out that if she had just twelve more graduate-level university credits, to achieve a master's degree, she would exit at a higher rank and command a fatter pension. That was what led her to Wesleyan, to which she came for mercenary purposes, but with whose rhythms she quickly fell in love. She wrote a play about Rais, called *An Eye for an Eye*, as part of her coursework, and, to her great surprise, it won the university's prestigious Rulewater Prize.

Her husband, Dick, was also once a teacher. He had, in retirement, remade himself as a wedding and family photographer, with an elaborate studio overflowing with cameras and lights just off the kitchen; now, proud as ever of his "famous Napoletano omelets," he was flirting with the notion of setting up a bed and breakfast in their house.

The Napoletanos belonged, in a way, to the same America as Rais:

the country whose governing faith is reinvention, the country that sees its essential trait as an ethic, not an identity. They were an older Christian white couple out in central Connecticut; Rais was a younger Muslim brown bachelor from Dallas. But they saw in him a devoted striving and a small, gentle greatness and a habit of defying odds that seemed to them profoundly American, and they wanted the country to possess these traits long after they were gone. Rais offered a chance to keep their America alive.

When Rais arrived at the Napoletanos' home that week, he found among its floral, woody, homey Americana decor a prayer rug, arranged to guide him toward Mecca, in the guest room. He had come to speak at a Christian church, and there was a prayer rug in his bedroom! He couldn't believe it.

"They are Christian, I'm Muslim, and I'm staying in their house and praying in their room; they made a special rug for me," Rais said. Their example made him wonder why the larger society was perpetually up in arms. "Why can't it be this entire country like this house?" he asked. This idea appealed to him, and he returned to it later: "We can take this as an example and just multiply, increase the size of this house—make it this country."

⋇

AT DUSK, RAIS and the Napoletanos drove to Christ Episcopal Church for the first installment of the two-night presentation. On the way, they passed a white house with a small shop on the premises. Staked in the yard was a three-line sign. The first and third lines were in small, regular type; the middle line was in a larger font and all capitals:

We sell
AMERICAN GIRLS
dolls and accessories

Out of nowhere, this angered Rais. He sniffed that the sign was clearly trying to make people think that the store sold American girls rather than American Girl dolls and accessories. He seemed to believe that the shop owner was playing on some sinister fantasy. Moments like this were a reminder that Rais's faith, which seldom came across as rigid or doctrinaire in his everyday dealings, was the lens through which he regarded everything. It accounted for his tendency to perceive in the most ordinary events the tragedy of degeneracy. It had helped him to see America's situation with some insight, but it could also make for stranger reactions.

The church was small and old, wooden and white, set in the dense forest of Middle Haddam. Upon arriving, Linda was nervous. Would people come? It wasn't like she hadn't pamphleted and e-mailed enough—but would the parishioners show to see her Muslim Texan friend? She warned Rais, who was relaxed and milling about in his blazer and khakis, that attendance might not be what she'd hoped. "Perfect," he told her. "Even if just two people show up . . ."

Rais had gotten the routine down pat. He set up his Toshiba laptop on the table, hooked it up to the projector, and fired up PowerPoint. On the screen appeared the logo of World Without Hate. Behind the screen happened to stand a statue of Jesus, which Rais later marveled at as yet another example of the mashed-up tolerance the world needed. He fiddled with the assortment of computer files he had gathered for his presentation—videos of Stroman, TV clips, news articles, pictures of himself before and after the day of the attack. Linda and Dick, meanwhile, were fussing over the audio, trying to get just right the connections among the amplifier, microphones, computer, and projector. There was a brief panic over whether they needed the headphone-jack-to-headphone-jack cable, or the one with red and white on one end, or the yellow one. Yellow, it turned out.

Then they began to trickle in, the parishioners of Middle Haddam, most of them older, almost all of them white, none of them anything like Rais. But here they were. They filled the pews, whispered and waited.

Rais began his show: first a video presentation about the shootings in 2001 and his campaign many years later, followed by an onstage interview of him by a visiting pastor from New York. Rais opened with a blessing, explaining that it was a tradition of Muslims when they addressed others: "I begin in the name of almighty God, the most gracious and most merciful."

He told his strange, sweeping story: his origins in Bangladesh; his journey into and out of the Air Force; his American fantasy-turned-reality; the fiancée he once had; his victory in the Diversity Visa lottery; his move to Dallas; that rainy day in September 2001, when he was not supposed to be working; his rebuilding and recovery, piece by overwhelming piece. He spoke also of his campaign to save Stroman, and now his effort to save Stroman's children from becoming their father. His organization, he said, was dedicated to interrupting the cycle of hate, violence, and lack of education.

When the time came for audience questions, hands shot up across the church. Rais deftly took them one by one, charming the audience, honoring their faith as much as his own, deflecting when he didn't want to go there.

A woman named Rose stood up and apologized, first of all, for stepping out during the interview. She was cooking for the reception afterward and had to check the oven. "My question goes back to something a little more personal," she continued. "You had said in your early discussion that your father had a stroke, that you had a fiancée, and I don't know if you married. How did your life go from those very sad events, which compounded your sorrow and misery, to where you are today? It would be a comfort to know that you are with someone who loves you and nurtures you, and that your father's well—where do things stand in your life and relationships?"

"It's a very good question," Rais began, though his considerable practice with Q&As had taught him how to avoid answering it. "Well, I was taught by my parents that whatever happens, happens for good reasons. There are good reasons behind, and God loves us so much, He doesn't want us to go through any kind of pain and sufferings. But sometimes we go through—it's a test for us."

Rais then reprised a favorite theme of his, the idea that God had saved him for reasons that he was only beginning to understand: "God could have taken me on September 21. He took two others; He could have taken me. But He did not. Definitely there are important reasons behind. That's why He kept me alive. Maybe there is something that could be done through me in the future in course of time. That's why He put me through that."

Rais often spoke of himself as God's instrument, and as he built on the idea in the church, he had to catch himself. "If you look at the life of Abraham," he began, "if you look at the life of all the—I'm not a prophet, so don't get me wrong. Just saying that I was taught all these stories at my childhood. Look at their lives—they went through one after one test—pain and suffering in their lives. God could have stopped that right away. But there was a reason behind. So because of those teachings, when I was going through all this disaster, I never asked God, 'Why I was shot?' "

Rais added, "Definitely God wants me to go through these hardships. It's a learning curve for me. Maybe something good is waiting for me."

✳

W<small>HAT AWAITED HIM</small> the next morning was a great deal of work. The Air Force man who became a Buckner Food Mart man who became an Olive Garden man who became an entry-level IT engineer was now a big-shot manager in the universe of databases and servers. At 11:30 a.m., he was sitting at the kitchen table, after a night of uncharacteristically long sleep, remotely conducting his global orchestra of engineers.

A short while earlier, he had received an e-mail about a sales promotion in the works. The Customer Delivery Team sent word to the Advance Support Team, which in turn informed the Operation Team, on which Rais served. In roughly a week, one of the travel company's websites would unveil a new sale: €99 flights from Brussels to various European destinations. They were expecting maybe three times the normal volume of visitors to the site, which would crash if nothing was done. Enter Rais's squad.

He knew his role by heart now. He would look at the spreadsheet that informed him how much of the computing power, memory, and bandwidth were consumed by normal usage. Multiply that usage by three, and you could calculate how much additional memory had to be freed, or what applications had to be shut down, or whether the system had to be restarted, or whether more servers were needed. In the latter case, Rais could deploy his team to prepare servers in London remotely from Bangalore. They would be online by the time the sale went live, and then thousands of users would somehow find their way—via ads, via word of mouth, via news coverage—to the website, and their arrival would, fingers crossed, be entirely uneventful, so that they had no idea of all the work being done just to let them look up the price of a ticket.

Rais sat in the kitchen quietly doing this work, talking to faraway places on his phone, running his miniature global fiefdom. He was part of the weightless new world that had brought much promise to many people and places but that could also, as he well understood, be profoundly threatening. Here he sat in a spacious, well-appointed home on a well-proportioned lot, paid for by two teachers in public schools. Jobs like theirs—once the vertebrae of so many communities—used to buy houses and lives like this without much trouble. In a changing country, though, no one Rais's age, embarking on a career like Linda's and Dick's, could reasonably expect this kind of life—the family home they shared in Rhode Island, the retirement condo they had bought in the Century Village development in southern Florida, the photographs of countries they had visited on the walls.

In his wits and his grit, Rais was not ordinary, and he was part of the sweeping changes that were making this a harder country for the ordinary: the "hourglass economy," some called it. Rais understood how the squeezing out of ordinariness would complicate his battle against resentment. The new virtual world had done so much for him, but it wouldn't for everyone. And it placed distance between people. It made it possible to sit at this kitchen table and work with four different countries, it was true, but it made it rarer to have the kind of face-to-face contact that melted brittle incomprehension— the kind of melting that Rais had begun to achieve with Amber over Starbucks coffee and Chipotle burritos.

He was equally torn over the merciless American economy that had served him so well. It could be a cruel country, with a fetish for the idea of lone wolves. Rais had seen that when the hospital kicked him out after the shooting. He had seen it at work, where full-timers were often hired as contractors, so the company could kick them out at will. He had experienced the lone-wolf fantasy most acutely, of course, by getting shot in the face by a self-proclaimed one-man allied brigade. Yet Rais grasped that this fantasy and the harshness of American isolation were not unrelated to the country's possibilities. When Rais went to Europe on business, the coddled employees of the same company came across so differently: conscious, above all, of their rights and hours and vacation days, more worried about what the company owed them than the other way around. It was difficult, Rais observed, to get them to work. The Americans on his team worked as hard as the Bangaloreans, because in America, as in a poor country, the consequences of failure were too dire. Harshness raised the cost of falling behind. It propelled you onward, though perhaps only if you were blessed enough to be the onward kind.

✳

Of all of Rais's new aspirations, perhaps the most momentous had gone unmentioned until lunchtime on the second day. In recent months, Rais had decided that he was ready, once again, to turn his attention to women and the possibility of marrying.

His family had consistently applied pressure to this end but had by now more or less given up. It had been nearly a decade since Abida left him, and he hadn't been with a woman since then.

Linda, who was the kind to volunteer matchmaking services without having to be asked, was thrilled at this new customer. She was already thinking of women she knew, already bringing Rais up to mothers with unmarried daughters. To help her search, she had asked Rais to define, however precisely he could, his criteria for a wife. He was still working them out, but in their incipient form they spoke to how he had, and had not, been changed by his American remaking.

Now thirty-nine, he wanted someone thirty or under—not least because, like Robert Stroman, he dreamed of starting a family. It didn't matter to him whether the woman worked or didn't; Islam, he said, accepted either. What was important was that she be unlike all those people Rais knew whose conversation amounted to "nothing but car, their clothing, the jewelry, the ornaments, the vacation." He was open to any background, but she had to be free of materialism and worldly concern: "The person—I don't care who she is, Latino, Hispanic, white, Bengali, whatever—but a person who has the kind of mentality that life should not be defined based on what you have, what you had, what you're going to have."

Despite his own restraint, Rais had no expectations of marrying someone, particularly if she grew up in America, for whom he would be the first: "I cannot expect that I'm going to go and marry a virgin. I don't expect that. I have to be practical. Finding the right person is more important than what she did in the past."

Rais's wife also didn't have to be Muslim. Of course, if she was willing to convert, "that would be very good thing," he said. This idea, like many of his ideas, had derived from a close study of how the Prophet had lived.

Rais understood from the Koran that Muslims were permitted to marry any person of the book—Jews and Christians as well as those of their own tradition. "Even our Prophet, he married a Christian. A couple of his wives were Christian," Rais said. Then he told his version of a story about one of the Prophet's gestures that had given him an idea for his own life.

"There was a war about to be started," Rais said. "For a peace treaty, He did not go and tell that tribe or that people, 'I want to marry so-and-so.' He said, 'I'm willing to make this peace treaty, and I'm offering myself—that let's build a relationship. I'm willing to marry anyone from your tribe.'" In other words, the Prophet "did not marry for his pleasure," Rais said, but for bridge-building.

Rais wondered if he could achieve some bridge-building of his own, between the Muslim world and his adopted country, through marriage.

"That is one of the thoughts," Rais said. "I don't compare myself with the Prophet. But what I believe is that there's another way of bridging among people, among cultures. And also it's one of my thoughts that if I go back to Bangladesh and marry someone, then I have to bring that person here, and I have to babysit that person for several years to adjust herself with this culture, with this language, with the environment. Whereas if I married someone here, then I don't have to go through that."

Having reached these realizations was one thing; getting from realizations to wife, quite another. The truth was, Rais had no idea how to proceed. On one hand, he knew that God would look out for him and that his fate was predetermined; on the other, he knew that was no excuse, not in America at least. "If I find someone and when that person will come, it's already decided," he said. "That doesn't mean I should be sitting tight."

But he wasn't going on dates, either: "Are you crazy, that I have the time to go on dates?" Even at work, he tried to avoid situations in which he and a female co-worker ended up alone at lunch time. "In this country, one-on-one means a date," he said. "At least more than two person, then it's safety. You're off of the pressure."

Because of the campaigning he was now doing, he had negotiated with his company to let him work from home three days a week. That was great for his campaign but further deprived him of encounters with women. Another complication was his history with Abida, which he mentioned in all his talks. After his lecture at DePaul, a bunch of young women, taken with his story, had come up to him and asked about Abida and whether they now had children.

"Since I tell that I had a fiancée, they think that I am still with my fiancée," he said, unsure of how to correct the record. He wondered if he should start using "ex-fiancée" instead: "I always thought about that—that I had to clarify. Because it also closed a lot of doors."

The one thing Rais refused to adopt from America was this insatiable consumption of partners on the supposed path to true love. He knew that women weren't cars, and that it didn't work to treat them as if they were: "You switch your partner like a new car came to the market, and you have to test it, drive it." Wasn't it this behavior, Rais added, that had so punished the Stromans?

But why not at least go on a few dates? Nothing too intimate—just dinner and soft drinks?

"Here's the problem," he said, finally just putting it out there. "In this culture, once you go for a date, the way girls—women—behave in this Western culture, then they expect that you will go and sleep with them. Maybe not the first date; maybe second or third or the fourth date. They expect, right?

"But I can't do that. I cannot cross my boundary before I find that person that's my wife. So if I go for a date, and then next date it doesn't happen, then they will think, 'What is wrong with this guy?' And the dates are like that: you have to expose yourself that you're a guy, you're manly. You have to expose yourself in that way—sexy way—and then increase the expectation of your female partner that you will take her and there will be something. And I cannot do that."

Rais was a man of technology, though. Surely the Internet, with its florescence of dating and matrimonial sites, had overcome this problem. Were there not sites for Muslims who hadn't slept around and didn't want to date in the American way? There had to be women out there with the same dilemma.

"Where do I find them?" Rais said with a nervous, hopeful giggle.

Hula Hoop

To get to Stephenville from Dallas, you drive west across the city until, for the briefest time, civilization vanishes. It quickly reappears, though somewhat diminished, in the form of Fort Worth, whose gripe with Dallas is that it is inadequately western. Then you fall out of Fort Worth into country made for horse chases: endless flat land, hilly at times, most of it ranches. You can count the number of animals you see in a few hours' drive—a lot of land for not so much meat. On the highway, mirage after mirage spreads and dries up in the 100-degree July heat. From time to time, you cross some town redolent of afterness: just a lane or two, maybe a store, maybe a crossroads.

Erica Stroman emerged from the horseshoe of apartments where she was living. She wore white bug-eyed sunglasses with fake diamonds on the edges and was joined by her cousin Desireé. They were headed to Brownwood, sixty miles to the southwest, to see Tena and

Amber. In two days, it would be the one-year anniversary of Mark Stroman's passing.

It had been a good year for Erica, considering. "It's doing better," she said. "I mean, I'm looking up. Little by little. Just as far as being able to work, pay things. You know, I got a vehicle—a truck. I'm not dependent, really, on anybody else. It's kind of being on my own a bit, really."

Not long after her father's death, she had taken the graveyard shift at McDonald's for a month. Then she got 6 a.m. to 2 p.m., which was good because it gave her the rest of the day free. There was a lot to learn very quickly: how overtime works; how the registers were checked and the employees docked for shortfalls; the three-warning system for misbehaving; how to wash your hands at the start of your shift and only then clock in, because they're not paying you to become clean. Yet what began as a drudgery in Erica's mind had quickly turned into something else.

McDonald's was not known as an engine of mobility, but in a place like Stephenville it could seem like the closest thing. All her life, Erica had dreamed of an altered end state, but she had never been able to figure out the intervening how. Now, at McDonald's, the future felt real and malleable. She had already been promoted to junior manager, and if she kept rising, she could get a transfer to Fort Worth or maybe even Dallas. The way you got promoted was by studying. Erica wasn't a big book person, but McDonald's made it straightforward and step-by-step. You could take online McDonald's classes and even earn college credits doing it. You could, if you were lucky, get picked to go to Hamburger University, a training center for managers and owners. Erica's boss had recently gone, and she was now clearing $40,000 a year, just working at McDonald's.

When Erica explained to outsiders what she was studying—subjects like food cost, waste, hygiene, and the like—she zipped through it so quickly and energetically that it was hard to follow: "OK, it's like we sell a McDouble for $1.08. Well, it costs us 60 cents. But if you make a McDouble the wrong way, then you gotta make it again. Then you throw it away—that's waste. The nuggets are 6 cents. You know, 24 cents for the four-piece nugget that we sell for $1.83. But when it's busy, we'll make a lot, and all that's waste, waste, waste. So that's 6 times 60. Plus everybody goes by, because on the grill they like to press the timer, so you go by and open it, check it or just pick up one and 'O.K., that's old.' So that whole tray—that's waste."

Life had often left Erica callous and surly, but the customer-service training had helped her keep it together for the sake of business. "Even on a bad day," Erica said, "nobody's gonna wanna come in here with me being pissed off."

She knew, more clearly than in earlier phases of her life, what the next steps were and what she had to do to take them. She was assigned the cash registers these days, counting down the drawers. If she finished the class she was currently taking, then she'd get a twenty-five- or fifty-cent raise. If she continued, she would soon set her own shifts. After the next set of classes, another boost of twenty-five or fifty cents. It wasn't out of the question to grow into a general-manager role within a few years. Erica's boss did it within four, and now she owned her own house, had bought a used Camaro for two grand, and paid for school on the side while also managing the restaurant.

"It's like a climbing ladder, really," Erica said. The job had filled her with hope: "I'm not at the bottom anymore."

Desireé was Erica's cousin on her mom's side; they were rooming together these days. Desireé was eighteen but could easily have passed for ten. She was short and scrawny, to the point of appearing malnourished, and wore little rectangular metallic glasses. The only hint of her age was the sizable diamond she wore on the fourth finger of her left hand. Her fiancé, Chance, had proposed recently, on

Valentine's Day, in the middle of their junior year. They planned to wait a whole year after high school before marrying, to stress-test their love.

Desireé had a spark and vibrancy and thirst for the world that distinguished her from her family. On paper, her options were just about as lousy, but she had an aspirational quality. She had a lot of questions about the world. She was keen to share the story of her Indian friends in school, who, she helpfully explained, were from Pakistan. She made sure to tell people that Chance came from a family with money. He bought her a $5,000 ring, supposedly, which she claimed to have thrown into a field after a fight. They never found it, she said, and so he bought her another. In a place full of half-men, she'd found herself a diamond mine.

Amber had, of course, gotten out of the desert of good men by going over to women. When she and Maria got together, four years ago, it had shocked everyone, including her sister. Amber, as far as anyone knew, had never been with a woman before. Some in the family had been resistant at first, but Maria had proven herself, Erica said, by not cutting and running all the times when that would have been the smartest thing to do.

As for herself, Erica was dubious about settling down, which often seemed to involve a lot of settling. Girls like Desireé were the lucky exceptions, happy and in love and well tended. The reality was, the women Erica knew worked harder than the men. Far from here, governors and senators and presidents spoke of a crisis of the family, of a breakdown in marriage. But Erica sensed what they didn't: that for people like her, taking on another person wasn't always the stabilizer it was cracked up to be. "It's just, you can do bad on your own, and then when you get with somebody that's just doing the same as you are, or worse than you are, you can't—my grandma used to say that you can't hang around with trash or it gets in your eyes." The country's marriage enthusiasts often had the fortune, unavailable to Erica's class, of being whole to begin with. They multiplied with other whole people to form still greater products. What Erica intuited was that a fractional being like her multiplied by another fractional being equaled—in matrimony as in mathematics—a smaller fraction than either person was before.

✲

Amber's new home in Brownwood was in a so-called clean house, with subsidized rent, strict rules of sobriety, and required attendance at recovery meetings. The building was various hues of brown and beige, decorated with seashells and cross-sections of trees. Amber had a well-ordered upstairs apartment. The one-bedroom place had a small kitchen, in which dishes recently washed stood neatly in a rack, drying, and a poster over the stove advised "serenity." The kitchen spilled into the living room, which was dominated by a sofa whose stretchy cover kept coming off. A television with its own built-in DVD player sat unplugged; Amber and Maria carried it into the bedroom when they wanted to watch in there. The air-conditioning was set at 64 degrees and on all day, since electric was included in the rent. The smell of cigarettes, perhaps in violation of the compound norms, hung in the air, mingling with the scent of simmering hamburger meat, which was cooking on a plug-in griddle on the kitchen table.

Amber Stroman had, for the first time in the longest time she could remember, been sober for four months now. The entire apartment was a temple to the conquest of addiction. A calendar advocating drug-freeness hung on the front door, as though to remind Amber where not to go every time she left. On the fridge, beneath a chart detailing the proper schedule for children's vaccinations, was Amber's "Daily Moral Inventory," a document obtained from her sobriety meetings, which told her which traits to avoid and which to cultivate:

LIABILITIES	ASSETS
Watch for:	*Strive For:*
Self Pity	Self Forgivness
Self Justification	Humilitay
Self Importance	Modesty
Self Condemnation	Self Valuation
Dishonesty	Honesty
Impatience	Patience
Hate	Love
Resentment	Forgiveness
False Pride	Simplicity
Jealousy	Trust
Envy	Generosity
Laziness	Activity
Procrastination	Promptness
Insincerity	Straightforwardness
Negative Thinking	Positive Thinking
Vulgar, Immoral Thinking	Spiritual, Clean Thinking
Criticizing	Look for the good!!

Tena was sitting on a big, soft chair that was her favorite. She was in her early forties now. She still had that gash the length of a carrot running vertically down the left side of her neck, from the time that either she cut herself as a teenager or Mark Stroman cut her. After all these years, and Mark's passing, she was still sticking with the story that she had cut herself. She was short and round and sweet to a fault, and given to making impolitic jokes, many of which she had learned from Mark and held on to. She was a person who laughed easily—sometimes she sent out a bit of her laughter after something she said to elicit some more from her interlocutor, which would convince her to unleash a great deal more of hers. She was still wearing the purple Jerry's shirt from the burger joint where she now worked.

Like Amber, she had been clean for a while, almost a year, for the first time in a long time.

Amber seemed less anxious than a year ago. Her gaze had a new focus. She wore around her neck a red-white-and-blue flag-patterned locket, on a thin black string, containing her father's ashes. Things were solid between her and Maria, who was also in recovery and who remained pretty much silent.

The five women had much catching up to do.

Erica was complaining about money: owing $400 for her truck payment that week, another $120 for insurance, then the elective but essential $30 for Friday after-work drinks at Montana's.

Desireé, meanwhile, was somewhat insensitively talking about floating down some river with Chance.

Tena said she was working forty-nine hours a week or thereabouts serving Jerry's burgers. Erica was getting thirty-eight to forty, but she was often allowed to get an extra hour in here and there.

Erica was now criticizing Desireé for her spending habits, saying that she never saved. Desireé countered that she had no bills to pay that month (perhaps the advantage of having a fiancé like Chance) and that she had plenty in the bank. Erica said her bank account contained $93.

Desireé said something admiring about Amber's coffeepot, joking that she just might have to take it with her.

"You cannot take an alcoholic-in-recovery's coffeepot!" Tena said. Besides, "coffee will put your ADD ass to sleep."

In March of that year, eight months after her father left for good, Amber had quit Stephenville for this clean house in Brownwood. Tena was already in the city and sobering up, and Amber somehow realized that it was time: "I just got to, getting high wasn't even fun anymore. I'd get high, and I'd feel guilty. I was tired of being worthless. I was ready to be Madyson's mama again." She still remembered how clear it became to her the last time she used, writing in her diary, taking stock of what she'd become: "I was done."

She had remained in Fort Worth for a time after the execution, but it had thrown her even farther off the track. She started using again. Eventually she and Maria returned to Stephenville and lived for six months in the same trailer park where a friend had taken them in on short notice a year before. One day the man they were staying with, a meth head in his own right, told them they had to go. Amber called Tena in desperation.

"I told her, 'If you don't come and get me, then I'm going to a motel room and there's gonna be plenty of dope,' and that's what my way of thinking was," Amber said. "So she came and got me." In just three weeks, sequestered from everyone she knew, in a place with rules, she and Maria both found jobs and Amber got into a free out-patient rehab program paid for by the state. The migraines she had suffered for years would soon cost Amber her job at a dry cleaner's, but Maria had kept working to support them, and Amber felt herself being reborn: "Next month, on the third, it will be five months clean. Clean. Nothing: no drinking, no pills, no dope, nothing. Clean. Only thing I'm doing is smoking cigarettes and drinking a shitload of coffee. But that's OK."

What had most helped Amber through recovery was arriving at a deeper understanding of where her addiction came from. The AA meetings had taught that what she had was an illness, not a habit, and that there was, in her God, a power great enough to pull her out of her morass. The program had, Amber said again and again, helped her to "get out of self," to overcome the inwardness that for her nourished addiction. To be whole and healthy was not to be without affliction, but to be even more aware of one's place and duties in a world of others.

Amber was starting to sense her role in the family change. All her life, she had known that she was failing them, especially Erica. She should have been there for her little sister; instead, she had been strung out or semihomeless or in prison. In the last few months, though, she had detected a momentous change in the family dynamics: Erica and the others had started calling Amber for advice.

"They take what I have to say," she said. "I guess it's different today, because I've got my shit together. I'm sober. I'm not the fly-by-night family member like I used to be. I've got my head on my shoulders. So, yeah, I'm not gonna be their best friend, and I'm not gonna tell them what I think they want to hear. I don't care if they get mad at me. If I can save them any pain, if I can keep them from going through the shit I had to go through, I would."

Still, in Amber's mind, all these things were fringe benefits. The only prize that mattered was Madyson, and that prize now felt closer than ever. Yes, like her mother, Amber had lost hold of her baby. Unlike her mother, Amber now had the opportunity to win her baby back before she was old enough to know too much.

Like Erica with McDonald's, Amber had the steps laid out in her mind. She needed to upgrade the apartment so that by the time she went to court and reclaimed Madyson, the little one could have her own bedroom. Grandma wasn't going to give Madyson up easily, but if Amber was clean and sober, living in a decent space, with a durable relationship and—not least—a good attorney, she could out-wit Grandma. There was a new urgency to her plan: she had heard that Madyson's father was getting out of prison in a matter of weeks. By law, he wasn't supposed to be around Madyson, because of his past behavior; in reality, he had nowhere to go but his grandma's. It pained Amber that she, after everything she'd done to turn around, would be here with her moral inventory and vaccination schedule but without her baby, and he, on what would likely amount to a brief vacation from prison, would "be with Madyson from the time she wakes up till the time she goes to bed."

At one point in the conversation, Tena sought to share in the blame for Amber's travails. Tena had, after all, been homeless for a couple of years before Brownwood, bouncing around friends' and relations' apartments, dealing meth, depending on the worst men. What had happened was not only Amber's fault but both of theirs.

"You know, if I would have been a better grandmother and if you weren't smoking methamphetamines, if you would have been a better mother and a better support system for your daughter, God wouldn't have let Madyson get took away," Tena said. "That's my perception of it—whether it be true or not."

Amber said that her mom was still living in the past and with regret. Channeling the lessons of the front door of her refrigerator, Amber told Tena that she had to forgive, not pity, herself.

Tena wouldn't have it. "I blame myself for losing Madyson," she said, "and we weren't even together when we were getting high. But I feel like, if I had been at home, doing this job thing like I do every day, being a stronger backbone, maybe she wouldn't have been out there doing that." Here she was looking at Amber.

This Amber didn't like. She said, "I would have been doing what I wanted to do, regardless of what you were doing."

Tena had been the family pioneer in discovering Brownwood. Back in Dallas, bumming around homes not her own, Tena had one day mustered the courage to check herself into the Green Oaks psychiatric hospital. They recommended a sober-living house in Brownwood, and she agreed. Tena stayed in that house for a time, until they discovered that she lacked insurance of any kind, which was a requirement there. They pushed her out to a government-financed treatment center, where she remained for twenty-eight days.

Finally, she had ended up in a different sober house from Amber's, but also in Brownwood, where she paid $100 a week in rent and lived with two others also in recovery. The house had an 11 p.m. curfew during the week, stretched to 1 a.m. on weekends. Even to stay at Amber's tonight, Tena had to obtain a pass.

For Tena, an essential part of recovery was getting her faith right. "I know there's a God," she said, "but sometimes I think God would do more for Desireé than He will for me. God will take care of Desireé and her problems before He will mine. And that's just because of the way I've lived my life. I feel like my God—I've turned my God to a punishing God, a strict God, a disappointed God, a God that's not happy with me." Sometimes Tena flirted with polytheism by imagining her unitary Christian God as more like a brand with franchises: "If I need to, I borrow Amber's God, because Amber's God answers her prayers; Amber's God takes care of her; Amber's God loves her. So if I have to, I'll borrow her God until I can identify who my God is."

The sober house was just transitional. It was training wheels to learn to get out on your own. Because of it, Tena felt the ground beneath her shifting as never before—and not only related to her addiction. She realized, when faced with the reality of things, that she had never, until now, understood the meaning of work and of independence.

"I always depended," Tena said. "I never depended on myself. And today I know, in order for me to have anything, I have to work. You know, nothing comes easy." She felt good: "I'm self-supported. I work every day. I pay my rent. Every two weeks, I pay my rent. I don't think I've ever done that. I've always handed off to somebody." The equation had become clear to her now: "If I work, my rent gets paid. If I don't work, my rent don't get paid."

The country often argued about people like Tena. What would right her path, or give her a chance to rise, or help her to help herself? What, ultimately, was responsible for her condition—social structures, underfunded rehab and psychiatric care, dismal parenting, a decadent culture?

The trouble with these arguments was that they so often forced a choice between caring for the weakest and honoring their agency. The left-leaning political half of the country that spoke most eloquently about the poor and vulnerable could be less comfortable judging their family structures and child-rearing habits, telling them the truth about culture and behavior, burdening them with the consequences of their decisions; the right-leaning political half of the country, more comfortable with such judgment and truth-telling, tended not to make underdogs their highest priority.

Here in Brownwood, for the time being at least, Tena and Amber seemed to have found a kind of middle ground—their own blend of judgment and compassion, structure and freedom. They felt themselves newly alive. "I have self-respect," Tena said. "I have my kids' respect. You know, for a long time, that one right there was real disappointed in me." She gestured at Erica. Then, on Father's Day this year, Tena had received a text message from Erica that floored her. It reminded Tena how far she had come. It said, "Thank you for being both."

Amber's cell phone rang. She had been planning to turn it off in the next day or so, to save money, but it was on today, and it was Grandma on the line from Stephenville, probably with some question about Madyson. Amber picked up. The call went on and on, and Amber sat looking progressively grimmer as it continued. Her side of the conversation didn't sound good.

"Yeah, he's her daddy—I understand that," she said to Grandma. "But she doesn't know him like that."

Pause. "Well, I'm sorry my family isn't as perfect as yours!"

Pause. "So you're saying Erica can't see Madyson? Well, if that's your choice right now. You are the sole conservator of Madyson. There's nothing I can say. All I can tell you is Erica's never put Madyson in any kind of danger. When I was fucking up, when I was off doing my thing, Erica was the only one there."

When Amber hung up, everyone wanted a debrief. As it turned out, it had been a strange call, and Amber needed the group's interpretation.

On the surface of things, Grandma had called to offer Amber some advice. She knew Amber wanted Madyson back, and she was calling because she had come upon some things that might complicate that wish. She purported to be telling Amber what to repair so as not to screw up Madyson's eventual return.

Grandma complained, for starters, about the dodgy apartment complex where Erica and Desireé lived, and where Madyson

sometimes spent the day. She had heard that there were people coming in and out of their apartment at all hours.

Erica countered that they went over to other apartments for flour,
sugar, toilet paper—stuff like that. Desireé was slightly more honest:
"Does she not understand I'm a teenager and my friends are going to
come over?"

Grandma also complained about a man named Ricky, who lived in
that same complex and who she heard was doing drugs.

No one contested Ricky's drug issues, although Erica pointed out
that Ricky lived in his own apartment. There was now some speculation about who was ratting out Ricky. This speculation converged
on yet another friend called Whitney.

Most ominously, and least baselessly, Grandma had complained
about Erica's drinking. She worried that Erica was often drunk
when taking care of Madyson, as she regularly did.

That pissed Erica off. She drank only a six-pack a day. "If I had
more money, I'd probably drink more," she admitted. (When Erica
later retold the story to her manager at McDonald's, her six-pack
shrank to a two-pack.)

Once Grandma's allegations had been detailed, and rebutted, the
group could step back and assess what the call had meant. It was sort
of random, out of nowhere, this sudden litany of worries. Amber,
though rattled at first, now reached an interpretation of the call that
left her very happy.

"What it is, is she's knowing and she's seeing that it's getting closer
and closer for me to get Madyson back, so she's starting shit," Amber
said. "She's nitpicking at every little bitty thing. And she knows that
she's taking a chance on letting Tyler move back, because she knows
if he fucks up one time, she's fucked. They will remove Madyson.
They'll come investigate me. And if they see that I'm doing what I
need to be doing, she's coming home. That's what that phone call was
about."

When Madyson's father returned, he could be randomly drug-tested at any time. If history was a guide, this was a test he was unlikely to pass. Grandma, everyone agreed, was worried and trying to generate additional reasons why Madyson should be kept from the Stromans. Perhaps she thought that if she registered the complaints now, they would predate any drug test and thus have greater validity.

The call persuaded Amber that her legal action against Grandma was going to be important. She had to have a good lawyer. Tena, hearing this, suggested one possibility. Maybe that nice Rais man would be able to help. Maybe he'd know how to find—or even pay for—a lawyer, so that Amber could get her baby back. Amber said yes, good idea, she would talk to him. She hadn't spoken to him in a while, but she felt confident that Rais would help if asked.

"He told me, 'You lost a dad, but you gained an uncle,' " Amber told her family. That earned a general, impressed murmur among the women.

Presently Annette walked in. She was Amber's sponsor in the AA meetings and the sturdiest pillar in her life right now. She was a lean, hard-bitten woman; life and chemicals had worn her down from the pudginess that endured on her driver's license. She blew into the room with the verve and willingness to kick ass that had endeared her to Amber and spared her charge uncountable backslides.

Amber told Annette about the phone call, and the idea of getting a lawyer and all the rest of it. Annette was of the view that Amber didn't need to mess with all that; she just needed to stick with the program. Annette, now well into middle age, had been in the program since age thirteen.

"God is taking care of this," Annette said, standing in the doorway. "When it's time for you to have a lawyer, it will come. Don't stress yourself right now. Anything that has to do with the law or any of that crap, it don't fit in your hula hoop. Leave it out there. Grandma having trouble with Erica, and her traffic there and her six-pack of beer or however much, the drugs going in and out—that don't fit in your hula hoop. Leave it over there. Let them deal with that mess. Don't put it up here; don't store it."

Annette had to go. She was only checking in. "You just keep doing what you're doing," she said as she walked out. "You're doing good. Look at it. It's all gonna fix and come back to you. Stay on the right path. Don't move backwards. And don't stray. I love you, too. Nine-one-one if you need me."

A FEW MINUTES later, Annette burst through the door again. One last thing: she wanted to tell everyone a story that she thought might help. They knew it already, but still . . . It was about Annette's son, and about the possibility of second chances.

From his earliest days, her boy wanted to ride in rodeos. That was what he wanted, and he couldn't be persuaded otherwise. His mom was an addict, of course, and not in much of a position to challenge him. When her boy was thirteen, the age at which she had first attended an AA meeting, they went down to the funeral parlor together and selected his arrangements. It was what young rodeo boys were meant to do. Better to do it with no real urgency. Mom and son were best friends. Then, two years later, because of her drinking and drugs, he cut her loose. He told Annette he was done with her.

Her boy's bull-riding career took off, and, praise the Lord, the funeral arrangements never became necessary. Until that day two years ago. Her boy had ridden four bulls without a helmet, and without incident, at the rodeo. The fifth bull somehow convinced him to put on a helmet. In that round the boy lost his way on the bull and the bull struck him, with all its ferocious weight, in the head.

Even with that helmet on, half the boy's face slid off—peeled off from the underlying meat like chicken skin. Rushed to the hospital, the boy fell into a coma. Annette received the news and rushed down there. She hadn't seen her boy in the longest time. She went anyway. The security guards ran her off, said she had nothing to do with this boy. She was only allowed to watch over him through a small window in a door. The boy's father was on the other side of that door. The boy had tubes running into his head; the room was bustling with doctors and machines. There was nothing they could do. The boy's father consented to pulling the plug, but it would still take hours for her boy to go.

All Annette could do was pray: "If You are out there, if You are really out there, don't do this to me. Let my baby walk back into my arms. Don't take my baby from me. This can't be real." Annette left the hospital, and as the hours passed hope turned to anger, and anger to doubt: "If there was a higher power, if there was a God, He wasn't gonna be no friend of mine because of what He did."

Then she got the phone call. Eight hours after they had pulled the plug, the boy had finally died. "They came and pronounced him dead," Annette said. "They pulled the tubes out of his head, pulled all of this off of him. They covered him up, and was ready to take him off to the morgue. They were fixing to transfer him from this bed to this bed. They seen something move under the sheet."

They lifted the sheet, and parts of the boy were back alive. Slowly more and more of him woke up, and he was reborn.

"And by the graces of God and the program we work on, and me following my program, my baby walked back into my arms for the first time December of last year," Annette said.

The story, already improbable on many levels, now grew more so. Not long ago, the boy had sent Annette a message—without knowing a thing about her protégé Amber or Amber's hair color.

"Mama, remember tools. You are a tool. Don't preach it; tell your feelings. Our Father works through you and in you. One soul, one heart saved, will one day save many. Our Father in Heaven, bless and keep my mama. She hasn't seen what You have shown me. Mama, your friend with red hair, she is safe with God. To believe is to be saved and have eternal life. Believe as my mother did the day I died."

✳

THE NEXT MORNING, sending off her guests, Amber was relish-
ing her new role as a bona fide big sister. A scrounger no more, she
packed a bag full of eggs, toilet paper, turkey, and other things for
Erica and Desireé, because who knew how they were living. The two
of them faintly protested, but Amber would hear none of it. It felt
good to be the giver.

It was July 19. Tomorrow Amber and Tena were thinking of doing
a small ceremony for the one-year anniversary of Mark Stroman's
death. For Amber every day remained a battle, but she felt surer now
than in a long time—certainly surer than a year ago—that she would
not turn out to be him.

They all said their good-byes, not knowing when they would meet
again. On the road home to Stephenville, Erica kept to herself mostly.
A year earlier, she had been the solid one, relatively speaking. Now a
piece of her felt deserted by a mother and sister who, in admitting to
their problems at last, made her stand out as the little family drunk.
But there was McDonald's and the classes and the coming raise and
Hamburger U. and that ladder she knew she could climb . . .

Desireé was chatty all the way back, full of stories about how
amazing she and Chance were going to be, trying to make connections between her life in Stephenville and the outside world she
didn't want to live in—because she loved Stephenville!—but which
she so longed to understand.

When Erica and Desireé got back to the apartment complex in
Stephenville, it was in the middle of some kind of situation. Two
police vehicles, lights spinning, stood near the entrance. The officers
had gone in to ask questions. Some listless young men lingered to
the side, winter hats pulled snugly over their heads in the sweltering
July heat.

The men were friends and neighbors of Erica and Desireé, some
just from the apartments, some all the way from school days. They

claimed they'd been robbed by one of Erica's other cousins. The police didn't show up until one guy threatened over the phone that he and his boys were going over to kill the culprits right now. This young man was beside himself with rage: the worst thing, he said, was that they stole his most personal shit—his porn, his court records, and, worst of all, his brother's death certificate. What kind of a person steals a bro's death certificate? Erica had gone inside to see what was happening. Desireé, still outside, whispered that this man and his buddies, in addition to being their close friends, were well-known Stephenville meth dealers.

Desireé wished to drown out these men and this scene. She wanted to feel important. She knew she was better than this place and knew she would never leave it. She wanted to change the subject. Standing beside a police truck, lights still spinning, she began to talk of things as distant from this time and place as possible. She meandered from one excitable claim to the next, paying zero attention to the chaos around her.

"I want to adopt a little girl from Africa!" she said at one point. And perhaps she would, and perhaps from her exclamation would, in time's fullness, grow another immigrant story like Rais's—another voyage to America, another brave and hard blossoming. Still, with the police still in the compound, with the meth dealers hovering, with Desireé's six-pack-a-day cousin sorting through stuff inside, with one day to go before the one-year anniversary of her uncle's execution for murder, it was strange to think of bringing a child from the deprivation that Desireé seemed to imagine far afield to the different deprivation that enwrapped her too fully for her to see.

"They always need a better home in Africa," Desireé said.

Arrivals

One morning that week, Rais lingered anxiously at the Dallas airport. For the first time since he landed on these shores thirteen years ago, his parents were visiting him. It was to be their first contact with American soil. His mother spoke almost no English, and his father was diabetic, and they had been scared of the coming trip. But it was a voyage that Rais needed them to make.

The flight seemed to have arrived, but no sign of them. He paced. He sat. He wondered if something had befallen them. He asked a guard what would happen if they had grown unwell. How would they even reach him? They didn't have a phone and didn't know how to do things in America. Would anyone help them? It was better not to think about it.

He was looking forward to the chance to serve them, to pay down some of his unpayable debt: "I've been praying for the last few years, 'God, give me a chance to serve my parents before they leave this world. God, help me take care of my parents the way they took care of me when I was a little child.'" He was hoping he would get enough time with them outside of work and his campaign. He wished he could take them across the country, show them what he'd seen. He felt guilty about all the work that would get in the way, especially because, as he rosily remembered it now, his parents had loved him without constraint: "When I was a kid, wherever I wanted to go, they took me."

He was worried about their ability to adjust to America, where they planned to spend some months. They were acquainted only with Bengalis and only with their neighborhood back home. They weren't used to these glassy towers and these wide highways. They weren't used to the food, so bland, so thoughtlessly, hurriedly prepared. Rais could already hear his mother's horror at the way he ate breakfast—only coffee and cereal, as though a war or famine had broken out. And why coffee to go? He didn't have five minutes to sit with his mother and drink coffee?

Rais had floated by his parents the idea of moving to America for good, of following in his footsteps, but they had their own lives. They lacked his leaving impulse. They wanted simply to be around close friends and neighbors, to sit and talk the years away, to bask in that familiarity. "They have their own gossip, their own newspaper," Rais said.

"What I want is to make them happy," he said. "The feeling's important that my son is in good shape and now he's trying to do something good."

The visit was equally important for Rais's feelings. Of his many leavings, leaving his parents had been the most wrenching; and being unable—then unwilling—to return when he was shot, harder still. He needed them to know, as he now knew for himself, that his wandering odyssey had been worthwhile after all.

"After I was shot, they'd been asking me to go back, and I said that, 'No, I wanted to give it the fight and maybe, by the mercy of God, things will change one day,'" Rais said, standing in the arrivals area.

" 'I will make you proud. Let me stay there, and I will do my best.' Once I look back ten years and I see myself now, God really helped me, and I accomplished something. I think they will see that it was worth it to let me stay here."

Then he saw them—or at least, at first, their luggage. A lanky porter emerged pushing a stack of four bags almost as high as Rais. Shuffling many steps behind was a small, veiled woman in a lime-green salwar kameez—and far behind her, and slower still, a man brightly hennaed on his head and beard. Their American boy, in jeans and a plaid shirt, hugged his mother. She clutched his neck with one hand and rubbed his back with the other. She looked at him, as though a little incredulous. Once again, she buried her head in his chest and held Rais, now with her husband awaiting his turn. Rais embraced his father, pulling him to his left, then his right, then his left again. Now Rais's phone rang. He looked at the number—the office, in all likelihood—and put it back in his pocket. It could wait. He slipped the lanky porter a tip.

"Are you happy?" Rais's father brokenly asked the porter, making sure it was enough. "Are you happy?" The father didn't want his American adventure to begin inauspiciously. Reassured that it hadn't, that the tip was ample, the father and mother followed Rais toward the electric doors and the searing summer light, and into their miracle boy's American life.

ACKNOWLEDGMENTS

I am thankful for many gifts of time and friendship that allowed the making of this book. I am particularly grateful to the people who let me tell their stories—above all, Rais Bhuiyan and the family of Mark Stroman. We would know so little about our communities, and ourselves, without those brave souls who answer the storyteller's knock.

If publishing is a marriage, I'm blessed with my in-laws at W. W. Norton. John Glusman, a true writer's editor, believed in this story from the start and possesses a judgment (and sense of humor) at once sharp and subtle. Thank you, too, to Tori Leventhal and Jonathan Baker, to India Cooper for careful and imaginative copyediting, and to the art, publicity, rights, sales, and marketing folk. Steve Wasserman, in a last hurrah as an agent, represented me on this book with his trademark fervor and curiosity. He has a gift for seeing what could be where little presently is.

I'm grateful to the *New York Times* for teaching me this trade and for supporting writers in a difficult era. Many thanks to Vera Titunik and Hugo Lindgren for their encouragement to tell the story that became this book. And to Jill Abramson, Alison Smale, Dave Smith, Richard Berry, Mary Jo Murphy, and Marc Charney, among others, for paving this path and making my writing better.

Many people, in Texas and beyond, went out of their way to help me report this story. Ilan Ziv, the filmmaker, was unfailingly gracious in sharing footage, contacts, and insight. In the book, most quotations from Mark Stroman come from his own prison writings, but some are from interviews done by Ilan and generously shown to me. Beyond the principal characters already mentioned, I'm appreciative of everyone who aided my reporting—whether by sitting for interviews, guiding me to files, or sharing letters and photos. Many people's names have been changed to protect their privacy.

A squadron of friends and family agreed to read the manuscript and comment. I have tried to live up to their high standards. Thank you, Nora Abousteit, John Blaxall, Marc Charney, Sam Dolnick, Nandini Giridharadas, Rukmini Giridharadas, Shyam Giridharadas, Andrea Harner, Kate Krontiris, Salma Merchant, Jeanne Moore, Deepa Narayan, Sue Parilla, Priya Parker, Brian Schechter, Baratunde Thurston, Emma Vaughn, Mariquel Waingarten, and Omar Wasow. Dr. Naresh Mandava helped me get my medical facts straight. Thanks, too, to Herman De Bode and family for the magical hillside where this book began to be written; to Beth Goff, for enlivening my Dallas reporting trips; and to my teachers and classmates in the Henry Crown Fellowship of the Aspen Institute, for challenging me to think hard about the writer's duty.

Vrinda Condillac was, once again, a master editor—careful, sympathetic, able to see past the words and into the characters' hearts. She brings skills from literary fiction to my world of facts, and has pushed me to make the people and places in this book leap more vividly to life. Sara Stroo and Katherine Marrone, both of the University of Oregon, were tireless and cheerful research assistants. They worked hard, over long hours, to ensure that the characters could be heard in their own voices.

I'd be nothing without my family. My parents have always spurred me onward in the pursuit of a profession that more calculating people would urge their genetic legatees to avoid. It is they who taught me to observe, dwell on details, tell stories, and never stop asking why and how. My sister is smart as a whip, an editor with heart, and the most loyal friend you could have. But you can't have her, because she's mine.

Then there's Priya. My wondrous wife told me, one sunny and confused morning, to write this book, and later that day I began. It's like that with her. She knows me; her only agenda for me is that I become the fullest expression of myself. She edits with vigor and ingenuity, and yet somehow also with love. How do other people get things written without her? This book is for her. Without her, it might never have been. Without her, even if it had, the experience would have been no fun.